REBUILDING
THE CHRISTIAN
COMMONWEALTH

New England
Congregationalists &
Foreign Missions,
1800-1830

Rebuilding the Christian Commonwealth

John A. Andrew III

The University Press of Kentucky

ISBN: 0-8131-1333-4

Library of Congress Catalog Card Number: 75-38214

Copyright © 1976 by The University Press of Kentucky

A statewide cooperative scholarly publishing agency
serving Berea College, Centre College of Kentucky,
Eastern Kentucky University, Georgetown College,
Kentucky Historical Society, Kentucky State University,
Morehead State University, Murray State University,
Northern Kentucky State College, Transylvania University,
University of Kentucky, University of Louisville, and
Western Kentucky University.

Editorial and Sales Offices: Lexington, Kentucky 40506

CONTENTS

ACKNOWLEDGMENTS

A number of libraries and librarians offered kind assistance during the manuscript research. For permission to examine and quote from collections I would like to thank the Houghton Library at Harvard University, Congregational Library, Connecticut Historical Society, American Antiquarian Society, and the Andover-Newton Theological Seminary. Mrs. Pam Autry and Mrs. Joanne Hawkins of the University of Texas at Austin always astonished me with their ability to acquire books on interlibrary loan. The Graduate School of the University of Texas at Austin provided financial assistance while this project was in the dissertation stage.

Throughout the course of my work at the graduate level I was fortunate to have some sound advice and criticism. Howard Miller forced me to reconsider my assumptions about nineteenth-century social reform, and Lewis Gould carefully excised a number of rambling passages, thereby tightening the manuscript. James Curtis proved a model dissertation director as well as a kind friend. Although they are responsible for nothing that lies within, my wife and two children contributed in other, more meaningful, ways.

INTRODUCTION

A small band of dedicated missionaries met in Park Street Church, Boston, on October 15, 1819. They were to sail four days hence to the Sandwich Islands (Hawaii) in the mid-Pacific and thereby usher in a new age of American religious activity. How did they get to Boston? Where did they come from? Why were they going? The answers to these questions reflect a society enmeshed in change—social, political, economic, and religious.

Forces of change—increased land pressure, improvements in transportation, competition from agricultural areas to the west, and growing political factiousness—moved to divide society and alter communities. This transition brought with it the erosion of traditional institutional structures and social values. Because the change was gradual, it went almost unnoticed until it had become well advanced.[1]

The New England clergy, always sensitive to social change, noticed the trend earlier than most. Blaming it somewhat too simply on the post-Revolutionary religious declension, they sought to arrest any further decline. Looking back on the problem in 1812 Lyman Beecher observed: "The progress of declension is also so gradual, as to attract from day to day but little notice, or excite but little alarm. Now this slow, but certain approximation of the community to destruction, must be made manifest. The whole army of conspirators against law and order, must be brought out and arrayed before the public eye, and the shame, and the bondage, and the wo [sic], which they are preparing for us."[2]

Beecher's attack on "conspirators against law and order" was an ill-disguised assault on those who were abetting the disintegration of the old order. Like Beecher, most clergymen were prone to find decline everywhere. Westward migration propelled by population pressure and declining soil fertility in older sectors, the disruption of commercial activities accompanying the Embargo and war, and increasingly bitter political conflict combined with a decline in religious uniformity, growing clerical impermanency, and the revivals of the Second Great Awakening to challenge traditional assumptions of order, stability, and communal integrity and responsibility.[3] Beset by these challenges, the Congregational clergy sought to recover Christian unity through new measures.[4]

To promote this unity and combat the evils of the age, pastors called on the youth of New England. They recruited young men with energy and commitment from villages, colleges, and theological seminaries. Their design was not solely to retain the hegemony of the Puritan church, but something larger: the preservation of a Christian America.[5] To bolster a sinking institutional structure and to meet the challenge of disestablishment these young crusaders turned to voluntarism and erected new institutional barriers to control the forces of change.

The foreign missionary movement was central to this effort. Generally apart from denominational hostility and removed from domestic political battles over disestablishment, foreign missions became the vehicle for a two-dimensional assault on heathenism. Foreign missionary activity would not only Christianize the heathen overseas, it would also revive and unify the religious at home. Both promoted the brotherhood of man and the Christian mission of American society. Speaking in 1800, the Reverend Nathaniel Emmons underscored the necessity of such action: "This is probably the last peculiar people which he [God] means to form, and the last great empire which he means to erect, before the kingdoms of this world are absorbed in the kingdoms of Christ. And if he intends to bring about these great events, he will undoubtedly make use of human exertions."[6]

Clerical efforts to curb divisiveness and disintegration in American life, however, achieved only partial success. This new commonwealth accommodated itself from the outset to the rampant economic individualism then so prevalent in New England society. It linked piety with prosperity in a prescription for national happiness. Evangelical religion joined with American commerce and domestic prosperity to spread Christian benevolence throughout the world. At the same time it sought to return religion to its original commitment to society and people: to the saving of souls.

Foreign mission societies attempted to transcend domestic religious division and political factiousness. Developing during the second decade of the nineteenth century, an extensive network of these societies permeated New England by 1820. They received their direction from the American Board of Commissioners for Foreign Missions (ABCFM) in Boston and carried its message across the region. A vast propaganda machine, aided by hundreds of agents and other warriors for the Messiah, gathered support for foreign missions. With a successful mission established in the Sandwich Islands by the mid-1820s, the ABCFM reached financial stability. By 1830 it achieved permanence—a point of stability in an era of change. The new institutional structure, however, rode the crest of change. It neither curbed nor consolidated it.

To historians of this enterprise, missionary activities have acquired an aura of glamor and romance. Missionaries appear as saints in their own time. Using the organization of the Sandwich Islands Mission as a case analysis, this study seeks to move beyond adoration and examine both the missionaries and the societies that supported them.

The Sandwich Islands Mission illustrated the objectives of this crusade, as missionaries attempted to implant New England culture and the Christian religion. Here, as elsewhere, social reform followed the advent of missionary activity, for Christianization meant not only attachment to a new religion but also reformation of fundamental social principles. For this the missionaries were criticized and condemned, but theirs was a dynamic Calvinism. They sought to transform and save and did not introduce change merely to enhance personal reputations and influence. Unless their efforts are interpreted with a sensitivity to their own world and their perceptions of it, one cannot understand their objectives and motivation. At the Sandwich Islands in particular, the early mission activities should not bear the charges of narrow self-interest and sectarianism that were more correctly applied to subsequent arrivals. Similar caveats might well be issued for reform movements elsewhere.[7]

1. THE SEARCH FOR IDENTITY

At the beginning of the nineteenth century the Second Great Awakening burst forth in New England. This Awakening affected all denominations, but was especially crucial for Trinitarian-Congregationalists. No longer complacent or secure about their influence on society and determined to preserve a Christian commonwealth, they sought to enlist new supporters and generate new interest in religion. The revivals provided the impetus for an effort to give new direction to social and communal values.

Revolution and its aftermath had stunted Congregational church growth, and the religious revivals were in part a response to shifts in the power and structure of community life since the Revolution. During the 1790s only fifteen new Congregational churches were founded throughout Massachusetts, the lowest total for any decade in the eighteenth century.[1] Something was needed to reverse this trend. But the Awakening was more than simply a response to specific problems at particular times and places. It marked a renewed concern for the future of Christian society and the religious foundations of the republic. Pastors sought to reinforce those values and found they could do so only through organization of the Christian public.

The Awakening, therefore, represents an American identity crisis. Where was the country headed? What principles would guide its development? The response was not a static one. Revivals emerged as continuing phenomena that persisted for an entire generation. Although they sputtered and flared in spasmodic flourishes, these revivals became so commonplace as to dominate the New England consciousness during the first three decades of the nineteenth century.[2] During these years Americans pounced on oratory as the lifeblood of their existence, devouring it in orgies of indulgence. They were, therefore, openly susceptible to the new appeals. The hammerlike attacks of the Congregational clergy energized the churches and moved parishioners to secure their religion.[3]

Confronted by a growing opposition and convinced that prolonged disregard of changes in New England life courted disaster, the Congregational clergy struck out at these problems. Their attack was more than a religious reaction; it was a search for new principles of action and new structures that might supply some solid foundation. This organizational response had been germinating for more than two decades, but deepened and spread with the revivals it sought to harness. Cause-and-effect relationships were at best indirect, for perceptions and reactions knew the limits of neither time nor place. At the same time, ideas did not direct nor events control the Awakening. The interplay between the two produced the excitement.[4]

Noah Worcester sounded the first alarm for the Standing Order. Aroused at Baptist successes throughout New England, Worcester issued a call in 1794 for a revival of religion among Congregational churches in the region. He decried the "great coldness of ministers and private professors, of our denomination" and urged Congregationalists to show more zeal in religious matters. Baptist ministers, he noted, demonstrated a concern for their listeners. This accounted for the progress of the denomination.[5] Never an ardent admirer of the Baptists, Worcester nonetheless recognized the effectiveness of their methods. A zealous pastor, he argued, could carry his congregation by the force of his arguments alone. Whether or not the audience understood the reasoning behind the arguments made little difference, so long as its attachment to religion was strengthened. Worcester freely admitted who should be the directing force in the revival.

A great part of hearers, in all societies, are of such low understandings, that they are incapable of duly examining the force of arguments; and may be confounded by the length or multiplicity of them, while no real conviction is afforded to their minds. And when a preacher, by his zeal and address, has gained the affections of his hearers, so far, that they esteem him to be a pious man, and one who is really seeking their good, they are, in a great measure, prepared to give credit to what he says, whether they can see the propriety of it or not. And if the teacher labors abundantly, to prove a doubtful point, he will overpower their minds, and prevail upon them to believe he is right, before they understand his arguments.[6]

Worcester found reason for this manipulation in the preservation of the Standing Order and was not reticent in defining the leadership responsibilities of the elite. Pastors should use revivals to stem Baptist incursions throughout New England. Such measures would provide a defensive mechanism against competitors as well as furnish a weapon to advance the Congregational cause. They were both a symptom of change and the vehicle for directing this change. During revivals, Worcester instructed his colleagues, "the minds of people are generally very tender; and they are easily led into the sentiments of such as appear zealous for their own good."[7] Without fully admitting all the Standing Order's problems, Worcester cautioned against divisions in religious societies and open dissatisfaction with settled ministers. Both aided the Baptists. Few readers, moreover, missed the implications of his remarks. Included was the recommendation that Congregationalists should shed their complacency and actively recruit new members.

A regularly settled pastor was the focal point of any community's reawakening. In 1812 Lyman Beecher observed "that settled pastors with a systematic itineration would be able to embrace all the benefits of stability with all the benefits of missionary zeal and enterprise."[8] Beecher was issuing a formula for future activity and drawing on the experience of the previous decade. Local churches sought out able ministers, who, through preaching and increasing church membership, became the instigators of the new revival impulse. An increase in church rolls lay at the heart of the Awakening's purpose, for such an increase would surely signify the continued popular influence of religion and the clergy. To get these men, however, churches had to recruit settled pastors. This stripped another church of a settled minister. Stopping the tide in one place meant opening a breach in another. Until the number of trained and able clergy was sufficient to fill every pulpit, this unfortunate process agitated Congregational ranks. The dilemmas involved are reflected in the appeal from the congregation in Harvard, Massachusetts, asking for the release of the Reverend William Emerson in 1799: "The Alarming attacks that are made on our holy religion, by the Learned, the Witty and the Wicked, especially in populous and Sea Port Towns, calls aloud on professing Christians to invite and support in places of the most eminence, such Spiritual Workmen, as are endowed with Talents to convince or confound the Wicked by their arguments and to allure them by their Amiable Behaviour; *such a person will do good anywhere.*"[9]

The clergy labored to produce revivals, but many congregations sat in utter indifference. Men who were opportunistic in commerce and business remained indifferent to religious appeals. They were, one critic argued, "as much *at ease*, as though they *knew* the gospel to be *a fable*."[10] This apparant lack of concern for religion and piety persisted throughout the region. William Tudor encountered one proper lady in Boston who took a pew "because it was a nice, cool place, to carry the children."[11] In many towns parishioners raised protests in a losing battle against the heating of churches, apparently fearful that any accommodation to comfort would dilute the message.[12]

This left most ministers only one choice: increase the tempo and volume of their sermons and tighten the tone of their deliverance. Pastors hoped that such measures might trigger a revival. It was, after all, what they were being paid for, and there were a few hopeful signs. New Englanders liked direction from the pulpit, even though they might later ignore it. "The good farmers around here, some of whom would like to serve Mammon comfortably, are rather in a quandary what to do. They never would bear the constant hounding which he [the minister] gives them . . . and the merciless manner in which he breaks in upon their comfortable old habit of sleeping in meeting, were it not that they feel that they are paying him an enormous salary, and ought to get their money's worth out of him. . . . Your Yankee has such a sense of values, that, if he pays a man to thrash him, he wants to be thrashed thoroughly."[13]

Revivals appeared in large numbers throughout New England in 1799 and substantially increased each year thereafter. Social tensions both produced revivals and found release in them. Pastors welcomed the awakenings and labored to prolong them. The revival of February 1799 in Farmington, Connecticut, was characteristic. The Reverend Josiah Washburn reported that it "began in an uncommon attention and concern among the people of God, in view of the situation of this society, and a disposition to unite in prayer for the divine presence, and a revival of religion."[14] Other revivals stemmed from similar convictions. Each awakening followed turbulent social change and a long-standing lack of concern for religion. This change was especially disruptive at the town and village level, at the very place that the revivals originated. Coming together in weekly prayer meetings and on the Sabbath, men and women sought to reestablish stability and recapture a sense of purpose. The clergy encouraged them.[15]

Pastors everywhere pursued their task with verve and dedication. The forces of religion lost their timidity and took up new discipline.

They did battle with the forces of the antichrist, and their advances gradually became less spasmodic. But the new commitment was still rather one-sided. People remained most susceptible to the Awakening when they had little else to do. In 1808 Edward Payson wrote that "the embargo has put a stop to every thing like business, and people have now nothing to do but attend to religion." Payson quickly took advantage of this forced respite from business and noted that "we endeavor to give them meetings enough, since they have leisure to attend them."[16] Two months later he again addressed the problem and announced that, health permitting, he would try to "multiply meetings, and take up as much of their time as possible in that way." Only this could preserve the people's morals, their "habits of industry and sobriety," and save them from mischief.[17]

In his effort to demonstrate the new opportunities for religious awakenings, Payson also illustrated some of the problems ministers faced. Men generally were too involved in business to devote much time or thought to religion. This left women and children as the most available targets for ministerial labors. But by the nineteenth century Congregational pastors had very little contact with young people in their parishes. This was, according to one observer, largely their own fault. Ministers did not actively seek youthful worshipers for their churches, preferring to concentrate on men of property. As a result large numbers of young converts drifted into Baptist ranks. During the Second Great Awakening Congregational pastors attempted to reverse this trend, but in many areas the effort came too late.[18]

The clergy's attempts to promote revivals were most successful during the winter months, when few worldly diversions competed, and a heated meetinghouse was always attractive. This coincidence led the editor of the *Religious Inquirer* to conclude that there "are strong reasons for believing that gloominess and leisure have some considerable influence in producing revivals." Ecclesiastical notices of new awakenings substantiated this evaluation.[19] Critics of the revivals also pointed out this coincidence and attacked ministerial claims of spontaneity. It "might well lead them," jabbed one critic, "to hesitate about referring all to that divine power, whose accesses they would scarcely dare to measure, by the declination of the sun."[20]

No orderly procession of revivals marked the Second Great Awakening throughout New England. Instead the outbursts appeared at varying intervals in different places. Addison County, Vermont, typified this experience, as residents witnessed these awakenings during each of the first three decades of the nineteenth century. Every new release of tensions increased the size of congregations, but pastors encountered difficulty perpetuating these gains. As each new revival brought additional converts into the church, it also reduced the pool of available persons for future conversions.[21] Ministers tried to carry the pietistic spirit from town to town through visitations and occasional travels, but most Congregational clergymen were formally settled in a particular town or church. Congregationalists generally frowned on itineracy, moreover, believing that it contributed to instability.

Local pastors, nonetheless, eagerly welcomed each new revival and worked to reap some permanent advantages from it. Upon sensing even the slightest religious interest, and carefully avoiding intemperate zeal, ministers encouraged the new spirit. They delivered public lectures or held prayer meetings almost every week night after dinner. The arrival of a new pastor, or perhaps a man the stature of a Lyman Beecher, often inspired a new outbreak of religious activity. Ministers traveling to a new pastorate preached in towns along their route. Each of these devices proved successful enough to repeat; and one or another could be found in most New England communities by the second decade of the nineteenth century. In 1812 Lyman Beecher surveyed all Connecticut and encouraged his fellow laborers. "We are," he wrote, "rather looking up with hope than desponding."[22]

The most fruitful innovation for Congregational clergymen was perhaps the simplest. As early as 1794 Noah Worcester had noted the Baptist practice of widely publicizing their progress and implied that Congregationalists should do the same. In 1800 the denomination established the *Connecticut Evangelical Magazine*, in an attempt to reach the public. This proved to be only the beginning of the move to publicity.[23] By 1816 most journals carried at least some religious news, and a few publications, like the *Boston Recorder*, were entirely devoted to the subject. Both journals and reporters were unflinchingly optimistic about the future of their cause. The *Religious Intelligencer* reported in 1816 that during the previous year more people had been added to the church than during any similar length of time since the Great Awakening in 1740. The paper rhapsodized that "sinners are flying to Christ as clouds, and as doves to their windows." The Congregational church in New England appeared to embrace more people than ever before. Future growth seemed limitless.[24]

One problem remained and agitated the Congregational leadership throughout the Second Great Awakening. This was the debate over the proper conduct of a revival and the measures to be used in exciting an awakening. Congregationalists opposed itineration as a steady practice. Their most famous itinerant, Asahel Nettleton, they found acceptable for reasons peculiar to his preaching. A rarity in Congregational ranks, Nettleton used his evangelistic labors to supplement, and sometimes direct, local religious awakenings. In all his efforts Nettleton's reputation for strict decorum remained impeccable. He never adopted the "anxious seat," the practice of segregating confessors in separate seats. Nor did he encourage "promiscuous assemblies" of females, loud "praying and exhorting," or hold meetings "to a late hour in the night." In short, he pursued the conventional, cautious approach, but without benefit of settlement. And he was successful.

Nettleton also displayed the traditional New England reserve and discretion in refusing to take advantage of youthful zealots merely to augment his list of conversions. He did not, noted his earliest biographer, "allow himself to denounce ministers and professors of religion, as cold and dead, and as the enemies of revivals." Such steps would only promote "fanaticism and delusion." Enthusiasm could only cause disorder. In his labors Nettleton did not seek to divide churches nor to sever relations between pastor and congregation. He believed instead that the power of preaching plain Calvinistic doctrines would stimulate religious concern and heal divisions. The standard of orthodoxy could not have been placed in safer hands.[25]

Congregationalists accepted Asahel Nettleton because he did not excite wild enthusiasm or pursue sinners individually. One could attend worship and still retain a comfortable public anonymity when the itinerant chastised backsliding and made general appeals for a new religious commitment. Since Nettleton supplemented, but did not replace, settled pastors, he did not seem to carry the evils of disorder with him. Congregationalists had long criticized Baptist preachers for their constant itineration, lack of a settled clergy, and poor education. They were an unsettling influence, and Congregational pastors were deeply concerned about order and stability. Baptist methods, moreover, appealed to the poorly educated, and Congregational ministers preferred to mingle with the educated. Here was part of their problem, for as Baptist and Methodist ranks swelled, Congregational clergymen found their constituency further circumscribed.

The issue of itineracy became even more troublesome by the 1820s. Although the Congregational clergy had been forced to tolerate Baptist revivals for several decades, in the 1820s a more disturbing problem confronted them. Still aligned with the Presbyterians in the Plan of Union, Congregationalists reacted with dismay to the appearance of Charles Grandison Finney in upstate New York. Finney's energetic outbursts horrified staid New England clergymen and kindled a lively debate over the proper conduct of revivals. To Congregationalists, the "new measures," as they were called, smacked of demagoguery. Pastors attacked Finney's practice of praying for individual sinners by name and looked askance at his bold and denunciatory preaching. Traditional community decorum decreed that sins remained speculative rumors in the local gossip mill, unfit for public airing.[26]

In 1827 these two paths collided. Asahel Nettleton and Lyman Beecher collaborated to write a series of letters warning their colleagues against the new measures of Finney. These letters were published the following year in a pamphlet entitled *Letters of the Reverend Dr. Beecher and Reverend Mr. Nettleton on the "New Measures" in Conducting Revivals of Religion*.[27] This unleashed a debate within the ministerial community. Religious men, the two Congregationalists argued, "delight in universal order." "To be the enemy of order," they concluded, "is to be the enemy of God." No statement issued from any pulpit or pen more succinctly summarized the orthodox position. Measures that sought to promote religion either through disorder or through enthusiasm only frustrated true religion and subverted godliness.[28]

Both Beecher and Nettleton voiced several specific objections to Finney's style and practice. Finney's age was undoubtedly part of the problem. Nettleton, who had been on the revival circuit for years, complained about this in a letter to a friend in Utica, New York. Too much confidence, he insisted, had been placed in the activities of young ministers. The result was that people "dared not attempt to correct any of their irregularities, for fear of doing mischief, or of being denounced as enemies to revivals." At this time Finney had been in the ministry only three years. Surely he had no conception of what he was doing to the profession. "I have no doubt," wrote Nettleton, "that he begins with astonishment to look at the evils which are running before him."[29]

The problem was obvious. Finney had not consulted with the older, more experienced members of the profession. He had allowed his recent conversion to lead him astray. In a sincere attempt to advance the cause of religion, he had gone too far, too fast. The consequences were tragically similar to the outbursts of enthusism that had occurred at the time of Whitefield and Edwards, and the outcome could only be another disastrous division in the churches and ministry of New England. Finney's denunciations of settled ministers, therefore, were inimical to the revival of a sense of community and fellowship. Churches would divide, with some members rallying to their pastor's defense and others following the lead of the itinerants. Whatever else emerged from this conflict, Nettleton feared that all confidence in a settled ministry would disappear.[30]

Lyman Beecher reiterated the stern fatherly advice of Asahel Nettleton. The new measures, he wrote to a fellow pastor, undoubtedly contained some good. Unfortunately they breathed an alien spirit into revivals. Surely, he added, those "who countenance these measures" must not be aware of this. What was this alien spirit? It was a spirit of "fanaticism, of spiritual pride, censoriousness, and insubordination to the order of the Gospel." Such hubris or delusion must be corrected promptly, for "it threatens to become one of the greatest evils which is likely to befall the cause of Christ."[31]

Finney might be unaware of the consequences of his methods, but both critics agreed that their warnings merited a prompt response. If none was forthcoming, then a continuation of these techniques must signify an attempt to undermine ministerial authority. No longer could Finney's preaching be written off as the innocent efforts of a young upstart, for if he persisted he would seriously damage the cause of Christ. What was needed was an increase in solemn religious dedication, not severe enthusism. "I have not found naked terror to do much execution," warned Beecher, "either as the means of awakening men, or producing submission."[32]

Professional debate over the efficacy of revival techniques was not new, but the Finney outburst in the late 1820s brought it to a head. Critics attacked the new revivalism, although frequently their criticism extended to all religious awakenings. Orville Dewey expressed doubts about the validity of these awakenings, arguing that revivals required no thought and that their promoters were generally men of little talent and reflection. Dewey's pompous snobbery explains some of his objections, for emotional appeals to the common folk disturbed him. It was unfortunate, he wrote, but "the most ordinary person in these scenes may rise to the highest consequences."[33]

The Reverend Edward Payson, a prominent member of the orthodoxy, complained that revivals too often unleashed "merely animal feelings" which rarely made lasting contributions to religion.[34] The Reverend Joel Hawes criticized pastors who used flamboyant style and produced excitement through "brilliant images and well-turned periods." In one of his more popular sermons Hawes concluded that this gave the impression that "he is more anxious to show himself than his Master."[35] But perhaps the most succinct critical observation came from a Quaker, who in 1823 confided to his diary, "It is to be hoped some good will result from them [revivals], but the contrary is much feared."[36] Congregationalists continued to express concern over technique, but not about the revivals themselves.

What significance did the Awakening have for the Standing Order? Revivals refreshed a people bewildered by change and tried to breathe meaning into what seemed an inexorable process. Amid economic, political, and religious diversity Congregational Christianity fought to retain its meaning. All sects benefited from the revivals; and all sects struggled for the attention of the people.[37] The revivals were the first phase of an effort to recast the nature and meaning of religion in New England. But gains were transitory at best. Something much more permanent, and less controversial, was needed. For despite Congregational efforts to close ranks around the new awakenings, factiousness within the denomination persisted. William Bentley, the contentious Unitarian from Salem, demonstrated how deep the division was when he lashed out in 1810 at two leading Trinitarians—Samuel Spring and Samuel Worcester. "Neither of the men," he charged, "are sufficiently acquainted with the subject [the Trinity] to deserve particular attention."[38] There seemed to be no immediate remedy for this division, and Trinitarian-Congregationalists turned to organizational efforts in an attempt to maintain their influence and encourage order and piety.

Lyman Beecher promptly announced that ministers should be "watchmen set upon the walls of Zion to decry and announce the approach of danger."[39] The clergy took heed. At the same time they hastened to establish institutional bulwarks to prevent further division. This organizational phase of the Second Great Awakening had a number of objectives. It sought to solidify and make permanent the recent increases in church membership. If something was not done to maintain the new interest in religious activity, the Awakening would be but a transitory phenomenon.

Another problem was the need for stability. Related to the issue of permanency, this entailed the ordering of religious activity through specific structures with clearly defined purposes. These structures were to harness change and tone down, if not eliminate, factionalism and competition among all Christians. That this order would be imposed from the top is undeniable, but the new organizations would also demand broad popular involvement at the local level. The best men might direct the effort, but its success depended on mass participation. Lyman Beecher indicated the direction of this process: "The revival . . . is probably, for the time, nearly concluded. There are one or two districts where I shall make an effort, and then the whole ground will have been gone over, and will probably yield no more fruit at present; so I shall soon organize a Bible class, and endeavor to make the most of what we have gained, and to prepare the way for another onset as soon as new materials shall rise up, which will not be long. . . . After one battle and victory, it remains to clear the decks and prepare for another."[40]

One final obstacle remained. The Unitarian capture of Harvard in 1805 spurred Trinitarian-Congregationalists to additional efforts to offset this influence. In the process of these labors they established their own institution for training members of the profession. A familiar pattern developed. Institutions replaced revivals as the method to preserve republican virtues and religious principles.[41]

The job of organization was a perpetual one. Lyman Beecher's sermon in 1803 on *The Practicability of Suppressing Vice, by Means of Societies Instituted for that Purpose* set forth the method to be adopted. He described organizations and societies then at work in England and the United States and stressed the need for improvements in Connecticut's efforts toward that goal. Fifteen years later Jeremiah Evarts, editor of the *Panoplist*, complained that the country still needed new institutions to shore up old values. "The tendency of the American character," Evarts noted, "is then to degenerate rapidly; and that not from any particular vice in the American people, but from the very nature of a spreading population."[42] The clergy's organizational reflex sought to provide an element of permanency amid the welter of change. It hoped to save the old social principles and rebuild a Christian commonwealth. "New England can retain her permanence," Lyman

Beecher argued, "only by upholding those institutions and habits which produced it. Divested of these, like Samson shorn of his locks, she will become as weak and contemptible as any other land."[43]

Of necessity, the preservation of orthodoxy came first. Unitarian advances threatened the viability of the revival effort. Several decades later Joseph Clark, secretary of the Congregational Library Association, recalled that "Like an electric shock on torpid nerves" the Unitarian controversy "energized the whole body of evangelical Christians. It awoke a spirit of religious enterprise which, if it could not restore lost endowments to their intended and original use, could found others on a broader and safer basis."[44] Despite their theological differences, the Edwardian and Hopkinsian schools united in the face of the Unitarian challenge and moved quickly to repulse the threat from within Congregational ranks.

This union evolved in three areas of religious activity. In 1805 the two schools merged their separate monthly publications: the *Massachusetts Missionary Magazine* (Hopkinsian) and the *Panoplist* (Edwardian). Both groups also united in a General Association. These changes represented a determined effort to halt the encroachments of Unitarianism, which by this time had captured Boston and Harvard College. Formation of a professional organization, moreover, indicated a determination to preserve doctrinal standards among future ministerial appointees. Then in 1807 Trinitarians set out to save Boston and began a project to establish Park Street Church. When the cornerstone was laid in May 1809, Trinitarians once again had an outpost in New England's major city. They also turned to offset Unitarian control of Harvard.[45]

From the moment of Henry Ware's election to the Hollis Professorship at Harvard, Trinitarian-Congregationalists discussed the plausibility of founding their own theological seminary. Dr. Jedidiah Morse led the early planning. In December 1805 he wrote his friend Ashbel Green that "these events may probably be the means of founding a new Literary and Theological Institution, on principles and for purposes similar to those for which Harvard College was founded. A phoenix may arise out of the ashes of this ancient Seminary."[46] But the fires of controversy that raged at Harvard excited more than hopes for resurrections from its ashes. The rising Unitarian influence demanded action. If the principles of orthodoxy were to survive, new pastors must be trained in them. Since this would no longer be done at Harvard, it must be carried out elsewhere.

The Reverend Leonard Woods proposed the most comprehensive outline for the new institution. In October 1806 he advised Morse to establish a seminary that would appeal to *"all evangelical men*," Hopkinsian as well as Edwardian. A union between the two should be promulgated on general principles. Woods urged Morse to write Nathaniel Emmons and "press the idea of *union* in the General Association and in the Theological School." A more urgent appeal was made to John Norris, benefactor of Congregationalism in Massachusetts. Trinitarians emphasized that *"our Calvinistic churches throughout New England, and even through the United States, greatly need a pious and orthodox Seminary to supply them with learned and faithful Pastors."*[47]

The General Association of Connecticut expressed a similar concern, warning that towns should not hire unqualified candidates. In an address on the subject in 1808, the General Association recommended that no association in the state license a candidate for the ministry unless absolutely sure of his qualifications. It fervently urged destitute churches to avoid hasty decisions in settling pastors. "We think that experience has shown," it warned, "that the employment of a great number of probationers, tends to confuse and divide a church and people."[48] The profession suffered enough from division and impermanency.

While some ministers exchanged private suggestions, others set out to solicit public support. At the recommendation of Jedidiah Morse, Leonard Woods wrote a series of articles for the *Panoplist*. In successive issues from June 1806 to June 1808, Woods argued that the prevailing state of ecclesiastical affairs in New England called for the establishment of a theological seminary. Such a seminary was essential to insure that future generations would benefit from an uncorrupted Christianity.[49] Public discussion soon led to offers of financial support. Four men underwrote much of the early funding. Samuel Abbott, a wealthy Boston merchant then living in retirement in Andover was the seminary's landed benefactor. Moses Brown, a Newburyport merchant worth over $270,000, donated $10,000. A fellow Newburyporter, William Bartlet, bequeathed $20,000. Bartlet, like Brown, had amassed a fortune in the neutral trade during the Napoleonic Wars. In 1807 his wealth exceeded $500,000. John Norris, Salem merchant and state senator, contributed an additional $10,000.[50] The new bastion of orthodoxy undeniably retained the old links with wealth and conservatism.

Andover Theological Seminary opened September 28, 1808. Since it was to be a bulwark against Unitarianism, its constitution rigorously prescribed the criteria for membership. Every professor was to have a college degree and be a member in communion with some Congregational or Presbyterian church. He should also be "a man of sound and orthodox principles in Divinity." The Andover Creed was to serve as a guarantee against heterodoxy, and all the faculty had to sign the creed every five years.[51] The Reverend Leonard Woods, a strict Calvinist, assumed the crucial position of Abbott Professor of Divinity. In an effort to attract "poor and pious youth," the seminary offered free tuition, room, board, and books. Although these students might be more appreciative of an education than sons of the upper class, little thought was apparently given to the possibility that this recruitment would radically alter the class composition of the clergy. Perhaps plebeian blood could be transfused with patrician habits. In the face of student riots at some colleges, deference and malleability had their merits.[52]

The Unitarians criticized the seminary. As usual, William Bentley crystallized Unitarian arguments and added his own fillip of sarcasm. For two years following the opening of the seminary Bentley recorded a series of pointed remarks in his diary. He criticized the financing of the new institution and depicted its supporters as vultures hovering over the deathbeds of potential donors. Attacking the faculty as "fanatic priests," he expressed fears that "this wicked work will not be fully exposed."[53] The vehemence of his criticism, however, indicates that the Salem pastor recognized the growing importance and influence of Andover Seminary even by 1811. He was not mistaken.

Other observers also saw its usefulness. While traveling through the region in 1819 William Tudor remarked that the institution was in a "flourishing state" and was proving an effective counterpart to Harvard. Two years later another British visitor, Adam Hodgson, concurred with this analysis. But perhaps the most significant comment was made only three years after the founding of the seminary. In a letter to the Reverend George Burder, secretary of the London Missionary Society, Samuel Worcester noted that Andover Seminary was "an Institution, which, though young, is fast rising in importance, and in which, both on account of the principles on which it is founded, and the ability and piety with which it is conducted, great confidence is reposed."[54] At the time Worcester was secretary of the fledgling American Board of

Commissioners for Foreign Missions; and these remarks presaged a long and happy union between the two institutions.

With the success of Andover Seminary, the Trinitarian future seemed more secure than it had for several years. The new institution would train pastors in orthodox principles, and these men would preach in pulpits across the country. Trinitarian leaders turned elsewhere in search of greater religious unity and public commitment.

At the first signs of awakening in 1797, Connecticut pastors had formed a missionary society to carry the gospel into the wilderness. Two years later Massachusetts established a similar society. This marked the beginning of a vigorous home missionary movement. Home missions aimed at the Christianization of America's western wilderness. They sought to make the West religious, stable, and as much like the old America as possible. In doing so a new sphere for denominational rivalry and hostility developed. Without established churches or state controls on religious activity, western regions witnessed intense competition for converts among all denominations. Methodists and Baptists reaped the greatest harvest, with their willingness to embrace all classes and accept constant diversity. The scattered settlements and mobile population of the western frontier were suited to the wanderings of their itinerant preachers. But home missions united neither the profession nor society.[55]

During the first decade of the nineteenth century, their search for unity turned some members of the profession toward foreign missions. Foreign missions, they argued, could spearhead the effort to recreate a Christian commonwealth. Overseas missionary activity would not involve participants in domestic politics; nor would it irritate the troublesome question of denominational rivalry and disestablishment. Americans would not be forced to suffer the stewardship of their own countrymen—perhaps even their own relatives. Instead they could once again test the universality of republican virtues by applying them to heathen societies in foreign lands. "Nothing is more apparent," a correspondent to the *Christian Spectator* explained several years later, than the need "to enable the Christian public, to act with due discretion and safety, and yet perform the full amount of their duty."[56]

The remedy was to conduct "an extensive scheme of operations." This technique found early acceptance and by 1809 Boston alone could boast more than thirty benevolent and charitable societies. Here was an effort to stabilize society through new structures grafted onto the old church. Such measures tried to preserve traditional religious influences, while at the same time broaden their appeal. Laymen as well as clergy participated in the new design and set out to construct devices that would preserve orthodoxy at home as well as spread Christianity abroad.

The American Board of Commissioners for Foreign Missions became the vehicle for this evangelism. Founded in 1810 and incorporated two years later, the American Board represented a new phase of organizing activity. It sought to join clergy and public in a religious crusade of global proportions. At the same time, leaders of the effort hoped that foreign missions would preserve the spirit of the Second Great Awakening at home, but remove competition and divisiveness. Trinitarian-Congregationalists now looked to their strength. They used their vast numbers of middle- and upper-class parishioners to fund operations, and allowed anyone who could donate even the slightest sum to participate in the venture. In this way they hoped to construct a new Christian commonwealth and avoid domestic controversy.[57]

The foreign missionary enterprise in the United States did not develop entirely from indigenous sources. There had been missions to the Indians during the seventeenth and eighteenth centuries, but the major stimulus for foreign missions came from Great Britain. Stories of British missionary adventures in India had captivated American readers for more than a decade before the organization of the ABCFM. As early as 1797 printed sermons of the London Missionary Society appeared in this country. New Englanders also eagerly read reprints of William Carey's letters from India in religious journals or newspapers.[58]

But Melville Horne's *Letters on Missions* exerted the greatest influence of any British publication. Horne, a former chaplain to the British colony at Sierra Leone, addressed these letters to the Protestant clergy of the British churches, but they found an eager audience in the United States as well. Reprinted in America, the letters argued that foreign missions would revitalize religion at home and abroad. Horne predicted, "The spirit of our religion, lulled to lethargic slumbers, will revive with the energies of the apostolic age; and the Church will again become illustrious, by her victory over the kingdoms of this world."[59] According to Horne, man was the same everywhere in the world. Given this supposition, it was both easy and natural to insist that since New Englanders suffered ills and vices when deprived of Christianity, the moral condition of those who had never been exposed to its principles must be truly dreadful. Challenges surrounded the concerned Christian, from Islam in the East to Roman Catholicism in the West. Horne urged an attack. "The God of Christians is baring his arm," he cried, "and exposing the nakedness of the Scarlet Whore with whom the nations of the earth have committed spiritual fornication."[60]

A growing array of religious periodicals addressed themselves to this question, and by the close of the century's first decade the *Panoplist* emerged the leading spokesman for foreign missions. Begun in 1805 by Jedidiah Morse amid specters of Henry Ware and an advancing Unitarianism, it led the effort to promote religious orthodoxy throughout New England. In 1808 it joined forces with Hopkinsians and became the *Panoplist and Missionary Magazine*. After still another name change, in 1820 it became the *Missionary Herald*, house organ of the American Board.[61] Throughout its early years, when many persons remained unconvinced of the need for foreign missions, editors and contributors repeatedly reminded readers that efforts abroad would aid those at home. Their publication of letters, anecdotes, and tragedies from foreign lands provided New Englanders with reading obtainable nowhere else. This propagandizing of foreign missions helped lead to the creation of the American Board of Commissioners for Foreign Missions (ABCFM) in 1810.[62]

The founding of the American Board culminated several years of organizing activity. Soon after the turn of the century officers of the Massachusetts Missionary Society had initiated correspondence with their counterparts in the London Missionary Society (LMS). In 1805 trustees of the Massachusetts society made the president of the LMS an honorary member of their association. From these beginnings a lengthy exchange developed.[63] The overseas example, combined with religious developments in New England, inspired a new concern for the unevangelized.

Andover Theological Seminary became the focal point for this early interest in foreign missions, as students at the seminary organized societies to promote the new endeavor. In 1808 Samuel J. Mills, Jr., son of a Connecticut clergyman, formed the Society of Brethren at Williams College. When Mills left Williams and entered Andover Seminary, he took his society with him and renamed it the Society of Inquiry on the Subject of Missions.[64] This was a secret society for missionary inquiry, and members transcribed their journal in secret code. Officers carefully screened prospective initiates, and section five of the Brethren Society's constitution required that all "information shall be acquired of the character and situation of a candidate which is practicable." Only committed evangelicals were admitted, since the society's purpose was to promote missions to the heathen.[65]

At Andover, Mills kept the society directed toward the promotion of foreign missions. In 1809 he wrote Gordon Hall, then a student at the seminary, "We ought not to look merely at the heathen on our own continent, but to direct our attention where we may, to human appearance, do the most good, and where the difficulties are the least."[66] The Society of Inquiry retained the principles of the Brethren, and its constitution proclaimed that support of foreign missions was the God-given duty of all members. Only then could they promote the "glory of our Redeemer and the eternal happiness of our fellow man." The society was to investigate "the state of the Heathen; the duty and importance of missionary labors, the best manner of conducting missions, and the most eligible place for their establishment."[67]

Notice of the society's organization and purpose reached the public through the pages of the *Panoplist*. This disclosure did not cause much immediate public interest, but began the flow of propaganda toward this end. Organization of the Andover society also led to the formation of similar societies at other seminaries, beginning with the establishment of one at Princeton Theological Seminary in 1814.[68] The most immediate result was to excite and inform their fellow seminarians about the possibilities of foreign missions. Along with the Society of Brethren, it represents the earliest effort to institutionalize the energies of the Second Great Awakening and carry them abroad.

In 1810 several students from the Society of Inquiry petitioned the General Association of Massachusetts to create an organization devoted to foreign missions. Four students led this effort: Adoniram Judson, Samuel Nott, Samuel Newell, and Samuel J. Mills, Jr. They acknowledged the difficulty of the proposed venture, but emphasized their commitment to evangelizing the heathen. In a series of questions designed to solicit procedural guidelines as well as to appeal to the pride and conscience of the assembled association, the students asked for advice and guidance. They particularly wanted to know "whether they may expect patronage and support from a missionary society in this country, or must commit themselves to the direction of a European society; and what preparatory measures they ought to take previous to the actual engagement."[69] The young men were determined to become foreign missionaries, even if it meant working under British auspices.

The assembled clergy quickly accepted the students' petition and approved their request. With the many problems that confronted ministers at this time, the General Association seized on any idea that held out a glimmer of success. Although there was no reason to expect any startling conquests, all remained optimistic. Preparations began immediately for the creation of the American Board of Commissioners for Foreign Missions, and the organizers issued appeals for public support. A deathbed bequest of $30,000 from Mrs. John Norris of Salem, Massachusetts, gave the undertaking financial stability from the outset, although litigation over her will tied up some of the money for more than a year. Throughout 1810 and 1811 the board struggled unsuccessfully for incorporation, for only when it became incorporated could it freely receive all donations. At the same time it tried to awaken public interest in evangelizing the heathen. In an address to the public in 1811 the founders argued that the new venture signaled the approach of the millennium. "The Lord is shaking the nations," they wrote, "and unprecedented exertions are making for the spread of divine knowledge, and the conversion of the nations." People are now "ready to go into any parts of the unevangelized world."[70]

Before sending out its own missionaries the ABCFM sought cooperation and advice from the London Missionary Society. In a series of letters to George Burder, his counterpart in the LMS, Samuel Worcester explained why Americans were entering the foreign mission field. Admitting that "millions of men" on the North American continent were still without the Christian religion, Worcester outlined the rationale for seeming to abandon them: "The attempts which have been made to evangelize the aboriginal tribes of the North American wilderness, have been attended with so many discouragements, and South America is yet in so unpromising a state, that the opinion very generally prevalent is, that for the Pagans on this continent but little can immediately be done."[71]

Throughout the year Worcester and Burder carried on an active correspondence, and the American Board tried to work through the LMS to send missionaries to Asia. In September 1811 Adoniram Judson went to England to visit the London society. He hoped to become acquainted with its methods of missionary operation preparatory to his own departure for Asia the next year and to convey this information to the board's officers in Boston. Samuel Worcester also asked him to

obtain information on a number of other topics, especially preparations, methods, and fields for missions. On his return Judson delivered
his findings in writing to the ABCFM. He also reported that he had
obtained LMS support for a mission to the East. At this point the
ABCFM assumed the initiative and decreased its dependence on Great
Britain.[72]

The last obstacle for the American Board prior to achieving full
operational powers was to become incorporated under Massachusetts
statute, since its headquarters were in Boston. Litigation for control of
the Norris legacy prompted the effort for incorporation, and in February 1812 representatives of the board applied to the legislature for a
charter. William Bentley, the irascible old Salem Unitarian, summarized
opposition complaints when he noted, "Religious frenzy needs only the
civil patronage to render it as active as it ever was in this or any other
country."[73] After strong opposition from several quarters the legislature approved the request four months later.[74] The charter granted the
right to receive bequests and estates, thereby removing the final barrier
to the board's immediate financial solvency. Under the direction of its
Prudential Committee the American Board could now manage its own
affairs as a legal corporate entity.[75]

In the years following the board's incorporation, the Congregational
clergy of New England labored diligently to enlist public support for
foreign missions. Like their ancestors, leaders of the new enterprise had
discovered a new wilderness to revitalize their religion. By transplanting
American ideas and institutions in "uncivilized" regions they hoped to
resolve a long-standing Puritan dilemma between cohesion and dispersal. Older notions of community were fast disappearing, but now the
mechanism to establish a new Christian commonwealth was at hand.
Almost all Americans could unite in the effort to promote "pious,
virtuous, and diligent habits." In the battle against "heathenism" it was
easy to be on the side of "good," for few in early nineteenth-century
America would argue the virtues of paganism.[76]

With this in mind the clergy launched their effort to awaken and
excite the interest of New Englanders in foreign missions. Pastors faced
two related problems in carrying out this task. They had to solicit
public support and then construct an organizational network to give the
venture permanency. Congregationalists set out to solve these problems
with the conviction that they were in the right and must therefore be
successful. A few years later, in 1820, the Reverend Sereno Edwards

Dwight outlined the task of the ministry: "The call of God on this subject is distinct and loud. It bids her train up, and send forth, these heralds of salvation to the nations sitting in darkness and the shadows of death. The Church of America has begun to listen to the call, and is waking up to life and action."[77] The pillars for the new order had been constructed; now the campaigning began.

2.   A PANORAMA OF CHANGE

Why was such a campaign necessary? What had happened to the
economic, social, and religious structure of New England? The Awakening suggested a catalog of ills, and closer examination exposed their
magnitude. During the early decades of the nineteenth century, fundamental shifts occurred in the economic structure of New England.
These transformations disrupted old societal patterns. Traditional ex-
tractive and household industries lost their grip as manufacturing developed.

A variety of problems confronted New England farmers. After
generations of settlement and exploitation the soil presented a major
obstacle to productivity. Even on the best land fertility declined. Crop
production failed to keep step with the increased opportunities for
marketing, and farmers emigrated to more fertile lands in the West.[1]
These changes hastened the isolation of the family farm. The American
farmer, tantalized for a few fleeting years in the 1790s by prospects of
increased markets, now faced uncertainty, often unable to pay the
interest on his debts or support his family.

Coming as it did in the midst of an agricultural revolution that was
sweeping the inland valleys and villages of New England, the war with
Great Britain further disrupted the region's traditional economic pattern. A relatively low standard of living, social stagnation, and a
reluctance to experiment with innovative agricultural techniques were
the legacies of this upheaval. Poverty bred fear: fear of foreclosure and
fear of violence. Debtors trespassed on proprietors, and in one region of
Maine people banded together to prevent execution of the law and
further foreclosures.[2] The movement toward economic self-sufficiency
waned, and the communal atmosphere of the region deteriorated. War
sharpened into focus the farmers' reliance on external sources of goods.
The myth of independence, however, died slowly.[3]

After the War of 1812 the fortunes of New England farmers
fluctuated. Weather, always an unreliable element in the region, refused

to cooperate; 1819 brought heavy spring rains, followed by frosts and snow across the northern tier of states throughout the summer. There were no grain crops, few gardens, and scanty feed for livestock. Sympathetic New Jersey farmers sent wagons filled with swamp hay for the cattle, but New Englanders suffered nonetheless.[4] Food prices reached record highs, and by the spring of 1817 corn had climbed to $2.00 per half bushel in New Hampshire. Prices rose and taxes remained high.[5] One newspaper correspondent complained, "Our farmers are taxed not only for their land, furniture, watches and carriages, but even for their leather, nails and shoes."[6] Natives thereafter referred to 1816 as the famine year. There seemed to be no escape.

The postwar revival of European agriculture and commerce posed yet another threat. British products flooded the American market. Advertisements appeared in eastern newspapers for beef, pork, ham, and wheat, all at prices that undercut the domestic farmer. This aroused a storm of protest. One critic noted that this "was not the case during the federal administration, but such is beginning, and only beginning to be the case, under the present order of things. Blessed treaty!"[7] While some protested, others emigrated. But the transition from war to peace was arduous, especially where it coincided with the move from household to commercial production.

Encouragement of agriculture seemed to advance the hope of a revived economy, especially in the older, settled regions. Lyman Beecher, always attuned to the winds of change, spoke for many New Englanders in his Thanksgiving sermon of December 1819: "Agriculture may be encouraged, by awarding honour to the employment, in accordance with its utility; by associations and premiums for the collection and dissemination of agricultural knowledge, and by the excitement of a spirit of improvement in all kinds of husbandry, or by the improvement of roads, the construction of canals, and the multiplication of the various facilities of inland navigation, and by wise acts of legislation, calculated to secure to the husbandman a steady market and a fair price."[8] So much for self-sufficiency. Beecher's remarks reflect the beliefs of many in the region that change was desirable and, indeed, necessary. Traditional methods were no longer profitable nor attractive. New crops must be introduced and new markets developed. Some farmers did adapt, but others continued to plod along the increasingly well-worn path to poverty. Those who adopted the new ideas turned to the production of hay, which was too bulky for western competition to threaten, or to the production of onions, tobacco, and dairy farming.[9]

The adventurous cultivated more exotic products. In the early 1820s a silk craze swept the Connecticut Valley. This speculative mania aroused a new interest in growing mulberry trees, but passed by the 1830s.[10] Much more important, and of far greater duration, was the speculation in Merino sheep. Advertisements for Merinos appeared in newspapers throughout New England. Hoping that in a few years New England wool would be a major export to compete with the cottons of the South, natives offered larger rewards for the return of wandering Merinos than for runaway blacks. The focal point of the craze was Connecticut, but few areas escaped. Sheep-raising appealed to many whose acreage could no longer tolerate the annual rituals of plowing, planting, and harvesting. The substantial initial investment, however, retarded growth of the industry.[11]

Central to New England's development in the postwar years was the new urge for internal improvements. Here loomed still another threat to the beleaguered farmer, although few perceived it as such. Lyman Beecher's argument that those "who improve the highways of their country, stand high on the list of national benefactors" found ready acceptance.[12] But most of these improvements reached out to the frontier, and only a scattering of the new thoroughfares aided New England farmers. The Middlesex Canal, completed in 1808, demonstrated the danger. Extending from Chelmsford to Charlestown, Massachusetts, it facilitated trade from the Merrimack Valley in New Hampshire to the rapidly expanding urban center and markets of Boston.[13] During the first decade of the nineteenth century, when 135 turnpike corporations gained charters, the future woes of the region became evident. Turnpikes connected the major towns, and travel was easier than ever, but the results were not always encouraging for local inhabitants.[14]

The new facilities opened up eastern markets, and western competition hurt New England farmers. Prices for farm goods fell, and as the new transportation network bypassed and undercut the poor village farmer just off the line it hastened the disintegration of the old rural life-styles. Family farms could not compete with specialized production at lower costs.[15]

By the 1820s agriculture no longer rewarded the majority of New Englanders. With the coming of the turnpike, location had become a crucial determinant of profitability. Travelers observed that few farmed on a large scale. Soil conditions and landholding practices precluded extensive commercialization, except in a few instances such as dairying. The small, semi-self-sufficient homestead could not compete for the new markets. Although prices for farms declined, abandonment was almost as frequent as consolidation.[16]

The rewards of urban life attracted many from the rural farms and villages of the region. Part of this magnetic quality was undoubtedly the presence of higher wages in the city, as well as the opportunity to escape boredom and family. The changing economic structure made rural life less attractive, and the turnpike rendered it less necessary. With the efforts of villagers to improve and work their separate properties, along with the improvement of transportation facilities, village cohesion largely disintegrated.[17] New England was on the move, and social stability waned.

By the early 1830s this decline had turned into a depression. Many farms were heavily mortgaged, and household industries declined in the face of an expanding manufacturing establishment. Spinning and knitting for village consumption became obsolete.[18] Weeds choked the once sylvan glades and rock-strewn fields. Paint peeled on houses in many small villages, and the wind whistled unobstructed through dark caverns that had once been windows from which small children peered. Stone chimneys stood amidst rubble, lonely sentinels against the encroaching wilderness. Man had moved because he could not afford to stay.

Part of the transition from self-sufficient to commercial agriculture was the transfer of the textile industry from farmhouse to factory. Harbingers of a new economic order, many entrepreneurs seized the opportunity. When merchants experienced commercial difficulties they invested their capital in manufacturing. Others, though still nursing a profit from their commercial activities, diversified their holdings and branched out into manufacturing. In the years before Jefferson's embargo, wealth increased rapidly and money became more available. This stimulated domestic industry.[19] Success in these new enterprises encouraged many to envision a new age of prosperity for the New England states. Yet these naive perceptions reflected an unawareness of the impact of industrial capitalism. In his important sermon, *The Means of National Prosperity*, Lyman Beecher observed, "The vital utility of manufactures consists in their subserviency to agriculture, by affording the husbandman a near and steady home market, and by diminishing the competition of exported produce in foreign markets, increasing the demand and the price."[20] The cocoonlike world Beecher envisaged was not to be, and its failure to develop contributed to the turmoil of the New England scene.

The new mill towns revamped the social and economic structure of New England. Occasionally these changes engulfed and revitalized entire towns. Brookfield, Massachusetts, primarily a farming area before 1810, enjoyed such a revival with the introduction of the shoe business. New money flowed into the community, and many inhabitants were able to escape their debts. Danbury, Connecticut, went through a similar transformation with the introduction of the hat industry.[21] Factory construction progressed steadily after 1805, but the real period of growth came during and after the War of 1812. Cotton factories led the boom. In the face of this competition, the New England homespun industry declined rapidly after 1820. By 1830 the end was in sight, as local variety in manufacturing gave way to centralization.

The textile mill debilitated the internal mechanisms of the old rural communities. Linked as it was to the introduction of Merino sheep, the inauguration of the new textile manufacturing hastened the disintegration of New England agriculture. Cloth equal in quality to that produced in England could be woven from the new wool. This encouraged factories to spring up adjacent to wool-producing areas.[22] The woolen industry received an added impetus when passage of the Embargo and Non-Intercourse Acts curbed British cloth imports. Prices of woolens rose at the very moment that the new industry most needed encouragement and protection. It was a convenient coincidence.[23]

Seacoast areas experienced the same social and economic turbulence that afflicted interior communities. The Embargo did more than stimulate the woolen industry; it effected a shift in the economic structure of the New England states. Foreign trade declined dramatically after 1807, especially commerce with the West Indies. The less fortunate merchants never recovered from this loss of trade. A chain of indebtedness appeared, extending from the villager to the corner store to the merchant in the seaport who imported goods on credit. Effects of the Embargo, moreover, were far-reaching and disastrous. By March 1809 some 60 percent of the people in the maritime towns of Maine were unemployed. In Portland the needy queued up at soup kitchens. Estimated losses exceeded one million dollars. Elsewhere along the coast merchants, sailors and mechanics found themselves unemployed. Men talked of the need and possibilities for political change.[24]

Those who were able moved from commerce or agriculture to manufacturing and finance. Rowland Hazard of Rhode Island turned from trade to the manufacture of woolens when the Berlin and Milan Decrees hampered his trading, and the Lee family of Massachusetts contemplated taking the same step.[25] Town assemblies petitioned the Massachusetts legislature for relief. Barter and credit replaced cash in the exchange of merchandise or labor, to the distress of creditors.[26] This setback, unfortunately, came at the very moment that New England was nearing full recovery from the exhaustive revolutionary struggle.

The close of the war with England brought further dislocation and readjustment. Foreign imports forced down American prices, compelling many small factories built during the war to close. Their employees, just beginning to recover from the Embargo, now found themselves out of work. Federalist papers shrieked in alarm at this influx of goods and the severe reductions in income in many port cities. Self-proclaimed prophets, these editors claimed a gift of prophecy for their opposition to the war.[27] But self-righteous justification did not alleviate suffering. Taxes rose, and most businesses and professions staggered under the effects of the peace. Stagnant markets paralyzed trade. Unemployment increased and the future appeared bleak. But, warned one newspaper, "bad as all this is, some intelligent and well-informed men seem to think we have not yet seen the worst of it."[28]

These turbulent economic conditions continued to undermine community cohesiveness. Daniel Henshaw, in a speech before one of the many foreign mission societies in Worcester County, Massachusetts, echoed the sentiments of his fellow New Englanders. Who would have predicted thirty years ago, he commented in 1826, that New England would shortly become a manufacturing country? If someone had ventured such a preposterous notion, "he would have been taken for a lunatic."[29] Timothy Flint, returning to his native region in 1825 after a tour as a missionary in the West, marveled at the changes he encountered. He was not, however, enthusiastic. Children in factories, he warned, "breathe a heated and unnatural air," and "the inhabitants of the great manufacturing establishments abroad are generally depraved." Despite the moral and benevolent provisions to prevent this from ever occurring in this country, it was likely that "the same result will take place here."[30]

Shifting economic patterns altered village growth and spurred changes in the population of all the New England states. The rate of population growth decreased in some sectors, especially from 1800 to 1830.[31] Emigration became a question of vital importance. Why did so many leave? Certainly the unstable economic situation impelled many to abandon farms and to seek a better life in the West. Fertile soil was a dazzling attraction to anyone who had tried to farm in New England. Several areas of New England, especially the older settled regions, also had a surplus of population. Further subdivision of homesteads through lineal descent was no longer practicable, nor was it attractive to younger sons. The increase in manufacturing undoubtedly encouraged some to remain, but this lure had small impact in rural agricultural areas. Other persons left to escape the dominance of an established religion. Connecticut, the leading stronghold of Federalism and Congregationalism, furnished the largest proportion of emigrants.[32]

How did the population of New England shift in these years? A variety of statistical evidence suggests some answers. Emigration coincided with the steady decline of the birth rate. After 1800 the number of white children under ten years of age fell in all the New England states. The decline was not dramatic, but it was relentless. The older regions had the lowest birth ratios, and the hill towns in particular experienced a steady loss of population.[33] At the same time infant mortality remained quite high. For those who survived into puberty, however, chances to live well past the age of fifty were good.[34] With many of the young leaving, New England's population grew steadily older.

In Vermont and New Hampshire depopulation accelerated in many communities after 1800. Although Vermont's population increased steadily from 1800 to 1830, townships along the New York and New Hampshire borders saw many of their young men emigrate westward. By 1820 there were more white females than white males in the state. After 1820 an increasingly large number of aliens made their way into Vermont, breaking down the homogeneity of the population. Net population growth, moreover, slowed from 41 percent (1800-1810) to 8 percent (1810-1820). It rose again in the next decade, but did not approximate the earlier rates of growth.[35]

New Hampshire's total population expanded only one-third as rapidly as did that of Vermont during these same years, but the trends found in Vermont were even more visible in the Granite State. After 1800 the ratio of females to males increased each successive decade.

The percentage increase of the total population also fell steadily after 1800. As in neighboring Vermont, aliens began to appear in New Hampshire, but in much smaller numbers. The influx of French-Canadians had not yet begun. Except for a few towns along the northern reaches of the Connecticut River, most of the emigration occurred in the south-central portion of the state.[36] Most towns seemed to follow a common pattern, experiencing population decline from 1800 to 1810, some substantial growth during the subsequent decade, and then a serious decline setting in after 1820.[37]

To the south, Massachusetts experienced similar problems. As early as 1790 there were more females than males in the state; and after the separation of Maine in 1820 this surplus became even more striking, increasing by six times the disparity of 1810. This statistical shift highlights the reality of male emigration to the frontier. County growth rates varied according to location. The rate of population growth in eastern counties ranged from 11 percent to 25 percent. In western sectors of the state these rates dropped off to around 2 to 6 percent. Throughout the Connecticut Valley population growth lagged behind other portions of the Commonwealth.

Rates also fluctuated according to the prevailing occupations in the towns. The population of sixty-eight leading agricultural towns stabilized from 1810 to 1830 and then began a steady decline. Connecticut witnessed a similar development throughout these decades. At the same time manufacturing communities increased in size. Aliens became a more important element in the population, and homogeneity diminished throughout the Bay State as it had elsewhere in New England.[38] Whether local inhabitants emigrated to the frontier or merely separated to form a new town, the shifts in population during the early decades of the century indicate a rapid decrease in village solidarity.

The course of population change in Connecticut paralleled that in Massachusetts. There was a continuous surplus of females throughout these years, and the number of aliens mounted steadily. Most of the latter settled near the coast, and the population of inland areas like Litchfield remained largely homogeneous. James Morris, while compiling his account of Litchfield County in 1815, noted, "Only two European families have settled in Litchfield. They came from Ireland, and were respectable."[39]

The turning point for population growth in Litchfield, like so many New England communities, came during the first and second decades of the nineteenth century. Thereafter the number of inhabitants in many communities decreased for the duration of the century. Americans had long rejoiced at the incessant expansion of their population. It seemed to augur future greatness. Little wonder, then, that in those areas that did not share in this growth, some became alarmed. Population decline signaled the beginning of stagnation and decay; and the nation was so young!

As many of the best young men were drawn to the frontier, others wondered what was to become of New England, with its long and comfortable tradition of preeminence. Men had moved in search of new opportunities, leaving empty farmhouses as dreary monuments to their defeat. Emigration altered New England's living habits and attitudes. Apprehension over political factiousness increased. By the close of the 1790s gaps had appeared in Federalist ranks and signs of insecurity surfaced among its leaders. Elsewhere in the country the Jeffersonians were on the march, and New England could not entirely escape the repercussions. Although the opposition had not yet penetrated the region, local leaders could not abide the possibility that Thomas Jefferson might sit in the White House. Newspapers, usually concerned with financial developments, the problems of death and general health, and religion, now emphasized political affairs. The increased political agitation disturbed Federalists. The diary of the Reverend Thomas Robbins, a Congregational clergyman from Connecticut, expressed the sentiments and fears of the Old Order. In May 1800 he noted that the Democrats would probably carry New York, thereby bringing Jefferson into the presidency: "Blessed be God that all things are in His hands, and may He avert such an evil from this country for His name's sake. I do not believe that the Most High will permit a howling atheist to sit at the head of this nation!"[40]

Doubts about Jefferson's religious convictions had long plagued Trinitarians. But throughout New England, where politics and religion were joined through an established church, the Standing Order opposed him on political as well as religious grounds. Robbins's diary entry for July 4, 1800, reveals the intensity of this repugnance. "In the morning," he recorded, "we had news of the death of Mr. Jefferson. It is to be hoped that it is true."[41] The fates disappointed Robbins, but this did not stop many from sharing his hopes. Federalists echoed the fears of Mrs. Mary White: "What will be the result . . . we cannot tell, but may easily conceive; if they [Jeffersonians] make the progress in this country they have of late. I may not live to see the devastation, but you, my children are my greatest anxiety. Did we not hope for the protection of Divine Providence, I know I should immediately give up all ideas of better times."[42]

When Jeffersonian ranks in New England steadily swelled after 1800 and Republican candidates captured a variety of state political posts, Federalists expressed alarm and dismay. Then in quick succession came the difficulties with Great Britain under Jefferson and Madison. For political and economic reasons New England merchants and politicians rose to attack the federal administration. Opposition to war emerged as part of the broader struggle for control of state governments, particularly in Massachusetts and Connecticut. The Standing Order of Federalists and Congregationalists faced a strong, and eventually successful, challenge from the ambitious, the discontented, and the excluded.[43] Criticism of the established hierarchy mounted with the appearance of Republican tracts like the following dashing title: *The Politics of Connecticut; or a Statement of Facts, addressed to Honest Men of All Parties, religious and political, in the State: Particularly to the mass of Community. A Bold and Hardy Yeomanry, who compose the flesh and muscle, the blood and bone of the Body Politic.*[44] Democracy, long linked with infidelity and licentiousness, now frightened fewer people and attracted more voters.

The Embargo, followed by war with England, further loosened traditional party loyalties. Federalists held on, but the arrival of religious disestablishment in 1819 capped the upsurge of the Jeffersonian party in Connecticut. Toleration provoked conservative Congregationalists to decry universal suffrage and to yearn for their previous domination. By 1819 they were most upset at the recent turn of events. This hostility was undoubtedly more imagined than real; but the opposition had triumphed, and the old hierarchy now had to carry its own weight. Novelty bred anxiety.

The decline of community stability also affected the religious structure of the region. Hostility to the principles of the Puritans gained strength, and many persons refused to join any established religious organization. The unity of church and state had long faded, but this now appeared to challenge the basic assumptions of Christian principles and public worship. The tradition of resting every seventh day became more difficult to enforce, and Sabbath mail deliveries raised an outcry in religious circles.

Disaffection was particularly rampant among the Congregational clergy throughout New England. With their power base threatened and disestablishment either close at hand or an accomplished fact in all states within the region, something had to be done. This uneasiness was not new; it had been lurking in many towns since the Revolution, when Baptists and Methodists had met the test of patriotism and gained followers. After the turn of the century, party politics and religious controversy split towns and even churches, imperiling future security.[45] The social crises in town and nation, although only loosely related, worked upon one another. The intimate relationship between religion and politics dissipated. Institutions, always the last to feel change, caught up with public opinion. Political and religious conformity within the community diminished further with each passing year. But even with their political machinery in disrepair, the arrogance and power of the Congregational clergy continued to politicize latent denominational hostility.

One consequence was a noticeable decline in the stability of clerical ties to their congregations. Impermanency and restlessness, active in some towns throughout the eighteenth century, now overtook the Congregational clergy across New England. The mixture of economic, political, and religious change aroused new alarms about the future.[46] Since the Congregational church existed for town inhabitants as well as church members, dissension in one sector soon engulfed the other. As religious heterogeneity pervaded communities throughout New England an increasing proportion of local inhabitants resented being taxed to support an alien church. The double lines of authority—church and town—were on a collision course. The spread of impermanency bared the problems to be encountered in achieving reconciliation.

3. THE NEW ENGLAND CLERGY
AND THE PROBLEM OF PERMANENCY

By the first decades of the nineteenth century the traditional ministerial world was in disarray. Ministers who had long enjoyed respect and
tenure in their positions of community leadership now found their
situation precarious. It became increasingly difficult to distinguish the
pastor from any other citizen.

This clerical instability reflected years of unrest and can be measured
in the noticeable decline of permanency among settled pastors throughout New England. A number of problems confronted the clergy during
these years, most of which were linked to the situation of impermanency. The issue of "waste places," or towns without settled pastors,
always evoked serious discussion at ministerial gatherings. For a number
of reasons a town might not have a resident minister, relying instead on
itinerants or the periodic loan of settled pastors from generous congregations in nearby communities. The profession bemoaned the necessity
of relying on such emergency measures. Empty pulpits must be filled,
for ministers' influence and "real weight" emanated from their office
and their conduct. To head off new community divisions and solve the
problem of instability, young men were needed to fill out the ranks.[1]

The ranks of Congregational clergy were alarmingly depleted in
several sections of New England. Few Vermont towns could afford to
support one church and minister adequately and frequently had to
share a minister with neighboring communities. Even more appalling
was the great number of towns without any pastor at all. As late as
1838 Addison County in western Vermont still had six of its nineteen
leading towns without any minister of the gospel.[2] Further north along
the boundary of Lake Champlain, in Franklin County, only six of the
thirteen most populous towns had *ever* had an installed pastor.

Great periods of time, furthermore, separated the death or dismissal
of one pastor from the arrival of the next. During the intervening years

most rural villages remained destitute of religion. By 1840, the Bakers-field, Vermont, church had retained a pastor for only four of its twenty-eight years of existence. Over a longer stretch of time, the church in Franklin had never enjoyed a settled ministry and was usually hard pressed to obtain a nearby preacher for occasional visitations. Other problems beset the county. The church in the shire town of Saint Albans had a continuous supply of settled ministers, but none remained in the town very long.[3] New Hampshire towns and churches experienced similar problems. Although the majority of churches had settled pastors, few of these ministers were installed and several years usually interrupted the continuity of supply. Church societies in the other New England states suffered too.[4]

Other problems beset the clergy. Many communities struggled to maintain financial solvency amid persistent economic fluctuations. Patronage and politics often received priority over piety, and ministers in economically marginal towns struggled for adequate support. Timothy Dwight noted that local governments had expanded the number of offices beyond their means to provide for their incumbents, thereby necessitating the appointment of mediocre men as well as reducing the resources available for support of the local pastor and church. This represented another step in the breakdown of the Christian commonwealth and reflected the growing secularism in New England society.[5]

Pastors attacked this secularism from the pulpit and warned all brethren that the times were not favorable "to the temporal interests of Christ's ministers." Too many, Joseph Lyman noted, "are greatly embarrassed in making a decent and competent provision for the subsistence of their surviving families."[6] These dismal prospects were not likely to entice young men into the ministry, and New England divines harped on the dire consequences of towns remaining long destitute of religion. In his report to the Society of Inquiry at Andover Theological Seminary in 1829, E. C. Bridgman concluded, *"Two hundred* would not be more than enough to supply the destitute places."[7] Not only could these communities not afford a trained minister, many could not afford any minister at all.[8] This was especially acute near the frontier. Towns were often founded more on hope than substance. But all immediately sought to construct meetinghouses and settle pastors. Clergy who moved to the locale, consequently, found conditions unstable, and the financial problems on the frontier retarded clerical permanency.[9]

Other parishes and societies could easily afford a settled pastor, but were so divided among themselves that they could not agree on whom to invite. Differences of opinion, along with some instances of general religious indifference, kept many pulpits only sporadically supplied. Taunton, Massachusetts, suffered these woes continually from the 1790s to the early 1820s. The Congregational Society in the town invited John Foster to settle there in 1792. Unfortunately the members of the society had not consulted the rest of their brethren in the church, and the two groups divided over the invitation. The church withdrew and formed a separate society, later incorporated as the West Congregational Society in Taunton. Until 1809 it was without a settled minister. The Taunton parish suffered another secesssion in the fall of 1821 when the members invited Luther Hamilton to settle over them. Again a segment of their membership withdrew and formed a separate body—the Trinitarian Church.[10] By successive factional disputes, therefore, community and religious unity steadily broke down as the town grew. Other parishes skirted similar difficulties by refusing to ordain a settled minister, thereby keeping all candidates perpetually on trial. This solved the problem of religious supply, but at the same time prolonged the instability of the pastoral relationship.

Churches also found on occasion that it was difficult to break the bond between pastor and church. In the mid-1820s Rehoboth, Massachusetts, struggled with its minister over the issue of dismissal. The society voted in 1825 to dismiss Otis Thompson from his post and to close the meetinghouse to him. It then called another pastor, Thomas Vernon, to replace him. Thompson, however, refused to relinquish his pulpit and continued to preach regularly to a segment of the church. He subsequently sued for his salary and won the case. After lengthy discussions, the beleaguered pastor agreed to relinquish his future salary in return for a settlement of $1,000. Unfortunately for the future of religious harmony, however, the prolonged disagreement permanently severed the two groups in the church and society. New Gloucester, Maine, struggled with much the same problem from 1798 to 1802, as parish members sought to avoid settling former Methodists. Such problems were particularly prevalent in areas where another denomination was strong enough to challenge Congregationalist control. Prospects for a settled ministry remained dim so long as the dissonance persisted.[11]

Conditions and compensation, furthermore, varied widely from town to town. New Hampshire typified states in the New England region. Some pastors were fortunate, like Otis Thompson, and received ample salaries. Others did not. There is no correlation between the population of a town and the money it expended for clerical salaries. In Rockingham County, Hampton Falls, with a population of 583 in 1830, spent $416. On the other hand, Hawke, with 520 inhabitants, budgeted only $100 for its resident clergyman. Other communities relied entirely on voluntary contributions and made no budgetary provisions whatsoever for their ministers.[12]

A number of variables may explain this fluctuation. Nonpecuniary rewards could more than compensate for monetary discrepancies between towns. The pastor might receive a house, a woodlot, or his winter's supply of firewood in addition to a salary. In the harsh New England winter, adequate fuel was often more valuable than cash, especially in northern regions. Invitations to dine in houses throughout the village could aid in satisfying clerical palates and presumably appealed to unmarried pastors. The age, experience, and training of the minister were also important in determining salaries. A recruit fresh from theological seminary would not receive the compensation of a more experienced minister.

Among other factors, the relative wealth of the town could influence local citizenry, as could more capricious sentiments such as the clergyman's popularity with his congregation. These extra considerations supplemented a meager salary and eased the burdens of basic subsistence. On occasion other circumstances also influenced clerical fortunes. A popular pastor might be invited to settle elsewhere, in a more populous or better provisioned society. This forced the parish to improve his current circumstances or lose him and possibly face a factional division over the choice of his successor. Frequently nothing could induce a man to stay. Rural churches often remained destitute for long intervals between settled ministers.

The greater frequency of removals from one congregation to another reveals a major shift among New England Congregationalists. As clerical mobility increased, pastors became job-oriented rather then congregation-oriented. The bonds of attachment loosened, and what remained of an earlier cohesiveness disappeared. Never a tribal community except in its ideals, New England society in the nineteenth century lost even this psychic unity.[13]

In addition to the problems of depletion, discord, and disbursements, the question of professionalism agitated ministerial ranks in the opening decades of the nineteenth century. God supposedly called young men into the ministry; yet entrance into the clergy often required family connections and resources. Efforts to recruit pious, though indigent, young men gained greater headway in each successive decade after 1800, but social origins retained their importance. The notion of a divinely inspired motivation clashed with the need for professional training, and reconciliation of the two became increasingly troublesome after the turn of the century. By 1827 the problem was sufficiently acute to provoke Samuel Miller, president of Princeton Theological Seminary, to write a book of *Letters on Clerical Manners, and Habits, Addressed to a Student in the Theological Seminary at Princeton, New Jersey.*[14] This guidebook was designed to instruct young theology students in proper clerical behavior, as well as to dispense counsel on a variety of subjects that might confront a clergyman. The advice was general enough so as not to apply only to Presbyterians but to future ministers of all denominations.

That Miller felt compelled to undertake such a venture indicates the changing nature of the clergy. Greater professionalism meant an increase in systematic efforts for ministerial training. Miller's efforts reflected this change. The older personal method was hasty, and in some cases superficial, limited as it was by a single clergyman's personal library and theological resources. Dependence on the vicissitudes of individual commitment, moreover, was too risky. Recruitment of "poor but pious" youth, systematic training, and student charity gradually supplanted older methods of ministerial education. All helped to preserve collegiate education as a standard for ministers among the Orthodox.[15]

These changes also affected local congregations. The interior composition of a Congregational church, which had long reflected prevailing patterns of social dominance, still did so. But the men who ran the affairs of the church became less central to the daily operation of the external community. Although the congregation might be bodily in the church once a week or more, mentally, and often spiritually, it dwelt more and more in the marketplace. The clergy was faced with the task of joining the new with the old.[16]

In this task the clergy faced many difficulties, for New England society still wanted religion to present a familiar face. People distrusted "everything which bore the appearance of innovation."[17] Religious excitements could only contribute further to the uneasiness of political and economic change. Even after the War of 1812, ministers cautioned worshipers against succumbing to the persuasions of imposters. Speaking before a gathering designed to buttress ministerial ranks, the Reverend Eliphalet Pearson warned in 1815 that new men need not seek new measures: "From ignorance nothing better, than ignorance, can be expected.—Enthusiasm is still worse. To ignorance an enthusiastic preacher adds imposture. To gain the confidence, and excite the wonder of his hearers, he has recourse to visions, voices, and revelations. . . . But our country, at this moment, furnishes many distressing instances of such imposters."[18]

These problems became obvious by the second decade of the nineteenth century. In the 1790s ministers still maintained an aristocratic posture and could usually expect to be settled for life. Within the span of a generation, however, control over the appointment and maintenance of ministers moved almost entirely into the hands of the congregations.[19] This gave the pastor less control over the terms of his settlement, his tenure, and his dismissal. All pointed toward greater instability and insecurity.

Perhaps the most pervasive factor at work in New England religion during these decades was the decline of permanency. Information and empirical data on this phenomenon are readily available and clearly illustrate what was happening to the clergy over a span of almost two centuries. At times they explain why shifts in settlement patterns occurred.[20] An increase in the turnover of clergy, especially in dismissals, would indicate the plausibility of increasing instability and dissension throughout New England towns and villages. Each turnover meant that the members of a particular church or parish had to decide on another pastor to settle over them. Such deliberations held limitless possibilities for divisiveness.

Long-term trends in Vermont were somewhat difficult to see, since settlement patterns of this predominantly frontier society were unstable and of recent origin. Statistics for Vermont reach back only to the 1760s, but even in the span of about seventy years some patterns emerged. Ministers who began their tenure prior to 1800 usually remained in office more than a decade before their death or dismissal; there are numerous instances of individual terms exceeding twenty years. Because the number of clergymen in the state before 1775 was small, there were some sharp variations in the average term for those years, but for the most part, term averages were between ten and twenty years. After 1800 a different pattern emerged. From 1800 to 1810 no pastor remained in office more than twenty years or less than ten. This decline in permanency accelerated further after 1810. A sharp break occurred in that year, and thereafter in only one year did the average climb above ten years.

The average of terms ending in any one year throws less light on the nature of permanency in the Green Mountain State. Because Vermont was only scantily settled and the number of ministers correspondingly small, the data are inconclusive. The frontier nature of the state, coupled with the relatively short span of the data, probably make Vermont less representative of general developments in the ministry than other states in New England. Yet the settlement pattern of the Congregational clergy, averaged by the year their terms began, does illustrate the tendency toward impermanency.[21]

Elsewhere in the six-state region, settlement patterns followed a similar trend. Maine provides another set of circumstances midway between frontier Vermont and the older sections of Massachusetts and Connecticut.[22] Although still largely wilderness even in 1830, the state had several large, thriving communities along the coast. Until 1820, moreover, Maine was part of Massachusetts, and consequently the information is fuller than that for Vermont.

Prior to 1780, average ministerial terms were uniformly long. Only on rare occasions did they dip below ten years, and most averaged well over twenty years. Two breaks altered this pattern in subsequent years. The first came after 1783, when all average terms dropped below thirty years and most were below twenty years. The overall picture, however, was one of a fairly permanent settlement for a pastor. The second and more significant break came after 1802. In no year thereafter did the average climb over twenty years, and it dropped steadily for the duration of the data (1829). By the 1820s the average remained consistently below ten years.

The steady growth in the number of pastors throughout the district after 1800 makes this second break especially significant, since it indicates that the turnover was not only rapid but extensive. After a severe decline in 1804, the average term never regained its earlier length. Although, in each year, there were one or two pastors who settled over a church or parish for a long duration, permanency declined precipitously for the vast majority of ministers.[23]

Permanency collapsed gradually for Maine pastors over a stretch of a

decade or more, again because of the persistence of a few aged ministers. The death in 1810 of a pastor after a permanent residence of
sixty-one years boosted the average for that one year alone from 11.5
to 21.4. Similar occurrences can be found for almost every year until
1830, when very few of these long-term ministers remained.

Massachusetts and Connecticut were the two strongholds of Congregationalism in New England, and it is here that the changing conditions
of permanency are most evident. Both states had a long tradition of a
settled ministry, and both therefore provided bountiful data for an
analysis of settlement patterns.

In Massachusetts the average term for a minister in any one church
was at first low. After the 1640s, however, it rose to over twenty years
and rarely fell beneath that figure for more than a century (see Graph
1). Although the longevity of one or two pastors occasionally produced
extreme variations, the pattern remained remarkably stable until the
late 1740s. At that time the average declined slightly, from over thirty
years to between twenty-five and thirty years. A slight climb in the
1760s mirrored the end of the Great Awakening, but not until the late
1790s did the average begin to settle below twenty with any consistency. The running average reflects this trend after 1800, when the average
length of settlement diminished steadily. It never again surpassed ten
years after 1820. Instability among Bay State clergy remained rife, and
the permanency established in the early eighteenth century must have
seemed a golden age. As in Maine, the number of ministers in the state
grew steadily and dropped below 100 in only one five-year period after
1770. The turmoil after 1800 was, therefore, much more widespread
and influential than any variations in the past. The amount of data is so
extensive after the mid-eighteenth century that occasional eccentricities
in the trend do not seriously distort the overall pattern.[24]

The graph for length of terms by year ended reveals even more
precisely the change in tenure among the Congregational clergy in
Massachusetts (see Graph 2). Until the 1660s rarely did the average
tenure reach twenty years, a natural tendency that reflected the short
span of colonization. After this it increased haltingly until the eighteenth century, when it stood consistently between twenty and thirty
years. From 1730 to 1740 there were some violent fluctuations, which
undoubtedly reflect the turbulence of the Great Awakening. Following
this outburst of religious and social zeal, there were few marked
changes until the early years of the nineteenth century.[25]

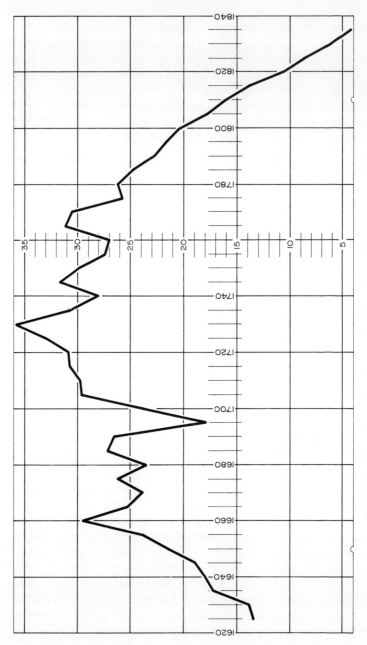

Graph 1   Massachusetts: Average length of terms by year term began

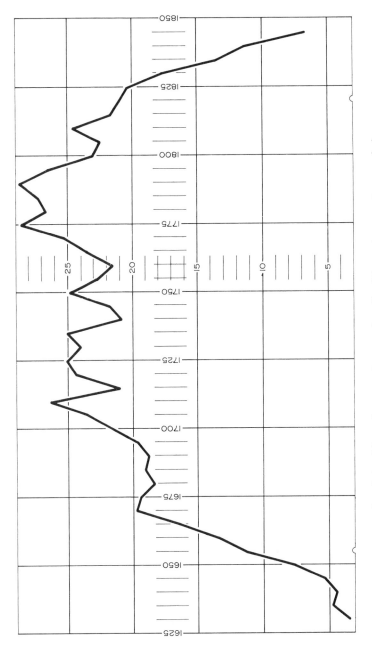

Graph 2 Massachusetts: Average length of terms by year term ended

After 1810 the average term declined slowly and continued to do so for the duration of the data. The sharpest break occurred in 1825. Thereafter the yearly average never again surpassed twenty, reflecting a drop of more than 50 percent from the high points of the eighteenth century.

The pattern for Massachusetts, therefore, resembles that for Maine. In both instances the statistical evidence indicates that the final collapse of permanency as reflected in the ending charts followed by little more than a decade the pattern demonstrated in the beginning charts. The figures for Massachusetts, like those for Maine, also indicate the impact of the longevity of a few ministers in the same pastorate for several decades. Almost without exception, averages rose substantially for the years in which these men concluded their tenure, although use of the ten-year running average smooths these aberrations. For most of the clergy permanence was becoming illusory by the nineteenth century.

To the south, in the Land of Steady Habits, much the same pattern prevailed. Connecticut, perhaps even more than Massachusetts, was a stronghold of Congregationalism. Accordingly, throughout the eighteenth century the position and tenure of the clergy in Connecticut remained more stable and permanent than in the Bay State (see Graph 3). The marked variations in the five-year average length of terms during the seventeenth century is the result of few ministers assuming new positions in any one year. As these numbers increased throughout the eighteenth century, the extremes narrowed and terms consistently ranged between twenty-five and thirty-five years until after 1775.

From 1740 to 1760 there was a brief interval of sudden jumps in the graph, when the Great Awakening eroded stability in Connecticut as it had elsewhere across New England. Not until 1775 did the average fall below twenty with any consistency. After 1794 it only surpassed twenty in one year, 1798, when only two ministers began their terms. Both enjoyed remarkable tenure and thereby distorted the prevailing pattern briefly. The ten-year running average, however, fell constantly. After 1815 the average term on the beginning chart never topped ten years. The trend that had begun in the late eighteenth century had now stabilized at its lowest ebb.

The ending chart for Connecticut reveals a pattern similar to those of the other New England states, but with much less dramatic fluctuations (see Graph 4). Throughout most of the eighteenth century the average term remained fairly stable—between twenty and thirty years.

From 1730 to 1750 there were the now familiar turmoil and accelerated turnover traceable to the Great Awakening, but no other severe or unexpected shifts broke the pattern until the 1790s, as term levels remained generally firm and high. Sudden yearly variations in 1792 and 1793 reflected the paucity of ministers assuming new positions and were inconsistent with former levels of permanence. After the erratic yearly high of forty-nine reached in 1793, there was a sharp downward trend. For the remaining years covered by the data the overall average term fell, although in 1810 and 1815 it again climbed slightly. In Connecticut a few pockets of permanency persisted far into the nineteenth century and at times interrupted the prolonged decline over most of the state. The great majority of towns and churches suffered under unstable conditions, and the increase in impermanency only slowed gradually.[26]

The above data clearly reveal that in all sections of New England ministerial terms declined after 1800. The disparity between beginning and ending charts does not vitiate these conclusions. Quite the contrary; it sharpens the contrast between eighteenth- and nineteenth-century conditions. Permanency seems to linger in the ending charts only until those ministers who assumed new positions in the more stable atmosphere of the eighteenth century died off. By the time religious disputes flared up in the 1800s these men were well entrenched and quite secure. It was the effort to replace these pastors that sparked controversy within local churches and communities. The earlier appearance of this instability in the beginning charts reflects both the increase in the number of churches as well as the failure of most eighteenth-century pastors to extend their earthly longevity beyond reasonable limits. As they expired after 1790, churches struggled to replace them and community divisions erupted.

One other influence on ministerial permanency is not measured in the graphs. That is the continued recurrence in almost every parish of intervals between the departure of one pastor and the settlement of the next one. Very few religious societies escaped this problem, and several were unable to settle a new minister for a number of years. Only infrequently true in the seventeenth and eighteenth centuries, this problem became particularly vexatious in the nineteenth. A number of difficulties produced these gaps. In the earlier centuries the dilemma was usually centered in finding someone to settle. Churches frequently had to extend several invitations before receiving an acceptance. During

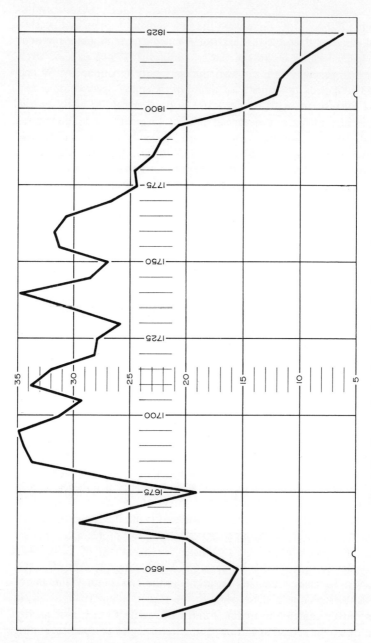

Graph 3   Connecticut: Average length of terms by year term began

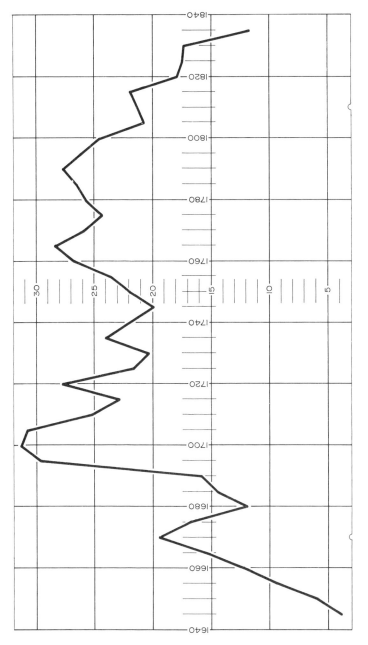

Graph 4   Connecticut: Average length of terms by year term ended

the nineteenth century, however, disagreements among parishioners over which candidates to invite usually caused the delay.[27]

The problem became so acute and widespread that the failure of a town to divide was an event worthy of comment. The Reverend Samuel Sewall of Burlington, Massachusetts, uncovered one of these rarities in neighboring South Reading. "In a day when dismissions of ministers have become matters of frequent and lamentable occurrence," he wrote, "it is refreshing to find a church, which has had no experience of the evil."[28]

Most communities could not avoid these divisions. Factiousness appeared everywhere. Although it might arise over the settlement of a new pastor, its real cause usually lay elsewhere. A quarrel in the First Church of Marlborough, Massachusetts, typified the disruptive potential of ministerial settlement. It erupted over the sudden dismissal of the Reverend Asa Packard in 1806. For twenty-one years he had successfully labored in the community, and with the apparent goodwill of all inhabitants. Further examination reveals that the issue in 1806 was not the preaching or doctrines of Packard, but a town dispute over the location of a new meetinghouse. This was resolved in 1808 and Packard returned as pastor of the new West Church, remaining until 1819.[29]

When faced with the prospect of a permanent division, less volatile congregations often agreed to disagree and thereby muted their hostilities. In 1828 the First Church in Westford, Massachusetts, split over differences in religious sentiments. A majority of the church opposed a minority of church members and a majority of the society. Since no future union was possible, the church voted to release all who wanted to join the new Union Church and Society. A sizable portion of the church seceded, and the two groups coexisted peacefully thereafter.[30]

Throughout New England during the nineteenth century, churches divided over a successor to a deceased pastor. Splits often developed between churches and religious societies. At stake was not only religious doctrine and domination of the local pulpit but also the right to occupy the meetinghouse as well as to control its use and contents. The decision of one party to secede, therefore, was not capriciously considered nor hastily reached. Yet many communities witnessed such secessions as dissension increased in the older churches. In one county in Massachusetts alone seven towns suffered divisions severe enough to provoke one party to separate and construct a new meetinghouse.[31]

Arguments arose over almost any imaginable grievance. Rights to a woodlot sent two religious societies to court in Sunderland, Vermont, to decide which minister was settled first and had thereby gained title.

The matter was continued in the county court for a long time, and a great deal of curious testimony was adduced from the clocks and watches of Sunderland, respecting the point in question. At length, with a discrimination which has seldom if ever, been equalled, it was decided that the ordination of Mr. Sherwin preceded that of Dr. Lee, about *two minutes.* This settled the matter in respect to the law, but not in respect to the gospel. The expenses of the law suit were heavy, and the alienation such as could not be healed. Some of the best men left the town. . . . the religious prospects of the town were ruined.[32]

More appalling for Congregationalists was the issue of correct doctrine and proper preaching, and many pastors were dismissed for changing their views on church doctrines. The spread of diverse doctrines occasioned clergymen to give careful attention to communal solidarity. The Reverend Edward Payson in Portland, Maine, found it necessary to ease the minds of his congregation after rumors of his doctrinal inclinations reached them. Although his parishioners pitied such a "shocking creature," he tried to convince them that his religion was not "morose" or "unsocial." A Hopkinsian, Payson was quick to inform them, "was not *quite* so bad as the devil."[33]

Political controversies often intruded on such debates as well. And when politics and religion combined, they severed society in a fearful division. Politics and political debate, moreover, drew attention away from religion and frequently drove pastors to despair.[34]

A smattering of other issues contributed to the erosion of ministerial tenure. Few were new, but when joined with other controversies all were potent. Salaries always provoked debate. The interaction of town, parish, and church drew the issue out of the shadows of religious prerogatives and into the arena of local politics. Most pastors enjoyed sufficient support, but their futures were rarely guaranteed. As politics intruded into church affairs, the question of religious taxation arose in many town meetings. To the dismay of critics, participation in town and church was not mutually inclusive. "If infidels and irreligious people are forced to sustain an equal proportion of the expense of supporting ministers," one critic lamented, "nothing can be more reasonable than that they should have equal influence in the choice of them." The dilemma was obvious; the churches had "either to have no ministers at all, or to have such as will please the taste of the carnal and irreligious majority." Prolonged salary disputes embittered pastors and undoubtedly drove some to take refuge in other pulpits.[35] The unabated emigration westward further undermined community resources and their ability adequately to support local clergy.

A number of other causal factors were possible influences on the problem of instability. Disestablishment, certainly an obvious consideration, had no measurable impact. In both Massachusetts and Connecticut, pastors with long terms in any one town were becoming scarce well before the disestablishment of the Congregational church in 1833 and 1818 respectively. What little acceleration did occur was largely the continuation of a preexisting pattern. Clergy in both states, moreover, had debated the issue for years, and when religious disestablishment did arrive it was neither sudden nor surprising. The frontier contributed to the persistent instability during the early nineteenth century. It did not, however, stand by itself. Economic and political changes in New England frequently forced men to look beyond the confines of their own community in order to prosper. In states that still retained sparsely settled regions, the instability can be traced to the preference of pastors to request dismissals and settle over more populous or more important churches. Their removal elsewhere agitated many rural churches for decades and contributed to the declining permanency. The new ministerial orientation toward jobs rather than congregations, moreover, added to the instability.

Not all the clergy, however, were migratory. Nor were most of them concerned solely for their own advancement and unmindful of criticism. Young pastors desired the approval of their congregations, but did not pursue it without remembering its costs. It was easy to succumb to the "thirst for applause," but religious societies judged their ministers harshly, and the rewards of such a course were tenuous. The Reverend Edward Payson was perhaps more introspective and candid than most and expressed his fears of a future surrender. "When I sit down to write," he confided to his parents, "I perpetually catch myself considering, not what will be most useful, but what will be most likely to gain praise from an audience." Payson preferred to remove himself from Portland, Maine, to a rural settlement to be rid of the "tattle of the drawing room." His yearning for plain Christian talk, however, did not induce him to compromise merely for public plaudits.[36] This was not always true with many of his colleagues.

By the early nineteenth century, therefore, the relationship between pastor and congregation was in disarray. Most pastors had signed contracts with their parishes, a fact that not only symbolized these changes but one that frequently provoked discussion itself. Delays in settling new pastors rendered the bond between minister and congregation even more insecure. But at the heart of the problem lay a contentious spirit. Political quarrels bred in part by economic diversity, disputes over church membership or doctrines, competition among several denominations, and struggles over meetinghouses and their contents divided churches. In their pursuit of unification or dominance, congregations sought ministers who met their own preferences.[37]

Secular relations governed ecclesiastical relations. When political and economic habits diversified and became unsteady, when geographic mobility increased, religion suffered. Apart from sundering existing congregations and churches, this new mobility created many new churches. All demanded ministers, but few possessed financial stability. This mobility, moreover, drained older parishes of their financial resources, thereby contributing to instability throughout the region.[38]

Ministers, too, felt the pull of opportunity and advance. Now more job-oriented than congregation-oriented, they increasingly asked for dismissals to move to more eminent posts. Whether or not a "thirst for applause" overtook the clergy, more populous or wealthier parishes held out promises of greater security, as did the escape from troubled communities. In this respect the problems of impermanency reinforced one another. Population growth and an increasing frequency of dismissals that created more vacant pulpits confronted ministers in unhappy circumstances with a choice of employment opportunities. These same vacancies also engendered a disposition among pastors to move rather than endure long-standing community quarrels. At the same time the greater supply of clergy emerging from the new theological seminaries also created a new freedom to move, bringing as it did the conviction on the pastor's part that a town could always replace him. The result was an unsteady and ever-changing ministry, one that perhaps unwittingly promoted disorganization.[39]

4. THE GLORY IS DEPARTED

That religion should become less central in the everyday lives of New Englanders was not surprising. Nor was it new. Since the arrival of Puritan settlers in Massachusetts Bay, the decline of religious fervor in the face of a mounting concern for worldly matters had beset the clergy. Local problems and material concerns repeatedly disrupted community relations throughout the eighteenth century. The ideal of the voluntary cooperative commonwealth dimmed as local factiousness grew. If ancient habits succumbed to pressing worldly and divisive impulses, traditional institutions might not withstand the storm. "Should these be changed, as I much fear this new order of things is changing them," one native cautioned, "it will then be written upon the tablet of our forsaken temples, 'the glory is departed.' "[1]

What was at issue was not only the religious sentiments of the people but the future direction of American life. Unlike those reformers solely concerned with the political purity of the Revolutionary heritage, New England ministers also drew their ideals of society from the Puritanism of early Massachusetts Bay and the Cambridge Platform. The former inculcated an evangelical Calvinism; the latter located ministerial authority. This mixture produced visions of an ideal commonwealth—stable, orderly, and sanctioned by God.[2] After the Revolution, however, the Congregational clergy became increasingly uncomfortable about the viability of the American republic as they understood it. During the 1790s, and especially after 1800, New England Congregationalists sensed several strong challenges to their republican ideals. This touched off a search for stability; a search that prompted them first to reassess their own position and then to reaffirm these ideals through a series of variegated responses. Ministers quickly discovered that their bonds to the populace were at best superficially secure. Beneath the protective apparatus of church and state, support at the local level was pitted, crumbling, and in some instances completely eroded. Efforts to realize their ideals sensitized the Congregational clergy to all but the faintest rumblings within the communal framework.

The clergy did not suspect all change. Instead they directed their attention to that which seemed to betray republican virtue and divinely inspired order. Disorder contradicted the ideal of a harmonious Christian commonwealth. The increasingly mobile character of New England society, coupled with a growing urbanization and complexity, frightened men born in a simpler time. Although the clergy certainly were not ascetics, like most of their fellow citizens they had some difficulty keeping pace with events taking place around them. Local problems formed the core of their despair.[3] Deference declined, and with it many old political and social assumptions. Age lost its accustomed preeminence, and children demonstrated a growing reluctance to bow to parental dictation.[4] These stresses and strains seemed all the more alarming because memories of bygone days remained strong. Critics challenged the prevailing system, and the orthodoxy writhed under the demanding scrutiny. Pastors in the Congregational establishment across New England had not yet come to terms with diversity and distrusted differences of any sort. The virulence of this criticism roused Congregationalists to alarm, and they rose to meet the challenge.[5]

In 1806 the *Panoplist*, voice of the Trinitarian-Congregational establishment, published a survey of New England's churches. The series of articles recorded some frightening alterations in the character and religious commitment of men and women throughout the region. The common cause of all people, the author argued, "should prompt them to a free and unreserved intercourse and friendship." But, to his dismay, he found that personal contact and sympathy were disappearing and that Christians were "strangers to the spiritual condition of their brethren." The old Christian covenant had changed, and the notion that one person's future welfare was intimately connected to the welfare of his community no longer prevailed. Internal decay plagued churches and congregations in all corners of the region. Men now appeared to reserve their energy for material pursuits. Unity waned, as did "all the comforts of social piety." There were exceptions to these ominous developments, but they were rapidly becoming remarkable in themselves.[6]

What had happened? Pastors carefully began to assess the drift of New England development. "If the want of Christian piety in church members; if the decline of gospel discipline; if the indifference of churches respecting the character and theological opinions of ministers; if the neglect or abuse of catechetical instruction and the growing contempt of creeds, are all evils of alarming magnitude, and of destructive tendency; then their removal is highly important to the good of the churches."[7] Similar warnings against declension or alterations in familiar habits and virtues came from other sources. In 1802 the Andover Association issued an alarm against the deterioration of family religion. Particularly disturbed at the factiousness that seemed to accompany the decline of family worship, it argued that those who prayed daily might expect to receive the blessings of God. Only family worship could excite "the members of it to love and good works." Both appeared to have less and less influence throughout New England as the new century dawned.[8]

Ball playing, drinking, and other recreational activities competed with family worship for attention on the Sabbath.[9] Such frivolities drew younger members of the family away from home, hearth, and Bible. Dissension and alienation, already exacerbated by changing patterns of settlement and wealth, now received an unneeded assist. Fears that parents foolishly coddled their children emerged in many New England towns. Critics noted an "absurd indulgence" of parents in their children's whims and wants. This was certain to produce "a habit of indulgence, fatal to future improvement." One anonymous critic stated the problem more boldly: "Why should they exert themselves to procure that which is ready at their call? . . . it is of the utmost importance to teach the youthful mind that enjoyment and self-satisfaction must be purchased by labor."[10]

Decline and decay seemed everywhere, and few corners of the region escaped clerical scrutiny. In 1812 the Reverend Benjamin Wood lamented, "A great portion of the New-England states is running over to briars and thorns, assuming the appearance of uncultivated fields in a moral point of light for the want of labourers." Discarding reason and moderation, he moved quickly from analysis to exaggeration and estimated that 600,000 persons in the region lacked religion. Wood was more accurate in his observation that many communities had churches without pastors and religious societies without teachers.[11]

Timothy Dwight corroborated these findings during his wanderings throughout New England. Although his apprehensions were not solely concerned with religion, his failure to discriminate between various activities indicated a persistent attraction to an older cohesiveness.

Among his many fears was the proliferation of newspapers, especially those not under the control of educated and talented men. That this expansion reflected the growth of political parties did not escape his notice. All pointed to a disturbing divisiveness. Too many people no longer embraced piety, at least as understood by Congregationalists. Instead they pursued rationalist doctrine, and "hail whatever will enable them to perpetrate it in peace."[12] The rush toward complexity and diversity appalled Dwight and his colleagues, especially since they saw their ideals as coterminus with those of the Republic.

There was good reason for this apprehension. Despite decades of control and dominance, Congregationalism by 1815 had not yet penetrated all sections of New England. The General Association of New Hampshire, meeting in Exeter during September 1817, found several of their local associations in disrepair. Amidst the exuberant optimism of some societies, "the moral and religious aspect of some parts of the state" were still "gloomy and deplorable." The report concluded that "the neglect of public worship, of the family altar, and the ordinances of the gospel, and the prevalence of vice and error, are manifest."[13] Coupled with the decline in ministerial tenure and permanency, the report's conclusions reinforced the growing knowledge that all was not well for New England Congregationalists. Few among the clergy, however, directed their concern to the problems of local churches or religious societies. Instead, their volume of criticism focused on larger issues: on politics, orthodoxy, and denominationalism.

The early decades of the nineteenth century witnessed a steady expansion of Jeffersonian power, which in turn produced local struggles for control or influence throughout the region. Since pastors saw society as an organic whole—each part dependent on another to produce a harmonious system—they could not divorce politics from religion. There was no state church, strictly speaking, but to Congregational ministers Federalism meant the familiar, slow progression and change that had served to mark the past.[14]

Against this background they castigated those whom they thought contributed to the increasing political factiousness. Their attack was not directed solely against Jeffersonianism, although many have narrowly condemned them for this.[15] They feared not change and innovation but the forces that this change and innovation unleashed. They did not oppose popular democracy itself, but the divisiveness of popular democracy.

Towns had frequently divided over ministerial salaries or the location of a new meetinghouse. Now, however, organized groups emerged which used such differences to marshal support against the established hierarchy. Since many community ties had been informal, this new spirit of division rendered them precarious. The coincidence of the new political contest with the proliferation and geographic dispersal of new towns heightened the clergy's sense of social fragmentation. Secular politics alone did not embody instability; it was their merger with communal religious discord that triggered Congregational protests. Ministers found competition with politics difficult.[16]

Across New England the Congregational clergy attacked the increasing importance of politics in the lives of their parishioners. Pastors assailed not only Jeffersonian ideas but the idea of contention and party itself. In his Fast Day sermon in 1815, the Reverend James W. Tucker of Rowley, Massachusetts, summarized the tendency of the past decade. "Newspapers," he lamented, "are read far more than the Bible; and men are more anxious to hear of the advances of their party, than of the triumphs of their Redeemer."[17]

Not only Federalists opposed the vice of party and faction. The Reverend Solomon Aiken, pastor of the First Church in Dracutt, Massachusetts, and a Republican, railed against Federalists, speculators, and bankers in his Fast Day sermon in 1811. He complained not only about the evil influences of these three groups but about discord and dissension in general. A good Republican, he of course blamed the Federalists for these vices. This dissonance, he argued, "will weaken the sense the People may feel of their moral obligation, to abide their national compact. . . . These effects of Federalism, are truly Pricks in our eyes, blinding and deceiving the People, and leading them into delusion."[18]

Other pastors also criticized the injurious effects of politics and electioneering, arguing that conflict was not a functional part of a healthy society.[19] In his Fast Day sermon for 1826, the Reverend James Sabine attacked the unfortunate perversion of traditional religious principles. Casting his eye across the preceding three decades, he observed that men seeking public office too often played to the caprices and prejudices of potential supporters. Courtiers flattered one and all, with total disregard to the "rule of righteousness." "The question then is," Sabine concluded, "not what is right, but what is popular, what will be most acceptable to the party looked up to?"[20]

These forces threatened the fragile unity of the parish. Such behavior spelled death to community moral standards and Federalist rule. It also promised prolonged instability while the several suitors courted the voters. Dalliance of this nature produced both diversity and religious declension. A sensitivity to these problems, as well as apprehensions for the future of the ministry, prompted Samuel Miller, a Presbyterian clergyman, to include a section on political behavior in his *Letters on Clerical Manners*. His comments were direct and dogmatic: "Never allow yourself TO BE A POLITICIAN. Never attend political meetings:—never harangue in political companies:—never scribble political paragraphs:—never connect yourself with political parties: nay, do not indulge in much political conversation, even with your friends. Ministers of the gospel, and those who are preparing for the ministry, have infinitely more important work to do."[21]

This was good advice, but in their pursuit of a Christian commonwealth ministers did not compartmentalize social, political, and religious activities. Although they wished to minimize conflict and division, pastors also wanted a Christian civilization and could not remain aloof from politics. Men like Timothy Dwight saw religion as the cornerstone of the political state and refused to restrain their inclination to combat. They hoped that contentious criticism somehow would eventually produce unity and that one party would absorb the other. Ironically, this process did work after 1815; however it was the Federalist party which disappeared. But amidst their apprehensions of turmoil, ministers stood firm with the observation of one colleague, "It is religion alone—revealed religion—which saves the world from this state of degradation."[22]

So long as Federalists contested Jeffersonians for political office these controversies persisted. They climaxed with the War of 1812. Pastors frequently found themselves unable to pray for the war effort; yet their congregations often demanded it. Patriotism had apparently overrun religion. "My congregation are chiefly of the Democratic party," one pastor lamented, "and expect their minister by his pulpit services to fortify their hostility to Great Britain. The most and the best that I can do, is with all my might to *pray for peace*."[23] Even William Bentley, usually critical of the Trinitarians, agreed that political polemics should not supplant pious sermons. "The other sects," he noted, "profit from this indiscretion and threaten the exterpation [*sic*] of the Cong. churches if this zeal continues."[24]

Unfortunately for members of the Standing Order, however, political controversy was not the only divisive note on the New England landscape during these years. More serious was what appeared to be a general assault on orthodoxy itself. Since the 1790s strong voices had clamored for the abolition of all state support for religion. Advocates of the change argued that only then could true religious liberty exist and all denominations join in the promotion of a Christian commonwealth.[25] So long as congenial interests dominated pulpits, political offices, and the courts, change could be forestalled. But as a second political party gained strength throughout New England the clamor for change became deafening.

The problem of orthodoxy produced more internal dissension among Congregationalists than any other issue. During the first decade of the nineteenth century, the debate over programs and piety became especially vexatious as Congregationalists encountered increased diversity within their own ranks. Some pastors followed the teachings of Jonathan Edwards and believed themselves strict Calvinists. At the turn of the century, most Calvinistic ministers in New England belonged to the Edwardian school. Attacking Latitudinarian theology, they argued that God would convert the pagan world according to his own plan.

A second group of clergy went beyond Edwards. Following the ideas of Samuel Hopkins of Newport, Rhode Island, and Nathaniel Emmons of Franklin, Massachusetts, they challenged Edwardian methods and techniques.[26] This group, usually called Hopkinsians, postulated varying degrees of sinfulness according to man's will. Total depravity became meaningless. Such revisionist tendencies impregnated New England Calvinism with seeds of conflict. Moreover, the injection of Hopkinsian notions of benevolence radically altered the course of religion in the region. The new moral emphasis attacked Edwardian ideas of depravity and led to conflict and confusion.[27] This lack of direction plagued New England Congregationalists off and on for decades. Only when they grappled with the problem of securing and stabilizing their ideals would it fade.

The division within Congregational ranks provoked some pastors to defend New England church history, as if to signify that this was an internal debate and not a religious secession. The defense reverberated across the landscape for almost three decades, climaxing in 1830 with the publication of *A Tribute to the Memory of the Pilgrims, and a Vindication of the Congregational Churches of New England.*[28]

In this series of lectures, the Reverend Joel Hawes argued that despite an increasing concern for material pursuits, New England remained the moral leader of the nation. Avoiding any direct reference to the religious controversies of the nineteenth century, Hawes directed his energies to a review of the region's religiosity during the seventeenth and eighteenth centuries. He implied that little had changed and that New England's moral preeminence reigned unabated. But merely reiterating the virtues of a godly commonwealth did not reinvigorate them. His defensive compulsions, moreover, betrayed his intent: "Though we may not infer, from the resemblance of our own churches to those of primitive times, that our's are the *only true* churches, yet may we justly regard that resemblance as a high recommendation of them, and as furnishing substantial ground for the preference we feel for the order and worship of our own denomination."[29]

All was not well. A great change had taken place "in the character and circumstances of the community."[30] By the end of the new century's first decade the ancient churches were no longer supreme, for a challenge had arisen from within Congregational ranks. Much more threatening to notions of a godly commonwealth than the Edwardian-Hopkinsian split could ever have been, the Unitarian controversy swept across New England and terrified Trinitarians. This debate was much more than a thoughtful theological discussion among intellectuals and theologians. Few persons in New England during the early 1800s misunderstood the alarming possibilities that might emerge from the controversy.

The city of Boston and Harvard College in Cambridge were the focal points of the Unitarian upsurge. Although Calvinists had long railed against Arminianism, Socinianism, and other deviations from orthodoxy, the appointment of the Reverend Henry Ware to the post of Hollis Professor of Divinity at Harvard College in 1805 caused much concern in the Trinitarian ranks. "The election of Mr. Ware," wrote Timothy Dwight from Connecticut, "has occasioned very serious sensations in this State and in the northern part of Massachusetts."[31] Several years later Dwight magnified his earlier lament and wrote, "Unitarianism appears to be the predominating system. It is believed that neither ministers, nor People, have had any reason to congratulate themselves on their change." This was a surprisingly calm response from the excitable Dwight. Many of his fellow Trinitarians reacted more harshly.[32]

In March 1806 Eliphalet Pearson resigned from Harvard and delivered a warning on the future of the college. Ostensibly addressed to the Overseers who administered the college, his remarks were really aimed at his Trinitarian colleagues. "In a word," he wrote, "such a gloom is spread over the University, and such is my view of its internal state and external relations, of its cardinal and constitutional maladies, as to awaken all my fears, and exclude the hope of rendering any effectual service to the interests of religion by continuing my connection with it."[33]

The Unitarian influence invaded one community after another. From Maine one observer reported, "Unitarianism has here many advocates . . . . Their situation is dangerous, let us feel the tenderest pity for them, they need it."[34] Pastors closer to the heat of battle, however, were neither so haughty nor so indulgent. They hoped for a change and cast about for auspicious signs that might give substance to these hopes. Lyman Beecher wrote his son in 1823 that he thought the end was near for the Unitarians. Taking heart from election results in Boston, which had gone against them, he optimistically predicted that soon Unitarians would be unable to "proselyte, and annoy, and defend by perverted legislation and judicial influence."[35] Beecher, who had been called to Boston's Park Street Church to help stem the Unitarian tide, tried to engender optimism in his colleagues. "Everything is shaking and changing," he wrote to a colleague. "If this assault on public opinion and feeling continues, the light will shine into darkness, and the darkness will comprehend it."[36]

Yet, another danger threatened. At stake in this struggle were not only the hearts and minds of the populace but also control over meetinghouses and tax benefits. The debate at Harvard concerned the profession; the debates in town and village concerned community institutional and social structures. Church members struggled with one another for control of the meetinghouse or for possession of church funds. Moreover, when they had to select a new minister for their church, Trinitarians had to contend with a new problem. Young clergymen coming out of Harvard to settle in pastorates across New England would be tainted with non-Trinitarian notions. New sources of ministerial supply had to be found.

But the question of who could, or should, control local societies and meetinghouses remained the paramount issue. The problem embraced politics as well as religion. Parish or town electoral politics usually determined the local religious establishment, and as the religious inclinations of residents shifted during the early decades of the nineteenth century, Trinitarians on more than one occasion found themselves suddenly cast adrift, the amenities of privilege gone along with the meetinghouse. Unfortunately for those evicted, the parish retained control not only of the meetinghouse but of church funds as well.

In 1833 the General Association of Massachusetts, voice of Trinitarian-Congregationalism, formed a committee to investigate instances where Orthodox Congregational churches had been driven from their houses of worship under the challenge of the Unitarian movement. Typical was the following report:

Turned out of their house of worship in 1811. At that time the church numbered about 300 members; not far from thirty of whom remained with the dominant party. . . . The funds of the church distinctively, were small—comprising sacramental furniture, money, etc., to the amount of $570. This was taken by the parish. The fund held in common by the church and parish, and given nearly two hundred years ago by a pilgrim father, or his immediate descendant, amounted to somewhat more than $13,000. This, of course, passed into the hands of the parish. . . . The majority that took possession of the parish property was but *three*—the vote, standing for the Orthodox minister 80, and against him 83. About one third of the tax paid before the separation, was paid by the church and their friends.[37]

A majority of qualified voters now appeared to control the church.[38] Beset by rising impermanency and social change, Congregational ministers now found their few remaining resources threatened.

The increasing intimacy between electoral politics and religion raised yet another question—that of disestablishment. This, too, was not a new issue; but the growth of Unitarianism had changed the nature of the problem. As one orthodox church after another fell to Unitarian control, Trinitarians became alarmed. The establishment was shifting. Now a Unitarian-Federalist alliance dominated eastern Massachusetts and threatened other sections of New England. The result was a new surge for religious disestablishment not only in Massachusetts but across New England. Lyman Beecher crystallized the issue for Massachusetts pastors in 1821 when he wrote: "We feel the danger of allowing the Unitarian heresy too much popular headway, lest the stream, like Toleration, once running, should defy obstruction, and sweep foundations and superstructures in promiscuous ruin. An early and decided check followed up will turn back this flood, and save the land from inundation.[39] By the time disestablishment carried Massachusetts in 1833, it had already arrived in the other New England states. Rumblings of the change seriously agitated Congregational ranks from the opening of the century.

In the twilight of the eighteenth century cases appeared on court dockets challenging the legal perquisites of established churches and religious societies. Although many of the plaintiffs met defeat in the courts, the mere appearance of these challenges frightened an already anxious and divided Standing Order. The tendency of the courts, moreover, to support the religious establishment further excited the opposition and increased the agitation for change. Congregationalists, whatever their theology, were unable to harmonize the "Revolutionary belief in religious liberty with the Puritan tradition of an established church."[40]

Two cases before the Massachusetts Supreme Court highlighted this dilemma. In 1807 a challenge appeared to the concept of parish settlement and permanent ministerial tenure. A Federalist court ruled in *Joseph Avery* v. *The Inhabitants of Tyringham* that a minister "settled in a parish for an indefinite term does not hold his office at the will of the parish."[41] Although Avery was settled for an indefinite contract in 1789, a town meeting in 1803 had dismissed the minister without either citing any cause for complaint or calling a council of other area churches. At stake was not only ministerial permanency but the broader question of control over church affairs. Could a majority of parish voters dominate church affairs through their electoral prerogatives? Even more ominous was the threat to the institutional structure of Congregationalism. By their unilateral action and failure to call a council of other churches, the voters of Tyringham had bypassed the Cambridge Platform. In a unanimous decision supporting Avery, the court ruled that settlement was for life. Dismissal must follow the guidelines of the Cambridge Platform. People did have the right to elect their own teachers, but only when a vacancy existed; for arbitrary abrogation of ministerial contracts endangered the stability of settlement patterns and leads to "mischievous" consequences.[42]

The case of *Thomas Barnes* v. *The Inhabitants of the First Parish in Falmouth* reached the same court in 1810.[43] Barnes, alleged to be a Universalist, was settled over an unincorporated religious society in the town of Falmouth, district of Maine. From all appearances, the unincorporated society was largely the creation of Thomas Barnes. He attempted to collect taxes for his support from the estates of two men, also Universalists, who supposedly belonged to the society. The court found against the plaintiff, much to the relief of local Congregationalists. Only public Protestant teachers of legally incorporated societies, the court ruled, could legally benefit from compulsory religious taxation. Moreover, "to extend this indulgence to a teacher of an unincorporated society, who is entitled to no support, would be to grant him a remedy where he has no right, and to encourage disaffection and divisions in regular parishes."[44]

The decision solidly buttressed the established hierarchy. No society could collect religious taxes unless it was incorporated, and no society could become incorporated without going to the legislature. Politics remained the portal to religious liberty. Both decisions solidified the ranks of dissenters, and soon Congregationalists confronted further divisions over the question of disestablishment.[45]

This issue agitated all denominations. In most New England states Trinitarian-Congregationalists retained control of the established churches. Baptists, Methodists, and a mixed array of other dissenters formed the opposition. Vermont was the first state to grant full religious liberty, with passage of an act abolishing compulsory tax support for religion.[46] Speaking in 1815 on the need to educate more young men for the ministry, to supply destitute areas, Lyman Beecher outlined the dangers inherent in such measures. "The overthrow of our religious institutions in New England, and the extinction of evangelical light," Beecher warned, "would render our circumstances calamitous."[47]

Here was the real threat that disestablishment seemed to pose. Without compulsory support for religious institutions, how could the Christian character of the republic survive? Serious dissenters had long been able to support the church of their choice, so long as they completed a deposition certifying membership in another society. But by the second decade of the nineteenth century even this had become odious to those who challenged religious establishment. Dissenters demanded complete religious toleration. "The *render of homage*," one critic of the Standing Order complained, "is so gross a perversion of every idea of rational liberty, such a base perversion of worse than feudal bondage, that we are astonished at finding it subsisting under a professedly free republic, and in the enlightened nineteenth century."[48]

Leaders of the Standing Order had not yet realized that a Christian commonwealth might be more stable and viable with voluntary support. The future looked ominous.[49] With the withdrawal of all state support, what would happen to the hundreds of local churches and religious societies throughout the state? The articulation of such fears was symptomatic of a more disturbing problem and illustrated that Trinitarian pastors had failed to entice large segments of their communities into the church. When legal support disappeared, where would these churches look for financial resources? Who, moreover, would serve as caretakers for the republic?

The new Connecticut Constitution of 1818 confirmed their worst fears. Article VII allowed all persons to withdraw from their present ecclesiastical society merely by registering their intentions with the clerk of the society. More distressing was the provision that persons who came of age after the constitution's adoption did not legally belong to any society until they formally joined. No longer could local religious societies financially benefit from those villagers too lazy or unconcerned officially to certify their withdrawal. The new law posed a stern test for Connecticut Trinitarians. Beset more by Baptists than by Unitarians, they feared for the future of religion throughout the state in the absence of a legal religious establishment. The new law, however, only revealed publicly how much the Standing Order had slipped in its popular support. Townspeople could now publicly abjure what many had long privately avoided. A few years later one pastor reminisced that the law "has not diminished the numbers of our Sabbath congregations," although it "has greatly diminished the legal numbers of the society."[50] Legal and financial support, not religion, declined.

During the next year New Hampshire passed a similar law. The outcome closely followed that in Connecticut, whose own example had stimulated events in the Granite State. Those who comprised the local congregations did not suddenly withdraw their support. Religion did not decline. What did diminish was the financial support that in many towns had provided the margin between solvency and indebtedness for local religious societies. Dwindling support, combined with challenges to Congregational control of meetinghouses and parish funds, made precarious the permanency of many settled pastors.[51]

To the south, the struggle to sever church-state ties in Massachusetts persisted until 1833. However, in June 1811 the state granted religious liberty to dissenters. This act did *not* disestablish Congregationalism, but did allow the legally certified secession so common elsewhere throughout New England. Religious taxes remained, but now could be paid to teachers in all societies, incorporated or unincorporated. The decision in the Barnes case had finally prompted Republicans to action.[52] When disestablishment did arrive in 1833, it did not seriously influence religious activities within the state. The long delay had exposed a welter of conflicting forces, and Trinitarian-Congregationalists greeted formal disestablishment with a measure of relief.[53]

These intense theological and political struggles were not the only worries that aroused clerical fears for the future of religion and society. Increasingly after 1815 pastors attacked the rise in "gross and barefaced instances of speculation," which "have a tendency to break down all barriers to common honesty."[54] Sermons reflected this clerical uneasiness. The attention of Americans, one minister complained, "has been anywhere, but where it should be. He grows up, he is intoxicated with pleasure and amusement. He plunges into business. His mind is *full* of the world. He has no relish for religious instruction." All Christians needed to exert themselves in "some systematic and efficient form" to remedy these ills.[55] A correspondent to the *Christian Spectator* advanced another cure. He urged all parents and ministers to induce "their young friends who go into the city to reside, to one Sabbath School, as the best guaranty of their moral safety."[56]

Joshua Bates, president of Middlebury College, also attacked this drift away from religious and community concerns. He urged that everything possible be done to advance the interests of religion in the community. This alone would ensure the peace and prosperity of society. Happiness inhered in spiritual well-being, not in the temporary accumulation of material wealth. "Without religious principles and religious hopes," Bates instructed his audience, "no man can be really and permanently happy; and, without a general prevalence of these principles and hopes, no society can long enjoy peace and prosperity." Only by advancing the "cause of pure and undefiled religion" could any citizen promote peace, liberty, independence, and prosperity throughout his community.[57] This invocation of the litany of the Revolution illustrated the intensity of these exhortations. By linking the past with the present, and then enveloping the whole in a cloak of religious principles, the clergy hoped to join both to the future. Their response also indicated a deep concern for the future of the country. The perils of contention and irreligion seemed to threaten the foundations of the republic. To save peace, prosperity, and all other republican virtues, ministers searched for some emetic to cleanse the body politic.

Pastors trembled at how easily the old standards seemed to erode. "Sudden wealth," Timothy Dwight warned, "rarely fails of becoming sudden ruin: and most of those who acquire it, are soon beggared in morals, if not in property."[58] Edward Payson expressed similar worries that he might be "overwhelmed by one wave of temptation after another."[59] Afraid that his congregation might condemn him for succumbing to applause and worldliness, Payson rejected resettlement invitations from the prestigious Park Street Church in Boston and Cedar Street Church in New York. He had preached against these very vices and concluded that refusing these invitations would "give me an opportunity to show the world that all ministers are not actuated by mercenary or ambitious views."[60] Not all pastors, however, were so willing to sacrifice their own ambitions and do battle with this new deviltry. The close of the new century's second decade found many ministers accommodating themselves and their actions to these new proclivities. The full extent of this accommodation would become evident in the organization of support for foreign missions.

What emerged from this change and disorder? Perhaps the most important development was a sense of crisis that prevailed among the Congregational clergy of New England. And judging from their actions and remedies, it would appear that only in a crisis atmosphere did the profession seriously undertake efforts for the continued preservation and propagation of a sense of a Christian community.

What was needed was not dull scholasticism nor pietistic asceticism. Ministers must instead appeal "directly to the understanding and conscience, and . . . to the feelings and wants of men."[61] Permanency had declined for ministers throughout New England. Religious and economic disputes divided parishes and communities. Geographic mobility had loosened family ties. All this indicated that new measures were demanded if the older notions were to survive. The need was for the enlistment of new legions in the Christian ranks. Everywhere pastors could agree with Lyman Beecher, who warned in 1812, "The mass is changing. We are becoming another people. Our habits have held us long after those moral causes that formed them have ceased to operate. These habits, at length, are giving way. So many hands have so long been employed to pull away foundations, and so few to repair breaches, that the building totters." "If we do neglect our duty, and suffer our laws and institutions to go down," Beecher concluded, "we give them up forever."[62] The sundering of the old traditions was one more indication that an undirected heterogeneity had supplanted the notion of the cooperative commonwealth.

5. ENLISTING THE PUBLIC

In the midst of this religious and social turbulence the new foreign missionary societies and their auxiliaries emerged. Under the direction of a leadership cadre centered in Boston and the American Board of Commissioners for Foreign Missions—men like Samuel Worcester, Jedidiah Morse, and Jeremiah Evarts—these societies attempted to insert new life into New England Congregationalism. In the face of growing denominationalism and religious division they sought, through voluntarism, to preserve the ideal of the United States as a Christian republic. They hoped to graft new forms onto an old order and consequently save not only the region but the world. Both the effort and the results were impressive.

Enlisting the public in such an enterprise was not easy. These promoters had to battle both atomistic tendencies in American society and a system of transportation and communication that was at best underdeveloped. Sermons, and later tracts and reports, became the first major evangelical instruments in the competitive struggle to capture the public mind and purse.[1] The art of persuasion was a vital force in the effort to rebuild the Christian commonwealth, for it was the primary mechanism for directing people to do good. Several years later, in 1827, Samuel Miller, the Presbyterian president of Princeton Theological Seminary, recalled this emphasis in his instructions to prospective pastors. "In every company and in every situation, be on the watch for opportunities to speak a word for Christ. And where you do not *find* opportunities, by a little address, you may *make* them: and you *will* often do so, if you have as eager, and as incessant desire to *do good*, as the miser has to turn every thing into the channel of gain, and the ambitious man to gather laurels from all quarters."[2] The enlistment of public support formed the heart of the new system, and the clergy overlooked few possibilities for its advancement.

Although only faint stirrings of clerical or public interest in foreign missions existed before the founding of the ABCFM in 1810, there had been a growing interest in the Far East for several years. New England merchants profited from trade with the Orient, and monthly magazines devoted space to exotic tales about distant lands and peoples.[3] In religious matters, however, most New Englanders remained preoccupied with the revivals of the Awakening and domestic missionary societies. At the same time there was an increased concern among deeply devout persons for religious duty and purpose. Was it simply to live one's own life, devoted to God but isolated from the rest of mankind? Or was it, perhaps, to convey to other peoples at home and abroad the religious feelings that seemed so essential in one's own mind? As the revivals of the Second Great Awakening spread across New England, more and more persons sought to affirm the second alternative. "I had been reading the *Life of David Brainerd*," one woman recalled, "and it had inspired me with a great desire to 'do good' to somebody."[4] Here lay the germ of a new crusade, and such a myopic view of benevolence gained adherents with each passing year. Its victims rarely had time to prepare themselves.

Clergymen throughout the region quickly set out to cultivate public support for the new benevolence. Hoping to capitalize on the tide of revivals, they preached the need for a new commitment, knowing full well, of course, that they would be the natural leaders for any new benevolent activity. People looked eagerly to the future, convinced that political and economic progress would continue to elevate and refine their lives and fortunes. Christianity had to keep pace or lose its vitality and relevance. The new benevolence sought to accomplish this. It hoped to join the traditional Puritan admonition to do good with the new wealth. Even a Republican pastor like Stanley Griswold could agree that "genuine Christianity is a system of complete benevolence."[5]

From the outset the clergy did not underestimate their task. Human depravity existed in all countries and must be eradicated if the world was truly to be a beneficent place in which to live. Pastors argued that progress, if it were to be genuine and lasting, had to alleviate the "wretchedness of fallen man."[6] As early as 1802, several years before the first appearance of interest in foreign missions among college students, ministers preached the necessity of saving the world, and of doing so through an extensive preaching of the gospel in distant lands. This was the duty of Christians, and the future of religion hung in the balance. "Those who have no proper conceptions of duty," New Englanders were admonished, "will not be led to religious acts."[7] The field was limitless and embraced "every creature capable of happiness and misery."[8]

What the clergy had done was to alter the nature of religious commitment to accommodate the values of the new nation. Deliberately painting a picture of veritable opulence for all Americans, they interspersed this encouragement to progress with warnings about prudent and temperate behavior and sought to demonstrate the uniqueness of this prosperity when compared to the problems of other peoples throughout the world. This very "ease and security," they argued, gave Americans particular cause to carry the blessings of the Christian religion to all corners of the globe. Pastors urged men and women alike to accept their responsibility for the poor and degraded. What they stated less frequently, but continually implied, was that religious commitment and social stability were somehow linked. The promotion of one would further the other.[9]

By 1805 some pastors had begun to exhort their congregations to devote more of their religious energies to foreign missions. Prominent among these promoters was Edward Dorr Griffin, who subsequently became Professor of Pulpit Eloquence at Andover Theological Seminary and later president of Williams College. Griffin, then a pastor in Newark, New Jersey, argued that there was much to be done throughout the world if the "heathen" were to be saved. Over 80 percent of the human race were unacquainted with Christianity. Moreover, "many of them are also suffering all the hardships of a barbarous state, without domestic or civil order, wallowing in the sinks of vice."[10]

In his sermon on *The Kingdom of Christ*, Griffin deftly correlated the future happiness of foreign peoples with Christianity and the enjoyment of social stability. All this, he concluded, depended on foreign missionary efforts for fulfillment. "Do not our hearts throb with desire to be instrumental in giving Christ *the heathen for his inheritance, and the uttermost parts of the earth for his possession*."[11] To fulfill such throbbings would entail great expense, and Griffin called his listeners' attention to this fact. With this concluding note he tried once again to equate acquisition and disposition of wealth with religious duty. Why else had man's material welfare improved if not to help advance God's purposes?[12]

Slightly more than a year later, the Reverend Joseph Lyman spoke even more optimistically about the future of the foreign missionary enterprise. He observed that although it would still be several years before all areas of the globe would hear the gospel, "all things in providence are in active preparation for this event."[13] Considering the few plans then extant for foreign missions from the United States, Lyman boldly overstated his case. Students at Williams College had only that year met to consider the plausibility of such a venture. No other organizations or societies existed to aid this cause. Even the colleagues of Samuel J. Mills, Jr., at Williams were not without reservations. Such a step, one argued, might be premature. Should not "christian armies" be sent to subdue the Asian natives before the sending of missionaries?[14]

If premature, Lyman was nevertheless prophetic. By 1806 New England clergymen were busily attempting to equate the accumulation of wealth with progress and foreign missions. Their method was twofold. First they illustrated the benevolent impact of happiness on a nation, implying all the while that pursuit of material gain accompanied such happiness. Pastors did not condemn wealth; they commended audiences for their productivity and then urged them to channel this new abundance into virtuous activities, such as foreign missions. Thus did they lay the foundation for a vast enterprise. While condemning pride and vanity, the clergy appealed to duty and benevolence. A truly happy people must be virtuous and holy and should go about the business "of reforming the world, and ameliorating the condition of men."[15]

The first effort to institute some broad system that would organize these promotional attempts came in 1807. In its survey of New England's religious condition, the *Panoplist* urged all churches throughout the region to adopt some comprehensive plan to advance the common interest of Christianity. This, the editor insisted, was the most important task facing the New England churches.[16] Agreeing with the proposal, the Reverend John Reed of Bridgewater reflected the attitudes of most Massachusetts pastors. Reed argued that unity among Christians, churches, and doctrines was essential for a stable society.[17] To promote this unity his colleagues formed the General Association of Congregational Ministers in Massachusetts.

The Reverend Joseph Lathrop of West Springfield quickly projected the ramifications of such systematic endeavors. Creation of similar general associations and societies throughout New England would in turn stimulate local churches to organize parallel bodies. A federal system of religious organizations would ultimately result—a system that would reach into every local community. Lathrop noted that "each *particular* church is to be an instrument of promoting religion within the smaller circle of its influence." The united efforts of all churches would carry the gospel to foreign lands.[18] Lathrop also recognized the value of foreign trade in facilitating entry into other nations and told his audience that "commercial intercourse" would be the springboard for foreign missions. He confided that "many causes were secretly operating" which would effect dramatic changes in the moral condition of the world. If all Christians did their part in support of Christianity, the "grand reformation" was not far off.[19]

Other ministers worked the same theme into their own sermons and emphasized the importance of everyone doing his part. Many of them knew that students at Williams College, and after 1808 at Andover Theological Seminary, had formed societies to investigate the plausibility of foreign missions. The general public, however, had no inkling of these developments. Since they had not yet determined public reaction to such an endeavor, organizers decided to veil their plans in secrecy. Too much promotional work remained to be done.[20] These men feared public opposition to any dilution of the domestic missionary effort, and of course they still had to contend with the prevailing religious factiousness and division. The Unitarian controversy had not yet expired. William Bentley and others publicly criticized efforts to promote the new theological seminary at Andover. Prudence and self-interest, therefore, dictated only the most general appeals for public support.[21]

For the next two years, while support for foreign missions slowly acquired adherents within the professional religious community, ministers preached personal piety, morality, and industriousness to the public. Few could quarrel with these bland pronouncements, and homilies of this sort were congenial to the prevailing tendencies of society. Pastors argued that "public happiness is *best promoted* by an adherence to religious and moral institutions." All men, the Reverend Nathan Perkins noted, were obliged to be industrious. Industry remained the key to wealth and virtue; and the prosperity of religion meant the prosperity of the nation.[22] Herein lay many of the clergy's difficulties. While on the one hand promoting industry as a step toward piety, they also encouraged the very secularism they were attempting to overcome. Blending the one with the other would not be easy, but it seemed to point the way to success.

In 1810 promoters of foreign missions publicly declared their commitment with organization of the American Board of Commissioners for Foreign Missions. For the next two years advocates of foreign missions scoured New England towns and villages to raise both funds and interest for the new venture. They encountered many obstacles, especially with the mounting concern over relations with Great Britain. The absence of any formal fund-raising techniques and the lack of systematic methods to distribute literature or recruit missionaries further compounded the difficulties of the ABCFM.

The value of such an institutional network was just beginning to dawn on these organizers. Appeals and exhortations to individual congregations remained useful, but something more extensive was needed.[23] The *Panoplist* urged its readers to join in this activity. In 1810 it instructed all Christians on the evils of heathenism and chastised the public for its neglect of these conditions. Depicting horrible scenes of gross idolatry, the editor told young men and women to "spend your days in winning souls from pagan darkness to your dear Savior." Only greater missionary exertions could save these poor destitute souls, and time was short.[24]

Pastors agreed that it was the time for missionary societies to go forward. They should recruit support from within local communities and discover some systematic method to collect funds. Timothy Dwight argued, "System gives to every concern of man importance, as well as method; secures the frequent attention of the mind, and the regular efforts of the hands; and therefore gives to human business the highest degree of energy and success."[25] Attention should be given to women as well as men. For although the "great transactions of society" fell primarily upon the shoulders of men, one pastor argued, women could perhaps contribute more to this cause. With deft psychological insight, the Reverend Joseph Lathrop emphasized that "their tender minds are more easily impressed with the solemn truths of the gospel. The troubles peculiarly incident to their sex render them more susceptible of religious impressions."[26] Closer to the truth was that society confined respectable women to a narrow role in the affairs of the world. Intellectually and physically confined, only religion offered women an outlet for their energies and talents.

After the Prudential Committee of the ABCFM decided to send out their first missionaries, it used all these avenues of appeal. Pastors aroused their congregations; letters left the board's offices daily; and the Andover professors dispatched several of their students to surrounding communities and their churches to solicit contributions.[27]

If the promoters of foreign missions hoped for a rapid and generous response from the public, they were disappointed. The board's coffers filled slowly. In the spring of 1811 the Prudential Committee issued an appeal for donations, although indicating that the enterprise was already a success. The appeal painted ugly pictures of a world without Christianity and urged New Englanders not to stagnate in their provinciality, but to carry the greatness of their civilization to all continents. That greatness, it noted, stemmed from a long and close affinity to the Christian religion.

Moving to blunt any criticism of the appeal, the board admitted a prevailing "derangement of public business, and loss of private property," but argued that "wealth enough can be spared from among us for the vigorous prosecution of this transcendently important purpose." New Englanders should not only freely contribute to foreign missions, they should also support other charitable institutions and societies already in operation. The authors of the address (Morse, Worcester, and Evarts) concluded with an announcement of plans to send a mission to Burma the next year.[28]

To facilitate and encourage donations, the ABCFM initiated a number of innovative measures. It sent out agents and published reports of British missionary activities and successes. Claudius Buchanan's *Christian Researches in Asia*, along with his sermon *The Star in the East*, provided the public with exotic readings of strange (and unchristian) customs and religions.[29] Both publications emphasized the humanitarian value and civilizing influence of Christianity and were partly successful in loosening New Englanders' purse strings. But agents had a difficult time. Travel was unpleasant, and few donations exceeded two dollars. Laboring to encourage greater liberality, agents played on personal and national vanity along with desires for community respect. Ezekiel Rich, writing in search of donations, argued that in most Protestant countries those who do the most to advance this cause "are generally considered the most worthy of respect by the citizens of Zion." Despite his appeal, Rich had trouble soliciting funds. John Frost, traveling through New England and New York in 1811 and 1812, experienced similar problems.[30]

In its report to the public for 1811 the ABCFM openly claimed that "the best way to raise the funds will be by applications to individuals, especially to the rich, but not to the neglect of the less wealthy, in all parts of the country."[31] No purse should be left unopened, and no scheme left untried. One temperate correspondent to the *Panoplist* urged readers to give up wine and spirits for the year and donate that sum to foreign missions.[32] A few followed his advice, but this was not the quickest way to put missionaries in Asia.

The most fruitful response to the board's pleas for support came from the Boston area. In 1811 citizens there formed a foreign mission society to act as an auxiliary of the ABCFM. This was but the first of many such societies that would emerge across New England in the next few years. Its organizers argued that the critical moment had come. Either money must be raised immediately to support foreign missions or the enterprise must be abandoned. This sense of urgency, self-generated for its propaganda value, became a familiar theme among supporters of foreign missions. Article 2 of their constitution clearly indicated their purpose: "The sole object of the Society shall be to raise money, and pay it over to the American Board of Commissioners for Foreign Missions." They set the membership fee at only one dollar so as to allow everyone to join, regardless of wealth. This was a brilliant step, for the larger the membership the greater the publicity; and continued awareness heightened the chances for greater donations.[33]

Another innovative proposal was a suggestion that before their departure, missionaries to India might first be sent to communities across New England "to call the public attention to the great object of their mission; and to excite a general interest in forms of missionary exertions." It was presumed that nothing would be more exciting or productive than for the populace to see one of these creatures firsthand. "I should think," the correspondent concluded, "that they might with propriety be directed to request contributions in those places, where they preached."[34] Apparently this barrage of propaganda was effective, for students as far away as Middlebury, Vermont, inquired about the possibilities of becoming foreign missionaries.[35]

But if these activities aroused support for the new cause, they also provoked some opposition. As might be expected, the Reverend William Bentley attacked the enterprise as merely one more scheme emanating from Andover to prejudice and mislead people who should know better. A correspondent to the *Panoplist*, however, evaluated these early labors much more perceptively when he noted that foreign missions were not yet fully supported because "the object is comparatively unimportant." The board was just beginning its activities, yet advocates of the undertaking exposed their colleagues to all possible objections so as to prepare them for future attacks.[36] They were obviously under no illusions as to the religious atmosphere of New England. The defenses were reinforced even before the attackers had gathered.

The turning point in this organizational effort came in 1812. Despite the discomforts that accompanied the war with Great Britain, pastors urged their congregations to imitate the example of Jesus Christ and send the gospel to the millions who were destitute, for the millennium was near.[37] The *Panoplist* now became the mouthpiece for the ABCFM. It dropped almost all notices of domestic religious developments not directly related to the board's activities and attempted to direct all public attention to foreign missions. In April 1812 the editor, Jeremiah Evarts, began a series on "Evangelical Exertions in Asia," designed to inform the public on the natives, history, and customs of the area. This was, of course, the very region where the board sent its first missionaries.[38] Evarts also instructed patrons that by subscribing to the *Panoplist* they could aid the cause of foreign missions, since all profits from the publication went to the ABCFM.[39]

Propagandizing efforts did not end here, but spread into local communities across New England. Pastors admonished congregations that their duty as Christians compelled them to propagate the gospel. The mere fact of war did not lessen the urgency. Laborers were needed, and preachers assured New Englanders that all who contributed would receive a reward. "Every cent," one pastor promised, "will be carefully registered in the records of heaven."[40] Students at Andover Seminary offered to sacrifice their vacation to solicit contributions and distribute missionary materials. The board accepted all aid and hoped to convince everyone that foreign missions were both practical and essential.[41] The *Panoplist* urged the creation of female cent societies for the support of these endeavors. The editor pointedly noted the real value of such groups: "The smallness of the donations in Cent Societies, so far from being an objection to them, is an argument in their favor. The greater the number of Christians who are personally interested in the cause of missions the greater will be the prospect of success. Those who give money to support a mission will pray for its prosperity, and will anxiously inquire as to its effects."[42] Benevolence and charity were the duty of all Christians, and no self-respecting Congregational pastor let his congregation forget it. If, as the Reverend Abraham Bodwell concluded, the millennium was to begin in 1866, there was extensive work to be done.[43]

This work was being done. Local societies formed to augment solicitations of the board and to assist in the moral reformation of society. Ministers quickly noted, and praised, their stabilizing influence on the "laws and institutions of our land."[44] The Prudential Committee circularized instructions to its agents urging that an efficient system be immediately established to secure "a regular and durable supply of the requisite funds." Agents should actively promote the formation of societies and attempt to unite "all classes of the community" in support of foreign missions. At the same time, however, no aspersions should be cast on the work of other benevolent organizations, since all these societies "are parts of one great system."[45] The committee also gave notice that without greater financial support the proposed mission to India would have to be abandoned. Only systematic efforts could save the venture.[46]

The last-minute appeal succeeded. More than one pastor imitated the example of Lyman Beecher, who hurried home from the meeting of the ABCFM and immediately set about establishing an auxiliary in Litchfield County, Connecticut. Aided by several colleagues, he circulated to pastors of all churches in the county detailed plans for the new society. A committee designated agents to make collections in each town and tried to interest local churches in the work of foreign missions. In November 1812 Beecher wrote to his friend the Reverend Asahel Hooker in an effort to broaden the institutional structure: "If we stand idle we lose our habits and institutions piecemeal, as fast as innovation and ambition shall dare to urge on the work. If we meet with strenuous opposition in this thing we can but perish, and we may—I trust if we look up to God we shall—save the state."[47]

Here lies the genius and broad sweep of the foreign missionary crusade. Its purpose was not only to evangelize the heathen in distant lands but also to combat religious division and political factiousness at home. Here was a cause in which people could submerge their individual discontents. Here was a chance to erect institutional safeguards against further dissolution of a sense of Christian community. These men saw themselves engaged in something far more important than petty denominational rivalries. At stake was their ideal of American society, grounded in religion and dedicated to orderly change. Charges that these men were reactionaries, committed to blocking all change and intent on preserving their own influence and status must be considered as a byproduct of the political and religious rivalries of the day. Once so considered, they must be scrutinized skeptically or cast aside. These organizations were a cross between the committees of the American Revolution and the more traditional parlor benevolence. They sought to combine revolutionary organization and activism with the stability and respect of the drawing room. Amid the confusion of voices in New England society they hoped to graft the new onto the old. In foreign missions these men believed they had found a cause that could demonstrate the verities of the old virtues while at the same time embrace the new. Religious piety joined hands with economic prosperity in the pursuit of progress and stability.

Success came rapidly in 1812. Ministers in Norwich and New London formed a foreign missionary society. Led by the Reverend Joseph Lathrop, citizens of Springfield and the neighboring Massachusetts towns organized another society. In Worcester, a Religious Charitable Society formed to support "poor men of piety and talents" also contributed to the ABCFM for support of the mission to India.[48] Elsewhere across New England similar societies organized to support the new cause. Each one circularized its patrons annually to solicit contributions. They also effectively propagandized each others' achievements in an attempt to increase donations. Yet, despite these efforts, rarely did anyone donate more than one dollar annually, regardless of his wealth. A ten-dollar contribution marked its donor as a truly liberal and benevolent man. Most societies bowed to this trend and instituted dues of one dollar, while encouraging members to give as much as they could afford. This trend disturbed patrons of the board initially, but in future years this broad base of contributors would be a valuable source of strength.[49]

Who led these organizing efforts? Men accustomed to authority and community leadership spearheaded this institutional growth. Jedidiah Huntington, collector of the port of New London, Connecticut, for twenty-six years, presided over that community's foreign mission society. Elias Perkins and Charles Lathrop assisted him. Perkins was for years a judge of the Connecticut court and a member of Congress, while Lathrop was clerk of the county court. In Norwich two well-known clergymen, Joseph Strong and Asahel Hooker, led the society, along with two Huntingtons and a Perkins. Timothy Dwight headed the local society in New Haven and vicinity.[50] In Massachusetts the same pattern prevailed. Names like William Phillips, Richard Bartlet, Jeremiah Evarts, Joseph Lathrop, John Hooker, Solomon Williams, and Joseph Lyman appeared as officers of local foreign missionary societies. The leadership of societies in Maine came from similar stock. Respected pastors like Edward Payson, William Jenks, Jonathan Cogswell, Eliphalet Gillet, and Jesse Appleton provided the direction for local groups in that district of Massachusetts.[51]

Not everyone favored the new undertaking, however. William Bentley, self-appointed spokesman for the opposition, bemoaned the growing network of foreign mission societies; for by 1813 they had appeared in almost every port town from Maine to Connecticut. Yet, considering Bentley's acute sensitivity to religious and political change, his mounting criticism of the venture in 1812 and 1813 perhaps measures its success. The Salem Unitarian also attacked the mission to India. "We have," he railed, "missions from every sect who follow all their prejudices into every country into which their zeal can penetrate."[52] Who supported this "fanatical design"? Most contributions, he insisted, came "from the most illiterate fanatics." Bentley could never understand why men would forsake their native land and own countrymen for foreign missions and remained adamant that the "mad scheme cannot be too much reprobated."[53] Few, however, spoke out against foreign missions. The Reverend Thomas Robbins stood nearly alone in his opposition to the cause in Connecticut, as William Bentley had in Massachusetts. Most pastors deemed any new attachment to religion, however synthetic, worthy of praise.[54]

After 1812 the organizing impulse spread rapidly from town to town. The Prudential Committee issued a public appeal for support through the pages of the *Panoplist* in an effort to increase its financial stability and hasten the growth of societies. Optimistically recounting recent successes, yet threateningly cautious about the future, the appeal urged a greater commitment from all Christians. The establishment of foreign mission stations, the committee warned, would not be easy. Many obstacles confronted missionaries, but their efforts brought greater rewards than those of "the most honored servant of Christ in a Christian country."[55] With this address, the board again demonstrated its promotional ability. It fully credited New Englanders for their accomplishments, but also prepared them for the possibility of future reverses. At the same time the board moved to rebut the demands of those few critics who urged priority for domestic missions. "On this subject," Timothy Dwight explained, "there can be no debate. The time for doubt is past. The work is begun."[56]

Local missionary societies cooperated in this effort. At its annual meeting, each society contracted a preacher to relate hideous tales of heathen superstitions and remind members of their duty to eradicate these evils.[57] These spiritual arousals quickened the stream of donations. Women especially remained a primary target for the crusade, and ministers lavishly praised their slightest contribution.[58] Each issue of the *Panoplist* carried lists enumerating all contributors along with the size of their donation, enabling New Englanders to measure their efforts against those of their neighbors. Few asked to remain anonymous. Religious zeal had truly accommodated itself to economic individualism. All could see who had done his duty, and who had not.

This promotional drive apparently peaked in 1812. Contributions to the ABCFM from its numerous auxiliaries and the public at large that year topped $13,000. For the next four years donations fluctuated, but did not exceed this figure until after 1816. If foreign missions heralded the approaching millennium, then the work had barely begun.[59]

During the next four years the board continued its fund-raising efforts, but the results were not impressive. A postwar recession tightened purse strings. With the end of the war people put their own affairs in order, and a lack of public excitement remained the greatest problem facing the Prudential Committee. The mission to India had departed, but the results were mixed. The missionaries had experienced difficulties in establishing a station. Some members of the mission had even deserted Congregationalism and joined the Baptist church! There had been no startling breakthrough with which to titillate the public imagination. The result was a steady decrease in donations. By 1815 the annual receipts of the board had fallen to $9,000, and the decline in several of the auxiliaries was even more abrupt. Two societies in Norwich and New London, Connecticut, donated $197.31 in 1815; they had raised $543.23 the previous year. In the Boston society, one of the largest and wealthiest auxiliaries, benefactors raised only $371.19 in 1815, compared to $1,223.72 two years before. This decline was repeated in foreign mission societies across New England.[60]

Through the pages of the *Panoplist* the Prudential Committee launched a counterattack; but it had nothing new to say. Again the committee pushed its old formula: the promotion of the general cause, the formation of societies, the preaching of sermons, the distribution of tracts, and the appeal to a sense of Christian duty.[61] But the system would not run itself. Some new animating spirit had to be found. The institutional structure was willing, but the people were not. An awareness of this moved the Reverend James Richards to ask the board: "Is this a time to sit still?" Richards questioned the sincerity of the commitment to foreign missions and reiterated various inspirational phrases and examples that had been used earlier at the founding of the ABCFM.[62] It was difficult to recapture the original zeal, and some had second thoughts about the enterprise. Elias Cornelius, agent for the ABCFM and later its corresponding secretary, was one who reconsidered its objectives in 1814. Admitting the need for foreign missions, he bemoaned their expense and argued that economy and duty impelled the United States to devote greater efforts to Christianizing the Indians in the American West.[63]

More ardent supporters of the new institutional network attacked this decline. Joseph Lathrop lashed out at critics of the crusade in an 1814 sermon in Springfield, Massachusetts. To oppose these societies, he warned, "is to rebell [sic] against God. The enemies of them will fall under awful guilt."[64] Lathrop defended the system and criticized New Englanders for not doing enough for charity. Benevolence, after all, was "an essential virtue" of religion. Moreover, it was "astonishing" that anyone would object to foreign missions or "manifest a reluctance to promote it."[65] But his moralizing had little impact. Despite the presence of collectors in nearly every town, local foreign mission societies could not match their earlier contributions. The crusading zeal had dimmed, and New England's ministers could not seem to revive its earlier fervor.[66]

The slackened public interest, however, only caused the clergy to increase their activity. Throughout 1815 pastors labored to awaken greater interest in foreign missions. Most of their efforts followed traditional methods and patterns and had little measurable success. The clergy seemed to have exhausted its resources. It had created a vast network of societies, but could not keep them in a state of perpetual excitement. Each new society encouraged the others to continue meeting and to solicit their members for donations, but failed to produce the expected awakening.[67] The stagnation of the previous two years persisted.

Gradually a few persons came to understand the problem. Several students at Andover Theological Seminary were among the first to realize the shortcomings of the existing system. In a meeting of the Society of Inquiry in 1815 Ebenezer Burgess, the retiring president of the society, noted that "the insinuation often made that the people know their duty in this respect, and have only need to be aroused to perform it, is not true." Exhibiting a wisdom beyond his years, he observed that mere exhortations cannot make people aware of their duty toward the heathen.[68] Something more substantial was needed. Other discussions before the society reflected this change of thought among supporters of foreign missions. James Kimball argued that foreign missions increased support for religion at home, since the number of clergy expanded to meet the new demands for ministers, and that the entire enterprise promoted greater unity among Christians.[69] Only one pitfall awaited supporters of the endeavor: the dangerous influence of improper motives. In his essay on the subject, Thomas Shepard warned that young men should not be "dazzled by the novelty of the subject, and urged on by public feeling." Dreams of travel, adventure, status, or denominational promotion should be cast aside.[70]

To augment these changes foreign mission societies once again encouraged patrons to donate whatever possible to the cause. Perhaps the most innovative suggestion came from directors of the society in Wiscasset, Maine. In 1815 they urged local farmers to contribute a Merino sheep or some lambs in lieu of money. During its first year of operation, the Wiscasset society succeeded in collecting $107.50, along with one half-Merino sheep and five lambs. It sold the fleece and sent the proceeds to the board's treasurer in Boston. Religion once again embraced the new economic progress to promote piety. Presumably these new exertions would enlist more people and encourage greater donations, and pastors preached the value of these gifts in helping to unify the church at home.[71]

Now, perhaps in an effort to resuscitate their cause, ministers openly praised the importance of religion and foreign missions to a well-ordered society. Suffering from growing impermanency, the clergy feared continued social disintegration and tried to prevent it. In its *First Quarterly Circular* in 1815, the Prudential Committee boldly stated the remedy: "It appears to be vastly important to the Christian cause, that the *social principles of our nature* should be consecrated to the service of God. It is necessary to a well-ordered and harmonious state of society, that the members should converse and act together; that they should feel their common interests, and be moved, as by a common impulse, to the promotion of a common end."[72] By diverting attention from divisive issues the clergy hoped to recapture a sense of Christian brotherhood. Unity of sentiment among town and church would mute, if not eliminate, local religious squabbles and thereby promote greater ministerial permanency. Congregational leaders thought they had uncovered the cause of their ills and sought to dispel them. Between their appeals to duty, stability, domestic influences of foreign missions, the millennium, and links between foreign missions and the cause of liberty, pastors tried to create a new excitement in the public mind. By 1817 they would be successful, but not because of these promotional themes.[73]

Success came slowly. Signs of a change in fortunes appeared with the onset of new revivals in 1816 and early 1817. By 1816 New Englanders were able to support the *Boston Recorder*, a weekly paper entirely devoted to religious news.[74] Cheered by these developments, the Prudential Committee mounted a new attack on the New England conscience and purse. In January 1816 the *Panoplist* printed a copy of the American Board's *First Quarterly Circular*, thereby placing its message in the hands of all its friends and subscribers. All persons, it claimed, can "exert an active benevolence" regardless of their wealth or position. The cause of foreign missions had no boundaries, and the board left no potential donor unmolested. Samuel Worcester wrote to Edward Payson in Maine and requested that he visit the principal towns throughout the district to "animate and strengthen" existing associations as well as "promote the forming of societies wherever it may be suitable."[75] Across the region the clergy once again instructed parishioners on their duties, and they again directed much of their appeal toward women. "Have your bosoms caught a spark of that heavenly flame," questioned one pastor. He then cited the appalling statistics that 80 percent of the world's population were still pagans.[76] The Prudential Committee, hoping that somehow the system would regenerate itself, increased its efforts.

In January 1816 the committee decided to further institutionalize the methods used to solicit contributions. This heralded the beginning of a period of rapid growth for the board. In a letter to all agents, Samuel Worcester summarized the progress to date and outlined the board's ambitious plans for the future. To support these activities increased funds would be needed. Citing the British example, he told the agents that the committee had decided to systematize the employment of agents along with the excitement and communication of the missionary spirit. He concluded by enclosing each agent's particular assignment under the new procedure.[77] Although the new system did not produce immediate results, the *Religious Intelligencer* noted that "the call for Missionary labors is louder than in preceding years" and hoped the new efforts would quickly succeed.[78]

A few women in scattered communities apparently felt the impact of these new exertions, but most societies did not witness any startling growth. One society suggested that a lack of information was the cause of the decreased zeal. Whatever the reason, local societies followed the lead of the parent organization and searched for new techniques to increase participation in the work of foreign missions.[79] Many groups instituted a prayer meeting on the first Monday of each month specifically designed to pray for foreign missions. They also found this a convenient time to raise funds for the board. Other societies used missionaries, recently returned from India, to attract large crowds for the purposes of praying and fund-raising, thus snaring the curious as well as the pious.

An adjunct of the alarmist sermon by a recently returned missionary was the decision to have some respected local pastor take a living example of heathenism from town to town. If the native had recently embraced Christianity his appearance was even more valuable. Any talent or bits of education he could exhibit made him a priceless addition to the board's promotional machinery.[80] New Englanders who did not have an opportunity to marvel at a representative of heathenism could read about heathen depravity in Melville Horne's *Letters on Missions* or Claudius Buchanan's *Christian Researches*. Both works were extensively reprinted and distributed throughout the region, and newspaper editors heartily recommended them to readers.[81]

The turning point in this struggle for regeneration came in 1816 with the establishment of the Foreign Mission School at Cornwall, Connecticut. This was a carefully devised plan to sustain interest in foreign missions. A meticulously orchestrated campaign to capture public attention preceded its formation, and the board thoughtfully considered all aspects of the scheme before its implementation. During the winter and spring of 1816 there had been some discussion in private circles about the desirability of raising money and organizing societies to support the education of heathen youth. Agents requested the board to provide tracts or documents on the state of heathen children. These would be used to promote the formation of societies to excite interest in this cause. "I hope," one agent wrote, "to form 2 associations in a Society—one among Females . . . and one among young men."[82]

At the same time, Samuel J. Mills, Jr., and other interested persons wrote the ABCFM, urging it to establish a foreign mission school in Connecticut. They noted the presence of several Owyhean (Hawaiian) youths in New England and recommended that the board support a school of this type.[83] Joseph Harvey and James Morris, leading citizens in their communities and later intimately connected with the school, also asked the board to assume responsibility for all Owyhean youths in the United States. They reported that a meeting had been held in New Haven on June 21, 1816, to organize a committee for just this purpose, on the assumption that the board would subsequently stand behind their actions. These self-appointed guardians included both Morris and Harvey, along with the Reverend Charles Prentice. Lyman Beecher, protector of Connecticut's morals, presided over the meeting.[84] This unilateral assumption of guardianship undoubtedly startled some of the Owyheans. Apparently no one thought that they might have preferred to be home in the Sandwich Islands than to be displayed throughout New England as some exotic exhibit. But this was irrelevant to those interested in their improvement.

Promoters of the new scheme lost little time in soliciting public support. In July 1816 the *Panoplist* published an article setting forth the advantages of training native missionaries. They would, the author argued, serve as good examples to their people, be fluent in native languages, find the climate agreeable, and know the local manners and customs. But they would be most useful for their ability to allay native suspicions about American missionaries. With native help Americans could ease themselves into intimate and influential positions in heathen nations, from which they could assert their "benevolent guardianship." Few could argue any of these points, once they accepted the basic notion of the larger scheme. The school would teach natives the virtues and arts of agriculture and commerce. The missionary experience was to be economic and social as well as religious. "Christianity and civilization," the authors concluded, "go hand in hand, and ever have been and ever will be mutual helps to one another."[85]

In their correspondence with the ABCFM, Harvey, Prentice, and Morris urged support for their plan. These students "might become eminently useful as instruments of civilizing and christianizing their countrymen."[86] The men carefully noted the beneficial domestic effects of their proposal. The proximity of large numbers of foreign youth receiving an education would influence New Englanders, and information on their progress would provide a continual flow of propaganda to aid in soliciting contributions for foreign missions. This school would also directly aid the ABCFM in its training of missionaries. Missionary candidates could spend some time there as assistant teachers, while learning the customs and language of the country to which they were assigned.[87] Unspoken, yet implicit in these plans, was the assumption that the guidelines being formulated for the Foreign Mission School represented the building blocks of Christian civilization. Its organizers hoped to realize their model of national glory and republican virtue. They hoped to establish a New England writ large. James Morris proposed to lay the project formally before the board at its next annual meeting.

Meanwhile the Prudential Committee increased its efforts to raise needed capital and assigned Elias Cornelius the task of promoting foreign missions throughout the entire New England region. The young agent quickly issued a circular to all clergy in Essex County, Massachusetts, alerting them to his plan to tour their sector, preach on various topics, and collect money for the new school in Cornwall. He asked for their cooperation and support.[88]

Throughout the summer and autumn of 1816 those with an interest in the new proposal kept the subject before the public. In October the school's agents requested the Prudential Committee to publish a tract suitable for public distribution "to facilitate the contributions." The same day a notice appeared in the *Religious Intelligencer* indicating that formation of the school was imminent. It only awaited evidence of "liberal support from the benevolent public." Readers were once again reminded of the advantages that this school would confer.[89]

While these preparations were under way, Cornwall authorities carefully examined the proposed property and estimated costs and repairs. They recommended that the board purchase the needed land and buildings and concluded that even if the institution failed land values alone would allow them to escape without a loss—concerned as these men were about foreign missions, they were also Yankees. Jeremiah Evarts, treasurer of the board, urged the building committee to solicit the wealthier classes for sufficient funds to purchase the lands and buildings. Evarts did not attempt to conceal the motives or methods for the solicitation. The campaign should concentrate on convincing wealthy farmers "in Litchfield County and other parts of Connecticut" to provide the Foreign Mission School with a handsome endowment. All possible inducements were to be used, and he suggested "that the first subscriber in each town will confer a particular favor on the institution by putting his subscription high."[90]

Religion had not only reached an accommodation with wealth, the two had merged into a corporate enterprise. By freely publicizing all contributions, promoters of the school joined forces with local class and status structures throughout New England. The request to put one's "subscription high" so as to set a standard of benevolence encouraged others to measure their present wealth and future ambitions against this standard, however false. A person's religious commitment was neither publicized nor cast aside; it was simply irrelevant. The system of societies was designed to collect money and propagandize the efforts of the board, and no one questioned an individual's motives for joining one of the associations. Although willing to accept donations in any form or amount, the agents' emphasis on the benevolence of wealth served to buttress the virtues of industriousness and frugality. Nowhere were the benefits of wealth more apparent, for they placed the blessed few among the first rank in the glories of evangelizing the world.

The activities of Elias Cornelius, agent for the ABCFM, illustrate these priorities. In November 1816 he hastily penned a letter to Samuel Worcester requesting immediate approval of his plan to visit every Congregational society in Essex County, Massachusetts.[91] His circular highlighted his objectives, and he even found a native of Hawaii to drag along. The collection methods of these agents were carefully planned so as to enable them to dine at homes where they did not expect to get any money. In this manner few persons escaped giving some aid to foreign missions, however slight it might be.[92] Cornelius's letters included no references to the piety of the contributors, but clearly implied that God would somehow smile down upon them once they had given to the cause. The clergy recognized only religious, not economic, poverty.

To systematize support further for the Foreign Mission School, the board issued another circular. This time it not only urged patrons to provide financial backing for the education of "heathen children" (presumably foreign) but also instructed them not to divert "their accustomed contributions from the general missionary object."[93] Perhaps each society could establish a special fund along with a separate constitution for this effort. The Prudential Committee soon issued still another circular giving further instructions on establishing "Societies for the Education of Heathen Youth." It also included a sample constitution to insure uniformity and encourage immediate action. Prospective groups had only to fill in the proper blanks and they had a finished constitution![94] The board's system of societies had woven a tight web across New England. Surely the mania for system and organization could go no further. It is a testimonial to the diligence and talent of the board's officers that they made this structural nightmare work. But there was no apparent dilution of effort on any project, and their reward was a significant increase in funds.

Meanwhile efforts to formally establish the school neared completion. One correspondent offered his town, Humphreyville, as a site. Other towns in Litchfield County extended sundry monetary offers in an effort to entice the school to their community. But the Prudential Committee settled on the rural Connecticut hill town of Cornwall. Agents for the board drove a hard bargain, capitalizing on Eben Maxfield's desire to sell his land quickly and emigrate in search of cheaper land and lower taxes.[95] The committee purchased approximately one hundred acres of land and two houses. Local citizens donated an academy building. The board seemed pleased, and certainly rural isolation had its merits.[96] If students suddenly discovered an urge to leave the school, there was no convenient place to go. They would be free from temptation, and the town itself seemed suitably religious.

The school opened in May 1817. Since many of the prospective students were already in the immediate vicinity, full operations began almost at once. Several Owyheans then in Litchfield came to Cornwall to attend, along with numerous American Indians and various natives from several foreign countries. The board chose the Reverend Joseph Harvey of Goshen to be the school's first principal, but his congregation feared a division over the choice of a successor and refused to release him. Board members then selected the Reverend Herman Daggett, who agreed to serve.[97] To assist Daggett, they selected Deacon Henry Hart of Goshen to superintend the teaching of practical agriculture. Students at the school were to be trained as missionaries, physicians, schoolmasters, and interpreters to aid both their own native peoples and American missionaries.

John Treadwell defined the object of the Foreign Mission School in his address at the inauguration of Herman Daggett. It was "to afford a hospitable asylum for such unevangelized youth, of good promise, as are, or shall be, providentially brought to our shores, and cast upon us."[98] This was a glorious vision, but the thought of natives from any land, barely literate in their own tongue, studying theology, Latin, Greek, or natural philosophy was a bit absurd. Nonetheless the board pushed ahead with its effort to transform the native youth into educated, pious, genteel New Englanders.

The establishment of the Foreign Mission School marked a significant advance for the foreign missionary enterprise. It created a permanent exhibit of "savable heathen" for New Englanders to marvel at. Potential missionaries could be introduced to examples of their future parishioners before embarking and perhaps lessen some of their apprehensions about strange lands and peoples. The inclusion of a few American youths in the school, moreover, would also serve to guide and influence the other students. In his sermon before the school and public in 1818, the Reverend Joseph Harvey emphasized the real purpose of the endeavor. He argued that it was "highly important" that some "heathen youth" be introduced to Christian society "and educated in it; that they may see the operation of principles which they are expected to inculcate."[99]

Here lay the power of Protestant Christianity in the nineteenth century. Religion preserved ancient values; but it was also a dynamic force that sought to transform American society, and even the world. Grounding their plans in the assumption that all virtuous political systems rested on a secure religious foundation, promoters of foreign missions sought to carry their message abroad. They judged New England's woes in the early nineteenth century to stem from an erosion of this connection between religious principles and republican virtue. Unable to roll back the tide of secularism and economic individualism at home, like their Puritan forebears they expected to provoke change at home by example abroad. That the crusade carried with it American values and institutions merely reflected the source of the Christianizing impulse. Many nations could lead, but few were chosen.

With the Foreign Mission School in full operation, the board hoped that contributions to the cause would increase markedly. Certainly this was not a time to relax. Jeremiah Evarts warned, "Our expenses greatly increase, and unless the liberality of the public shall keep pace with them, they cannot be sustained."[100] The central direction involved in the undertaking could not have been more succinctly stated. The board continued to develop projects for good Christians to support. Once a commitment was made, the board then asked the public for financial support. It mobilized its organs of propaganda and legions of agents to extract donations from a politely interested public.

Only a startling or fascinating phenomenon evoked an outburst of public enthusiasm and made support self-generating. The Foreign Mission School was such an event, and for the next year or two pastors and agents found that even their slightest efforts were well rewarded. The *Panoplist* contributed to this well-coordinated attack on the public's purse. In January 1817 it printed a front-page article urging "a grander display of benevolence on a large scale, than the world has ever yet seen." Every Christian should make "doing good" part of his everyday business. "It should be reduced to a system," the author concluded, "and have a large share of time and property assigned to it." Only then could pastors promote the "permanent good of others."[101] Statements like these perpetrated the dream of a Christian community and at the same time encouraged the public to participate through financial contributions. Donors could thereby feel part of the enterprise. Everyone could do something, and here lay the genius of the operation.[102]

In 1817 and 1818, after creation of the Foreign Mission School, donations to the ABCFM increased dramatically. Pastors throughout New England capitalized on this new concern for heathen education. Examples of hundreds of young Americans, eager to embark as foreign missionaries, became an increasingly common theme in sermons and discourses before local societies. The Bible, the clergy argued, was the only code of laws for men to follow.[103]

But pastors devoted most of their attention to the new facility at Cornwall. Heathen school societies formed in towns across New England, and donations to the ABCFM jumped from $12,501.03 in 1816 to $29,948.63 in 1817.[104] Some critics attacked the new efforts and complained that these funds "may be perverted to the propagation of *sectarian creeds*." But agents for the board discovered that in most sectors the prospect of educating heathen children diminished existing prejudices against foreign missions.[105] Agents appeared in all corners of the region in pursuit of money. Some, like Elias Cornelius, took along an exotic native to excite interest. By the close of 1817 the *Religious Intelligencer* concluded that "*action is the order of the day*." Indeed it was.[106]

After nearly a decade of promises, threats, and exhortations to do good by contributing to the ABCFM, New England consciences still were not exhausted. They did not have time to be. The Prudential Committee continually reminded them of their duty, and its network of agents crisscrossed the region so thoroughly that only a hermit stood a chance of eluding them. Joseph Buckingham, editor of the *New England Galaxy and Masonic Magazine*, criticized this "system of beggary," but he stood almost alone in his opposition.[107] Most New Englanders apparently assumed that since the regulatory and supervisory operations of foreign missions were directed at other peoples, they could reserve their criticism for societies that meddled in domestic affairs. The influence of the foreign missionary enterprise was either harmless or benevolent, if one could withstand the carping reminders to duty from its agents.

In January 1818 the Prudential Committee finally outlined the full extent of the system it sought to construct. Each county should organize a foreign mission society. If the county was large, it should be subdivided into districts, with each district forming a separate society. Finally, every town or parish within that district should also support at least one society specifically concerned with foreign missions. Any support given to the education of heathen youth or other related efforts should be channeled through separate societies formed for those purposes.[108] Figures documenting the growth of these societies filled the pages of the *Panoplist*. For those who needed personal reminders of their duty and the task ahead, a steady procession of pastors appeared before these societies to report new developments. Playing on the vanity and conscience of their listeners to elicit donations, these preachers bubbled with optimism and refused to acknowledge publicly even the slightest setback in their crusade. In this manner they glossed over or ignored the underlying urgency behind the board's appeals for funds. If the enterprise was flourishing, why did each new appeal seem more anxious than the last? Why did trustees of the Foreign Mission School continually request donations to meet *current* expenses? No answers were ever forthcoming, because the questions were never asked.[109] Indeed, religion thrived on cataclysmic pronouncements. The clergy's commitment to success, moreover, allowed no room for failure.

As if this system of societies and vast array of propaganda organs were not enough, the board flooded New England with yet another book of horrors and hopes in 1818. It was, perhaps, its most successful publication. Entitled *The Conversion of the World: or the Claims of Six Hundred Millions and the Ability and Duty of the Churches Respecting Them*, it complained about the shortage of ministers, but concentrated largely on demonstrating the resources then available to American Christians. At once a manual and a command, it reproduced intricate calculations to demonstrate how money could be raised to carry the gospel to the world.

The tract was the joint effort of two missionaries, Gordon Hall and Samuel Newall, and illustrated the commitment of these men as well as their attitudes of racial and cultural superiority. They called for more preachers for "the ignorant and careless heathen," for without civilized instruction even the Bible would not make sense to men of their "capacity and circumstances."[110] Much of the book called attention to native practices, estimated the number of missionaries needed, and suggested various schemes to raise funds. Most Americans undoubtedly read the numerous tales of foreign customs and superstitions with awe, shaking their heads at "their foolish ceremonies, and their obstinate attachment to the endless superstitions."[111] Truly something must be done, and quickly. If the flow of funds to the board is indicative of New Englanders' concern, then readers must have agreed with Hall and Newall that "the Missionary's usefulness will generally be in a great measure proportionate to the pecuniary aid which he receives in prosecuting the various methods of advancing christian knowledge among the ignorant."[112]

By the spring of 1818 this "hydra-headed" system was fully developed in all corners of the region. Even the Masons circularized their members, urging all to contribute to the board's projects; and Jonathan Greenleaf, an agent for the board, worked through their lodges with considerable success. An appeal also went out to women throughout New England, urging them to enlist their children in the cause.[113] Not even college students escaped the broad sweep of the clergy. Jesse Appleton bluntly told graduates of Bowdoin in 1818 that "the great design of every person on earth should be to do good."[114]

There could be no mistake as to the purpose of this campaign. The more the clergy sensed the coming of a new Christian commonwealth, the more they increased their solicitations. The most important branch of benevolence, pastors argued, was the promotion of community welfare. Benevolence knew no limits. New England should be an "irradiating point" for the world. Only through continued charity could the region prove to the world that she was not in decline.[115] The emphasis on monetary rather than spiritual contributions, furthermore, indicated the extent of the clergy's accommodation to the growing economic orientation of American life. It allowed people to participate in the venture in what was becoming the customary manner—giving money without making a personal commitment.

By 1818 and 1819, moreover, Connecticut and New Hampshire had moved irrevocably toward disestablishment. This spurred the Congregational clergy to increase their efforts to promote voluntarism. All signs indicate that clerical efforts had certainly become more efficient and more productive. Local associations remained the primary instruments of this effort, and by 1818 the Prudential Committee counted about five hundred auxiliary associations that were collecting money for the board. To be sure there were a few instances where local receipts declined. But these were rare, and it was difficult to be pessimistic about the future.[116] Each society tried to outdo the other, and this mutual excitement and self-stimulation further emphasized the benefits of systematic solicitation. Religious journals and newspapers printed letters and editorials suggesting numerous schemes to maintain public interest in foreign missions. Most of the recommendations reflected the success of earlier appeals and added little that was new to the campaign.[117]

But this spirit was evident elsewhere. Corner markets and general stores kept "missionary boxes" on their counters so that patrons could conveniently contribute. The flock of missionary sheep in Wiscasset, Maine, had grown to over twenty. Hundreds of families contributed household goods, clothing, and furniture to the infant mission school at Cornwall.[118] New Englanders, it appeared, agreed with the Reverend Samuel Gile's proclamation, "I love to plead for the poor; especially when I can do it in full faith and confidence of success." Certainly there seemed little doubt of the venture's success, for "if God be for us, who can be against us?"[119] Despite Gile's apprehensions that human means were not enough to carry Christianity throughout the world, the Prudential Committee seemed to be doing a thorough job of organizing the home front.

The ABCFM lacked only one ingredient to guarantee the perpetuation of its cause. As late as the summer of 1819 it had no foreign missionary stations operating independent of British control. The stations in India, moreover, had been only moderately successful. A new mission, entirely American in scope, was needed to assure permanency. The failure to achieve immediate success apparently discouraged enough supporters of the enterprise to provoke comment in the press. Tales of missionary hardship and heroic labors might well be true, but contributors longed for sudden successes and mass conversions. Quibbles over the justification for publicizing acts of charity would be forgotten if the board could redirect New Englanders' attention.[120] Until now the public's involvement had been largely one-way. People donated money to the board, and perhaps even saw their gifts acknowledged in print, but promoters of foreign missions had been unable to give them illustrious examples of success for this benevolence. By 1819 the auxiliary societies needed to see results, not hear more sermons on duty and organization. Contributors had been remarkably patient and wanted to see a return on their investments. The dream of recreating a Christian commonwealth had not materialized abroad, and without success overseas efforts toward that end at home seemed in danger of collapse. The ABCFM found the answer with their decision to send a mission to the Sandwich Islands.

6. THE SYSTEM AT WORK: THE SANDWICH ISLANDS MISSION

Until 1819 the activities of the American Board of Commissioners for Foreign Missions had been more domestic than foreign. The board had sponsored three missions: one to India in 1812, another to India and Ceylon in 1815, and the most recent again to India in 1817. All had gone to sectors that were under British control, and none had produced much excitement among New Englanders. Appeals for support reflected this inertia, as they continued to emphasize the numerous advantages and broad principles of foreign missions. News from these missions slowly filtered back to the board, and newspapers printed whatever seemed interesting. But most references to these early efforts dwelled on the hardships and struggles of the missionaries. They reported few successes. Even the most passionate supporters of the enterprise clearly recognized that their dream of millions of new Christian converts was far from realization.

In 1819 the board outfitted and dispatched four new mission companies. Two groups set out for Asia, one to India, the other to Ceylon. Levi Parsons and Pliny Fisk formed a third mission that went to Palestine to convert Jews and Muslims. The fourth, and largest, mission company departed for the Sandwich Islands, which lay astride the mid-Pacific trade routes. This last mission captured the attention of New Englanders almost at once. Its organization and support clearly demonstrated the effective power that could be exerted through the complex network of societies radiating from the board's offices in Boston. In its publicity, promotion, and organization of support, the ABCFM reached new heights with the Sandwich Islands Mission. Never before in the history of American foreign missions had so much attention been directed toward a single object.

New Englanders had long been familiar with the islands and their inhabitants. Traders and ship captains had frequented the area since the

1790s and occasionally brought back a native or two for the edification of the curious. In 1790 Captain Robert Gray of the *Columbia* returned to Boston with a Hawaiian prince on board. Bostonians clustered at the docks and along adjacent streets to catch a glimpse of the exotic visitor. They were not disappointed, as the prince appeared in his brilliantly colored native dress. He resembled a vision of paradise, dressed in full plumage with a feathered helmet and long flowing feathered robe that glittered in the sun. Although the prince returned to the Sandwich Islands after a stay of several months, Bostonians long remembered the sight.[1]

This was the first of several contacts with natives from these islands, and proposals for a mission to the region began more than a decade before the founding of the ABCFM.[2] Tales of Captain Cook's adventures and misfortunes among the Sandwich Islanders became favorite reading for youngsters. Bostonians were even treated to a stage play— "The Tragedy of Captain Cook." Among these eager thespians was a native youth that Captain Amasa Delano had shipped from Hawaii in 1801. He attracted public attention off the stage as well as on.

But most New Englanders learned of the Sandwich Islands from newspaper reports that detailed the activities of trading vessels and listed any native youths that arrived on board these vessels. Each year more of these natives entered New England ports.[3] Boston records even indicate that in 1807 Henry Brenneen, a Sandwich Island native, became an indentured servant for four years to David Nye of Wareham. This seems to have been an unusual occurrence.[4]

From 1804 to 1811, as American vessels increased their participation in the sandalwood trade, newspapers reported a concomitant increase in the number of Sandwich Islanders in New England. The local press published extensive notices on the customs and history of the islands. Both the curious and the business-minded eagerly scanned articles that described the growing foreign trade of the Sandwich Island princes, and New England merchant houses prepared to claim a slice of that trade.[5]

Not only traders cast a covetous glance toward these islands. Ministers noted the state of religion at the islands. That pastors were primarily concerned with religion, and not economics, did not render their schemes any less grandiose. By 1815 numerous Hawaiians resided in New England, and clerical discussions focused on the establishment of a foreign mission school. Efforts began to evangelize Hawaiian natives, concentrating first in New England and then in the islands.

Elias Cornelius, an agent for the ABCFM, wrote from Litchfield in December, "Our Hawaiian affairs are prospering."[6] The *Religious Intelligencer* confirmed Cornelius's optimism. In June 1816 the paper reported the presence of several Hawaiians in Connecticut and publicized their intention to return to their native land as missionaries. This news excited New England Congregationalists. Their grand design to evangelize the world clearly appeared to be nearing maturation. Pastors took some of these natives under personal supervision, helped them write pious pleas for assistance, and generally guided them to suit the board's purposes.[7]

In 1816 the board issued the first promotional material for a campaign that would ultimately send American missionaries to the Sandwich Islands. The *Narrative of Five Youths from the Sandwich Islands* briefly recounted the arrival of these young men in the United States and traced their educational and spiritual progress down to 1816. Their letters, which were included in the tract, presented positive evidence that the heathen could be "saved." More important, they provided exotic reading for romantic New Englanders and dutiful Christians. Since many of these letters discussed religious matters, they reminded all readers that there was a job to be done.[8]

The ABCFM carefully cultivated public attention, and through its annual reports intensively promoted a future mission to the Sandwich Islands. "Fortunate" boys would be turned into dark-skinned New England Congregationalists, and would eventually return to their native land and transform an entire people. When four of these youths renounced "heathenism" for Christianity, Americans were impressed. The goodness of American virtues had once again demonstrated its remarkable power to educate, transform, and save. Prompt exportation of this magic potion could save the world. The first step was to train these former heathens to assist in the task, and the Prudential Committee worked vigorously toward this end. In 1816 it announced, "Your Committee cannot but gracefully recognize the hand of God in bringing these lately pagan youths to our shores, placing them within the influence of Christian benevolence, inclining their hearts to the Gospel, and producing in them the desire of making known the unspeakable grace to their countrymen."[9]

In November 1816 the *Boston Recorder* reminded its readers that among the many natives then in the region was George P. Tamoree, son of a Hawaiian king. To New Englanders, Tamoree symbolized the potential goodness of pagans throughout the world. He had fought bravely for the American cause in the War of 1812 and had been severely wounded in several naval battles. During a brief period of recuperation he had come under the protective custody of the ABCFM. The commissioners sent him to Connecticut to be educated, hoping that he would prove useful in establishing a mission in his native land.[10] The *Panoplist* also devoted considerable attention to these Hawaiians, as did trustees of the Foreign Mission School. In a letter to the board's officers urging support for their plans, the trustees argued that one "cannot but view the hand of Providence in relation to the young men from the *Sandwich Isles*, as designed to draw the attention of the Christian public to the Islands, as an important missionary field."[11] Tamoree and the other foreign youths in this country were the new weapons in the orthodoxy's crusade to reestablish a Christian commonwealth.

Several other Hawaiians also received considerable attention in the press. One of them, George Sandwich, could scarcely be called a raw pagan. He had spent two years in Boston and ten in Enfield, Massachusetts, before reaching Cornwall in 1817. Thomas Hopoo had arrived in the United States in 1809. Like Tamoree, he had fought in the War of 1812. After the war Hopoo lived in Goshen and South Canaan, Connecticut, before venturing to Cornwall in 1817. William Tennooe had also arrived in Boston about 1809. In rapid succession a servant, privateer, and finally a barber, he went to Goshen in 1815 and North Guilford the next year. In 1817 he reached Cornwall.[12] There were other Hawaiians in New England, but public attention was drawn to those at the Foreign Mission School in Cornwall. The annual report of the school's agents for 1817 emphasized their presence and praised their religious and scholastic progress, concluding that a mission should be sent to the Sandwich Islands as soon as possible.[13]

Attention especially focused on one particular native—Henry Obookiah. This was no accident, but the result of fortuitous circumstance and vigorous promotion from ABCFM offices in Boston. This combination made Obookiah the primary symbol and instigator for a mission to the Sandwich Islands. He became the central vehicle for cultivating support for the mission and gave the ABCFM its first stirring success story. Consequently, his importance does not end with the Hawaiian mission experience. Through clever and opportune use of his example, the board extended his influence to the entire foreign missionary effort. A glimpse at his life will illustrate his value.

Henry Obookiah was born in Owhyhee, the largest of the Sandwich Islands. His parents and brother were slain during one of the frequent bloodbaths between local chiefs. Within a few years Obookiah fled the island and arrived in New Haven, Connecticut, in 1809 on board a merchant ship. He lived with Timothy Dwight, president of Yale, for a year. On a visit to Andover in 1810 Obookiah met Samuel J. Mills, Jr., who took him home to stay with his father in nearby Torringford. During 1812 the Hawaiian youth went to Hollis, New Hampshire, hometown of the Reverend Samuel Worcester, corresponding secretary of the ABCFM. In 1813 Obookiah spent the winter with James Morris in Litchfield. During these years he learned to read and write. His guardians also taught him basic agricultural techniques and directed his religious education. In 1814 the North Consociation of Litchfield appointed a board to supervise his education and personal development. At the same time they used his services at occasional religious meetings. Later that year he went to live with the Reverend Joseph Harvey at Goshen. By October of 1815 the young Sandwich Island native had left Goshen to reside with the Reverend Charles Prentice at Canaan.[14] These three men, Morris, Harvey, and Prentice, were later responsible for the establishment of the Foreign Mission School at Cornwall. Obookiah's influence on them was as profound as theirs was on him.

This constant change of residence benefited the board, if not Henry. Nathan Perkins, one of the board's agents, took the young Hawaiian with him as he solicited funds in Massachusetts and Connecticut during 1816 and 1817. Perkins reported remarkable results and observed, "It is truly astonishing to see what efforts are produced on the feelings of the people by seeing Henry, and hearing him converse. It opens the hearts and hands even of enemies. Many have contributed generously who never contributed before . . . . But the most pleasing is that it rouses a Foreign Missionary Spirit."[15] After Obookiah's death Perkins recalled that the native's visit "to this part of the country was of essential service to the cause of Foreign Missions. It has silenced the weak but common objection against attempting to enlighten the heathen, that they are too ignorant to be taught."[16] Herein lay the importance not only of Henry Obookiah, the Sandwich Islander, but of Obookiah, symbol of the essential goodness and intelligence of heathens everywhere.[17]

Yet, for supporters of foreign missions, his life was less important than his death. Henry Obookiah died February 17, 1818, of typhus fever and was buried two days later.[18] The Foreign Mission School was in full operation, and the large number of Owhyheans then in residence had begun to attract considerable attention.[19] Throughout New England there was already an undercurrent moving to assemble a mission to these mid-Pacific isles. The death of Obookiah furnished the impetus necessary to hasten these plans to fruition.[20]

New efforts began even before the youth's coffin had disappeared beneath Cornwall's rocky soil. Lyman Beecher launched the renewed commitment in his sermon at Obookiah's funeral. After noting the youth's hopes of returning to his native land, Beecher argued that his was a time for rededication to Obookiah's cause, not a release from an earlier commitment. Handwringing and pious lamentations would not suffice; this was more than ever a time to go forward. The churches of New England were obligated to outfit a mission "to bring the sons and daughters of Owhyhee, to glory." Always ready to use the slightest occurrence to advantage, Beecher insisted that "His death will give notoriety to this institution—will awaken a tender sympathy for Owhyhee, and give it an interest in the prayers and charities of thousands who otherwise had not heard of this establishment, or been interested in its prosperity."[21] For the next year the ABCFM mobilized its entire system of societies to produce this very result. Publication of Edwin Dwight's *Memoirs of Henry Obookiah* was the first step in this effort; the memoir eventually passed through twelve editions and sold over fifty thousand copies.[22] This first promotional measure was a successful one.

Efforts quickly multiplied. In his sermon at the inauguration of Herman Daggett as principal of the Foreign Mission School, Joseph Harvey reiterated the earlier message of Lyman Beecher. Arguing that the primary objective of the school since its inception had been "the evangelizing of the *Sandwich Islands*," he insisted that a mission to these islands would open the door for the introduction of Christianity to western portions of the United States. With this argument Harvey moved to blunt the anticipated criticism from proponents of domestic missions. Existing trade routes indicated that control of the Sandwich Islands afforded easy access to the western coast of North America. Since the Rockies blocked access from the east, ships sailing around Cape Horn could replenish their supplies at the islands before following

the prevailing trade winds to the coast. Contradicting his earlier statement of the school's objectives, Harvey concluded, "Our present establishment, while it may afford occasional labourers for other fields, has
for its leading object, the christianization of the western heathen of this
continent."[23] There was enough fuel in this address for advocates of
both domestic and foreign missions. Here was manifest destiny in a
grand manner.

Meanwhile, attempts to arouse support for both the Foreign Mission
School and the proposed mission continued to accelerate. Herman
Daggett recommended that the board allow pupils at Cornwall to teach
missionaries to the islands the native language. This would enable the
school to demonstrate its usefulness in the enterprise and probably
increase the mission's chances for success. Daggett also put his students
to work devising basic books for use in the missionary schools to be
established at the islands.[24]

During the spring and summer the board surged ahead with plans for
the undertaking. Except for a brief flurry of dissidence over the cost of
Obookiah's tombstone, no criticism emerged to blunt the effort. The
Foreign Mission School needed a successful venture as badly as did the
ABCFM, for the school was barely solvent. Expenses for Obookiah's
sickness had seriously eroded the institution's operating funds. Moreover, like most enterprises of the board, plans and purchases were made
in anticipation of future public support. Unless support was forthcoming its operations would be seriously circumscribed.[25]

In September of 1818 Morris and Harvey requested the ABCFM to
send an agent to the Sandwich Islands. This representative, accompanied by one of the natives at Cornwall, could make all necessary
arrangements for the establishment of a mission. Here was firm evidence that promoters planned to make the mission an immediate
success. They hoped to capitalize on this success to revitalize the
resources of the ABCFM. The two trustees of the Cornwall school
urged the board to learn from its problems with previous missions and
emphasized the need for thorough planning prior to embarkation.

Their rationale for these advance arrangements was many-sided.
First, the Hawaiian kings had demonstrated their liberality in the past.
Since they had assisted travelers, they would probably aid the establishment of a mission. A board representative might be able to procure a
grant of land to support the missionaries.

A second consideration, and perhaps the more perceptive, was that the arrival of an entire company might cause alarm. The trustees predicted that "the savage mind might not be able to comprehend the design, sufficiently to admit the experiment." More to the point, they concluded that "jealousies might arise, that political or mercantile interests were concealed under these fair pretensions."[26] The two men also noted the desire of Sandwich Islanders at the Foreign Mission School to return to their native land and particularly cited the desire of George Tamoree's father to see his son once again.

All these preparations would help promote a successful and permanent mission. An advance agent could bring back up-to-date information on the customs, climate, and inhabitants of the islands. The first missionaries could then become somewhat acquainted with what lay ahead. Finally, an agent "might select a number of promising youth from the chief and influential families in the Islands who might be desirable members of the school."[27]

With this last recommendation, Morris and Harvey bared the psychology and methodology of the board's future operations. Once it established strong ties to the ruling elite in the islands, the board would land missionaries at will and wield a strong influence over the conduct of local affairs. With the Sandwich Islands' crucial position astride the Pacific trade routes, the ramifications of such a step were momentous. Should the missionaries fulfill their dream of establishing an orderly, religious—and thereby virtuous—republic at the Sandwich Islands, its message could span the globe. The Sandwich Islands, like the New England of a glorious past, could be an irradiating point of religion, a beacon to the world.

In November Samuel Worcester wrote Herman Daggett that the Prudential Committee had resolved to outfit a mission as soon as it could find a suitable person to direct preparations. Worcester gave no indication when the mission would be ready to sail and said nothing about sending an advance agent.[28] Daggett assumed that the mission had been put off and acknowledged that perhaps his fervor for the undertaking had blinded him to the many problems involved. "I think we can see," he admitted, "that it would have been premature."[29]

After wishing Worcester luck in finding someone to conduct the mission, Daggett urged the board to begin preparing schoolbooks. The first task of the missionaries on arrival should be to establish schools. These could attract and impress the natives. Missionaries could befriend the natives and gain their confidence before attacking their religious system. "This will probably be grateful to the Natives," Daggett predicted, "& may serve as a cover to the ultimate object, which if too soon presented to their view, might excite prejudice & resentment."[30] This warning indicated that promoters of the enterprise were keen of mind and determined to achieve their goals. The natives would be "saved," whatever their religious preferences.

Advocates of the mission busily set about gathering support for its eventual organization. They publicized the "distressing" moral state of the islands' natives, emphasizing the poor example set by sailors who visited the ports. All hoped that these gloomy sketches would elicit new contributions. Daggett urged the ABCFM to invite pupils from the Cornwall school to visit Boston during their next vacation.[31] With its many sources of wealth, Boston seemed an excellent starting point for the new fund drive.

Only strenuous efforts would raise sufficient funds to send a company of missionaries several thousand miles into the Pacific Ocean. Newspapers sympathetic to the board's purposes tried to help fill its coffers. The *Christian Spectator* published a long review (replete with extensive excerpts) of the *Memoirs of Henry Obookiah*, highlighting Obookiah's piety and devotion. This was more than just another book review; it was an effort to evoke sympathy and garner financial backing for foreign missions. Obookiah's symbolic value was never more publicly displayed.[32]

This little memoir remained the vehicle for a renewed interest in foreign missions—and the Sandwich Islands' mission in particular. Samuel Worcester, primary director of the board's far-flung operations, quickly recognized this. Ever a cautious, careful planner, Worcester admitted that although he had not had time to look at the book, he was "persuaded it will be extensively interesting, and will help the cause."[33]

Despite his optimistic predictions for the book, he refused to succumb to the zealous advances of the men connected with the Foreign Mission School. They urged an immediate mission to the islands, but Worcester held back. Expressing concern over the sudden enthusiasm, he counseled delay until "the young men should be thoroughly furnished, and that our preparations should be in all respects, as complete as possible." The corresponding secretary instructed the trustees at Cornwall to keep the native youths quiet, cheerful, and studious until the right time arrived for their departure. "For this purpose," he admonished, "they should be kept, I think, as much as possible from communication with masters of vessels and others who have visited or are about to visit the Islands."[34]

Worcester insisted that nothing should be allowed to endanger the committee's careful planning. Not only the mission to the Sandwich Islands, but quite possibly the future of the ABCFM hung in the balance. He demanded that "if any boon is to be expected for conveying George P. Tamoree home to his father, it should by all means be secured to the objects of the Mission."[35] Worcester's instructions apparently cooled the ardor of the trustees for a while, although Joseph Harvey reminded him that the Sandwich Islands remained a prime location for a mission and that many persons desired to see one sent there as soon as someone could be found to take command of the necessary preparations.[36]

The Prudential Committee diligently searched for the right man. In April Worcester reported to Herman Daggett that he hoped the mission could depart by autumn. Although the committee had not engaged a superintendent for the mission, it had someone in mind. Worcestor instructed Daggett to be kind to a "Mr. Bingham" should he visit the Foreign Mission School during the next week. This was not an ordinary request, and the committee appeared close to a decision.[37] A few weeks later the board placed Hiram Bingham in charge of organizing a mission to the Sandwich Islands.

In 1819 Hiram Bingham was thirty years old. He had just graduated from Andover Theological Seminary and had no administrative or missionary experience. The task before him was awesome, yet there was little to distinguish him from the other men selected for the mission. Born and raised in Bennington, Vermont, Hiram was the fifth son and seventh child of Calvin and Lydia Bingham. Bennington was farming country, and the Binghams tilled the rocky Vermont soil. Calvin Bingham was a respected citizen and influential officer in the local Congregational church. Since Colonel Samuel Robinson, "the first and most influential proprietor of the soil" sold land only to Congregationalists, members of any other religious denominations had to go to Pownal or Shaftsbury for worship. Calvin Bingham's importance in the town, therefore, was presumably equally as significant as his influence in the church, for the First Congregational Church remained the only regularly organized religious body in the town until 1827.

Hiram professed religion in his twenty-first year and joined the

Bennington Congregational Church in May 1811. That same year he began preparatory studies with the Reverend Elisha Yale of Kingsborough, New York. Two years later he entered Middlebury College as a sophomore. In 1816 he began his studies at Andover Theological Seminary. Over six feet tall, angular, and "spare of build," the Bennington youth concealed within his gangling frame a rugged constitution and iron will. In appointing him to superintend the Sandwich Islands Mission, Samuel Worcester recognized these same traits that his parents had seen years earlier, when they chose Hiram, from among thirteen children, to provide for them during their declining years.[38]

Although a strong revival swept through students and faculty his first year at Middlebury, it was at Andover that the Bennington farmer's son acquired a lasting interest in foreign missions.[39] He joined the Society of Inquiry in 1818 and was soon elected vice president of the organization. Until graduation in 1819 Bingham remained active in this secret society of missionary inquiry and prepared a course of missionary reading for the members. By the time he graduated from Andover he had acquired a lasting commitment to foreign missions.[40]

Throughout his years at Andover, Bingham maintained occasional contact with the offices of the ABCFM in Boston, showing a concern for Cherokee land cessions in this country and in publicizing heathenism in India.[41] During his vacation in 1819 Bingham visited the Foreign Mission School at Cornwall. This solidified his commitment to bring religious and social change to the heathen. His appointment to superintend the mission to the Sandwich Islands gave him the opportunity to fulfill this desire. Years later, while compiling a history of his Hawaiian activities, Bingham recalled that following his visit to Cornwall, "I freely offered myself to the American Board for that purpose, and was accepted by their Prudential Committee, in the summer of 1819."[42] In his acceptance letter to Samuel Worcester he urged the board to send at least two educated missionaries in case the mission should be divided.[43]

Everything appeared ready for the organization of the mission; now the full complement of workers had to be obtained. Through marriage Hiram Bingham acquired an energetic and devoted co-worker. Sybil Moseley Bingham effectively complemented her husband's dedication to foreign missions. Born in Westfield, Massachusetts, and educated at Westfield Academy, she was orphaned in 1811. Two years later she embarked on a teaching career to care for her three younger sisters, organizing a select school for women in Canandaigua, New York, that was prosperous and successful. During a visit to Connecticut in 1819 Sybil Moseley heard about the ordination of the missionaries for the Sandwich Islands. Her attendance at the ceremonies introduced her to Hiram Bingham.[44]

This was not her first exposure to foreign missions. After joining the Westfield Congregational Church in 1812, she had spent many hours discussing the subject. These conversations formed the basis for a lasting commitment to the effort, and Sybil Bingham was always more than just a missionary's wife. Throughout her teaching career she sought to convey this interest in evangelism to her pupils, successfully encouraging them to contribute to foreign missions.[45]

The excitement of the ordination and her introduction to Hiram Bingham rekindled her desire for personal involvement in the cause. After a whirlwind courtship the two missionaries married on October 11, 1819, less than two weeks before sailing to the Sandwich Islands. Before her departure, the new bride donated all her remaining property (about $800) to form a permanent fund for the support of the secretary of the ABCFM.[46]

In accordance with Hiram Bingham's request, the Prudential Committee appointed another educated missionary to the mission company. He was Asa Thurston of Fitchburg, Massachusetts. The son of a founder of the Calvinistic Congregational Church in Fitchburg, Asa Thurston was born in a house overlooking Falulah Valley. The Thurston family was deeply involved in church affairs. His father, Thomas Thurston, was for many years the leading musician in the town and, indeed, throughout the entire region. In addition to duties as music teacher and leader of the church choir, his father was also a good shoemaker. A sturdy and athletic youth, Asa boarded in town and learned the trade of scythe-maker. For seven years, beginning at age fourteen, young Thurston diligently studied his trade. At the same time he attended school and developed an athletic prowess known throughout the neighborhood; an ability that undoubtedly assisted his development as one of the best ballroom dancers in the region.[47]

From the 1790s to the early 1820s Fitchburg was a bustling center of commercial and industrial development. Farwell scythes had an enviable reputation among area farmers and shopkeepers, and the shop remained the primary business enterprise in the town until after 1800. During the first two decades of the new century residents witnessed the construction of saw and grist mills, the development of soap and candle manufacture, and the introduction of chair manufacturing in 1816. Blessed with good water power, the town seemed to have a bright future. Paper-making commenced in 1805, and a cotton factory appeared two years later.[48]

Despite a generally prosperous economy, however, Fitchburg town affairs were not always harmonious. From 1786 until 1823 bitter theological dissension wracked the town. After 1801 this controversy became especially heated, causing divisions within both town and church. A divisive doctrinal dispute in 1801 forced the dismissal of the pastor—the Reverend Samuel Worcester, later corresponding secretary of the ABCFM. Universalists, Baptists, and Methodists challenged the divided Congregationalists and gained the rights to the meetinghouse for two-thirds of the Sundays during the year.[49]

Four years later the town suffered once again, and the Thurstons could not escape tragedy when typhoid fever swept the region in 1805. Near death for a while, Asa finally recovered; but the sickness claimed his mother, as well as a brother and sister. Although still apprenticed to Joseph Farwell, Asa turned to religion and began to pursue the ministry with a view toward foreign missions. No longer a frolicsome youth, at age twenty-two he chose the ministry for his future career and studied under the Reverend William Bascom of Fitchburg. In 1812 he entered Yale.

That same year a young boy from the Sandwich Islands lived in Fitchburg. George P. Tamoree, son of a Hawaiian king, resided with Cutting, the Baptist minister, for a short time. He later lived with Thomas Litch and worked in Litch's tannery. Although neither Thurston nor Tamoree would live in Fitchburg again, they would both be members of the first missionary company to the Sandwich Islands.[50]

Thurston's college career paralleled that of Hiram Bingham. Like Bingham, he went to the theological seminary at Andover, where he also joined the Society of Inquiry to further his interest in foreign missions. In his middle year at the seminary Thurston delivered an address on Christian theology at the annual examination exercises. He seemed a promising student.

After graduation he asked the ABCFM to include him in the mission company being outfitted for the Sandwich Islands. A few days later he wrote another letter to the board, outlining his views on foreign missions and expressing his personal commitment. He granted the need for exertions at home, but added that "there are millions of wretched pagans who have no *Bible*, no *sabbaths*, no *Saviour*, & no *Holy Ghost* . . . . Surely these wretched pagans have claims upon our compassion & benevolence."[51] Against the strong opposition of friends, who thought him foolish and suicidal, he dedicated himself to success among the Sandwich Islanders. Before his departure, Yale honored its intrepid alumnus by conferring, as it had upon his friend and Andover classmate Hiram Bingham, the degree of Master of Arts.[52]

Asa Thurston's early marital career, like his collegiate career, paralleled that of Hiram Bingham. His first proposal failed, when the girl's mother refused to allow her daughter to reside among the heathen. In the face of such strong opposition, Thurston gave up the girl and resolved to make no more proposals "without some degree of certainty as to success."[53] Only a month from departure Asa's chances for marriage appeared slight. Then he met Lucy Goodale.

Lucy was the daughter of Abner Goodale, a "substantial farmer" and deacon of the Congregational church in Marlboro, Massachusetts. Educated at nearby Bradford Academy, she was teaching school when her cousin approached her in September 1819 with a proposal that she marry Asa Thurston. With little delay she seized the opportunity to fulfill her desire to evangelize the heathen. The two missionaries married on October 12, 1819, only one day after the marriage of Hiram Bingham and Sybil Moseley.[54] These four individuals remained dominant forces within the mission for the duration of their lives.

The board now faced the task of filling out the mission company. One man stepped forward to volunteer his services even before the final decision had been made to outfit the company. In March 1819 Captain Daniel Chamberlain requested to "go as a Missionary Farmer to Owhyhee." His request raised a difficult question—the first of several the board would confront before the mission's departure in October. Chamberlain volunteered not only himself, but his wife and children as well; and the Prudential Committee questioned the wisdom of sending Christian women and children to a pagan land.[55]

Board officials had been discussing the advisability of including women in foreign mission companies for several years. As early as 1811 Samuel Worcester exchanged opinions on the subject with George Burder of the London Missionary Society (LMS). Burder advised his American counterpart that the LMS preferred not to send women to new missionary stations. But, he concluded, since the young men then in question were going to India, "a civilized country, where they will enjoy the protection of a regular government," married couples might go.[56]

The subject arose again with respect to the Sandwich Islands Mission. Parents and friends raised numerous objections, as there was no "civilized government" in control of the islands. The board never opened public discussion on the issue and eventually concluded that it was not only permissible, but highly desirable, for the missionaries to marry before departure. The happy Christian homes of the missionaries would provide useful examples for the lusty pagans. Married missionaries, moreover, would be less susceptible to the temptations and sinful conduct of voluptuous native women. New England piety, after all, was not indomitable. Out of sympathy for the women, however, the board shipped the frame of a house along with the first company. It also offered free transportation back to the United States for any woman who found herself unable to tolerate life in such a barbarous nation.[57]

With these decisions behind it, the Prudential Committee accepted Daniel Chamberlain's application. Captain Chamberlain, a prosperous farmer then in his late thirties, lived in Westboro, Massachusetts. Until the railroad arrived in 1834, Westboro was a rural, isolated community heavily dependent upon agriculture. There was little to disrupt traditional life-styles. The Congregational church remained the community's guidepost, its pastor the patriarch. The mission village in Hawaii would closely resemble the Westboro community.

Captain Chamberlain's two oldest children, Dexter and Nathan, found the mission a chance for service as well as romantic adventure. Throughout the summer of 1819 both youths attended the Foreign Mission School, where they proved able students of the Hawaiian language. Later, in the islands, they served as interpreters for the missionaries. The family was a welcome addition to the mission company.[58]

For its next recruit the committee had to look no further than the school at Cornwall. Samuel Ruggles, "a pleasant man of small stature," was probably the first missionary to embrace the notion of a mission to these islands. Only in his mid-twenties by 1819, he had already experienced a troubled life. Born in Brookfield, a western Connecticut town known primarily for its marble and granite quarries, Ruggles was the youngest of nine children. Both his parents, pioneer settlers of the town, died when he was very young, and his brother Isaac guided him to adulthood. Never in robust health, Samuel entered Yale but had to withdraw because of ill health. The young orphan then became an agent of the ABCFM, touring New England, to solicit funds for foreign missions and the school at Cornwall. He applied for admission to the Foreign Mission School soon after it opened and asked to be sent to the Sandwich Islands. When the proposed mission became a reality, the school's executive committee urged the Prudential Committee to send him with the first company as a schoolmaster. Few were better qualified, and the committee quickly accepted the recommendation. Like the expedition's two leaders, Ruggles married shortly before the mission's departure.[59]

Thomas Holman was a far different, and more troublesome, recruit. A native of Brookfield, Connecticut, like Samuel Ruggles, Holman graduated from the Cherry Valley Medical School in New York. After graduation he practiced medicine in Cooperstown, New York. There he met his prospective bride, Lucy Ruggles, orphaned sister of Samuel Ruggles. In May of 1819 Thomas Holman joined the Foreign Mission School. His medical practice had been unsuccessful; the young doctor was in debt and without any financial resources. He quickly offered his services for the Hawaiian mission.[60]

Only a few months elapsed between his arrival at Cornwall and departure for the Sandwich Islands, but his brief tenure at the school was checkered and turbulent. Two months after Holman's arrival the school's principal, Herman Daggett, complained to Samuel Worcester that "he has discovered a disposition to complain of his accommodations, & to dictate in the concerns of the Institution, which has not been very becoming; but we hope he will learn wisdom & humility."[61] Apparently Holman, then in his mid-twenties, convinced observers that he had reformed, for the visiting committee of the school recommended that he be included in the mission company.

This recommendation later came under criticism from Hiram Bingham. Soon after arriving in Hawaii, Holman struck out on his own and flaunted the authority both of Bingham and the board. In a mild letter of reproof to his superiors in Boston, the redoubtable Bingham criticized their judgment in the selection of Holman. He noted "that animosity was felt and manifested by the Dr. against Tamoree, & Tennooe & Mr. Loomis" at the Foreign Mission School. Bingham also recalled Herman Daggett's criticism of Holman's behavior at the school and argued that this alone should have disqualified him as a missionary candidate. Samuel Ruggles had tried to dissuade him from embarking with the company, but to no avail. Bingham concluded that the agents of the school "did not *know him*, but relied principally on recommendations from *unknown men*."[62] Rising to his own defense, Daggett insisted that he had assumed that Holman's poor behavior at Cornwall rendered him unfit for foreign missions. However, he lamented, "the agents, upon his making some concessions, & taking into consideration all circumstances, thought proper to present him as a candidate."[63]

Wherever the blame lay, Holman's selection later placed the ABCFM in a delicate position and threatened to jeopardize the success of a massive undertaking to which much time and money had been devoted. Perhaps his prospective wife influenced the decision-makers. Lucy Ruggles, sister of one of the missionaries, provoked favorable comments wherever she appeared. A schoolteacher, and later the first American woman to circumnavigate the globe, she enthusiastically committed herself to the enterprise and married the young doctor less than a month before sailing to the islands. Lucy remained loyal to her husband throughout the controversy.[64]

No mission company could be effective without a printer to turn out native dictionaries, sermons, and pious tracts for native minds. The printer for the Sandwich Islands Mission was Elisha Loomis of Middlesex, New York. Not quite twenty years old when the brig *Thaddeus* left Boston and destined to be the youngest adult member of the mission, he volunteered in May 1819 and spent the summer in the Foreign Mission School. Loomis reiterated his commitment in a letter to the Prudential Committee the following September and prepared to embark. Following the pattern of the other missionaries, he married only three weeks before his departure. His was perhaps the most crucial position in the mission, and he served admirably until his health failed in 1827.[65]

The final member of the little band was Samuel Whitney. Whitney's early career paralleled that of his colleagues in the mission company. He had attended Yale College, but withdrew in his sophomore year to join the mission. During his brief stay at New Haven, however, the youth met several natives from the islands. Never a brilliant student, Whitney nonetheless worked diligently to realize his ambition of becoming a preacher to the heathen and pursued that goal at every available moment. This undoubtedly pleased his mother, who had suffered through his youthful rowdyism while her husband was at sea. At one point she nearly gave up hope of reforming the boy, and at age fourteen

Samuel found himself apprenticed to a shoemaker. Seven years' residence with a "pious family" finally suppressed his youthful antics, and
at twenty-one he made a public profession of religion. Zealously attacking his studies, in 1819 this crusading spirit carried him to the Sandwich
Islands with his young bride of less than three weeks.[66]

All members of the mission company had to pass a number of tests
before being accepted. The Prudential Committee demanded that both
candidates and wives produce letters from their respective ministers
testifying to their good standing in the local church. The committee
encouraged pastors to include everything they knew about the appli-
cant and to evaluate his potential. At the same time, the board required
each candidate to submit a formal letter of application to the corresponding secretary in Boston. This letter was to explain why the man
had applied and set out his thoughts on foreign missions. Naturally all
professed a deep piety and sincere commitment. But in 1819 there were
no other attractions to encourage a young man to place himself at the
disposal of the ABCFM. Several applicants traced their interest in
foreign missions to the writings of Claudius Buchanan or the widely
popular *Claims of Six Hundred Millions.*[67] Most indicated a real concern for the heathen and acknowledged a dutiful sense of responsibility
for their welfare. This was not an easy admission, for missionaries were
expected to remain in the field for life. The board told candidates to
expect only "personal sacrifice, privation, exposure and suffering."[68]

The first missionaries to the Sandwich Islands drew their commitment from a wellspring of hope, piety, and duty. To this they added a
youthful exuberance born of innocence and the promise of success. The
structure of the mission company reflected the family background of
the men. Hiram Bingham and Asa Thurston, the two leaders, came from
pious, respectable families. Most of the remaining missionaries, however, looked back to a poor, humble, or troublesome childhood. Yet
one influence touched all of them. This was the experience of Henry
Obookiah and the other Sandwich Islanders who had come to New
England. Not all these young men had known Obookiah personally, but
they knew well the story of his trials and hopes in pursuit of the gospel.
Many had read his memoirs, and others had studied or taught among his
native friends at the school in Cornwall. Even Hiram Bingham, who
traced his commitment to the years preceding Obookiah's death, admitted that the tragedy refreshed an earlier interest in going to the
Sandwich Islands. Bingham confessed to Samuel Worcester that he

"became more deeply interested than before in that cause for which he desired to live, & from that time it seemed by no means impossible that I should be employed in the field which Henry had intended to occupy."[69]

These men, accompanied by their brides, had volunteered for an uncertain adventure several thousand miles from home. Except for Daniel Chamberlain, none left behind any substantial worldly accomplishments. Bingham and Thurston were committed to a life in the church, but in 1819 neither had yet embarked on his career. Fresh from theological school and unattached (until just before departing for the Sandwich Islands), their most promising hopes for service lay either as an assistant pastor to some established clergyman, or perhaps as the shepherd of their own church on the frontier. Whitney, only a sophomore in college, faced several more years of training before he could hope to be ordained. With his financial resources strained to the breaking point, doubt clouded his future. Samuel Ruggles, orphaned and poor, was already attached to the Foreign Mission School. His best hope for future success appeared to lie as a teacher of the native youth at the school. Thomas Holman, although a certified physician, possessed little more than several debts and what appeared to have been a failing medical practice. Only Elisha Loomis, trained as a printer and barely twenty years of age, appeared to have a secure future. There was, therefore, little to deter these young men from committing themselves to the cause of foreign missions.

On the other hand, a number of factors coalesced to draw these converts to the missionary field. The religious revivals that swept the Northeast after 1800 caught many of them up in an infectious enthusiasm for religious rediscovery.[70] Amid the fluctuation of economic fortunes and the welter of political and religious change and controversy that was New England in the early nineteenth century, the prospects of arduous and perhaps dangerous labors in a far-off land seemed more appealing than in placid times. Most of these men had arrived at a crisis in their lives. Bingham and Thurston, no longer under the protective mechanisms of school or seminary, had to forge their own careers in the ministry. Many of the others were too poor to expect a college education and lacked the perquisites of family or wealth to reach economic security. Thomas Holman, although a professional physician, had fallen on bad times. Only Chamberlain enjoyed economic security. Yet Westboro closely resembled many rural New England towns that were just beginning to stagnate. At this particular juncture in their lives, the evangelical impulse of the Second Great Awakening engulfed these men in its fervor. The Awakening was particularly successful among those most susceptible to its message. In search of a career, these young men embraced the new revivalism. Theirs was a commitment and not an escape.

As summer waned preparations for the mission's departure quickened. The Prudential Committee worked overtime in an effort to raise sufficient funds. In late August Jeremiah Evarts, treasurer of the ABCFM, instructed Samuel Worcester to release a list of estimated expenses to the press. At the same time, he recommended the publication of a notice "that presents in kind will be received."[71] This marked the beginning of an intensive fund-raising campaign. Such efforts were essential, for Hiram Bingham had not yet become a shrewd financial manager and assumed that the board could supply whatever he requested. Total expenses for the missionaries' outfits, equipment, supplies, and passage to the islands topped ten thousand dollars.[72] Four days after Evarts advised Worcester to publicize the mission, the corresponding secretary wrote an open letter to the press and the Christian public, meticulously describing the materials needed for the mission and their approximate cost.[73] Only through extensive public solicitation could the ABCFM hope to meet the unprecedented expenses necessary to send an entire company of missionaries to the Sandwich Islands.

The monetary response was disappointing. A few large donations reached the board's treasurer in Boston, including one for fifty dollars from Arthur Tappan in New York. A Colonel Williams of Greenwich, Massachusetts, left a legacy of three hundred dollars, apparently the result of reading the *Memoirs of Henry Obookiah*. But these were unusually large bequests. Despite the board's use of Sandwich Island natives and the complex structure of societies, donations for 1819 surpassed those of the previous year by only $3,200. This was a far cry from the additional ten thousand dollars being spent to organize the mission.

The prospective missionaries scurried from town to town in an effort to augment the mission's financial resources, but produced only meager results. With no reason to expect greater success from this mission than from previous efforts, contributors remained unwilling to increase their donations. Many did specifically earmark their annual subscription for the new mission; but it is apparent that people used their regular contributions in this manner, thereby diverting them from previous objectives. At best, the shift seemed to indicate a growing interest in the venture.[74]

The request for tools, articles of clothing, and other useful implements for the mission produced a much more substantial response. Articles ranging from lead pencils to Bibles to cheese poured into the board's offices in Boston from families and friends of missions across New England and, occasionally, from outside the region as well. A few of these gifts were quite valuable, while many could be called frivolous except for the sincerity of their donors. Most of them, however, represented basic supplies for the mission company—clothing, tools, food, and books.[75]

The board welcomed these gifts, but some of them caused a problem. Many well-meaning persons gave small presents and trinkets to the Sandwich Island natives who were going with the company. These were intended to be presents for the heathen, but, as Herman Daggett noted: "Receiving such things in this way would, I should suppose, lead the heathen to conclude that a christian people judged them important & commendable, & would give them wrong expectations with respect to the benefits which they were to receive from us."[76]

In October 1819, with the mission outfitted and plans matured, the missionaries met in Boston. With them were their brides, friends, and an assortment of curious onlookers. Prayers and speeches preceded their departure for the Sandwich Islands. Only a few weeks before, on September 28, Asa Thurston and Hiram Bingham had been ordained in Goshen, Connecticut. On that occasion public excitement and interest in the undertaking had filled every corner of the town's old meeting-house. Dignitaries of all descriptions attended, with officers of the ABCFM perhaps most conspicuous among the ministerial elite. Many onlookers no doubt came merely to catch a brief glimpse of the band of intrepid missionaries who were about to venture among the fierce and warlike heathen. This might be the last time any Christian would see them alive![77]

At the ordination, the Reverend Heman Humphrey of Pittsfield, Massachusetts, delivered a lengthy sermon on foreign missions and the missionary field. Like most exhortations, it reiterated the obvious and dispensed gratuitous advice on piety and personal behavior. Unintimidated by the immensity of the task, Humphrey claimed the world as his dominion. The Sandwich Islands Mission was just the beginning, and he argued that gains there would be "scarcely sufficient" to provide missionaries "even a precarious resting place for the soles of their feet."[78] Promoters of the enterprise sought an ever-wider horizon. Whether or not the "chosen" natives welcomed these harbingers of the new order made little difference, and Humphrey was quick to make this point. "The ultimate conquest and possession of all the heathen lands is certain. The heathen themselves may rage—Satan may come down with great wrath, and in his convulsive struggles for empire, may yet shake the foundations of the earth; but the promise cannot fail."[79]

The Pittsfield pastor warned that the struggle would be difficult, for missionaries would have to overcome dark and evil forces opposed to their goal. In his charge to the newly ordained men, the Reverend David Perry of Sharon, Massachusetts, commanded that their primary object was "to promote the instruction, the conversion, and edification of the Heathen."[80] Infused with a new burst of missionary enthusiasm, the crowd at the Goshen meetinghouse dispersed to carry the message home. Since their presence at the ordination probably indicated a commitment to the enterprise, it is doubtful that many new converts could be counted among those in attendance. But the large crowd and the dramatic tension preceding the detachment's departure helped publicize the board's objectives.

The week before embarkation bustled with activity and excitement for supporters of the project. On October 15, 1819, the small band met in Park Street Church, Boston, to organize the Mission Church. This was to be the vehicle for the conquest of paganism in the Pacific islands. Three days later Asa Thurston told an audience at the same church, "The present is emphatically styled a day of action." Concluding his parting address with a survey of the present excitement and benevolence, Thurston tried to stimulate greater financial efforts.[81] The board never satisfied its need for funds.

Just before departure the mission company received its final instructions from the ABCFM. After smothering them with advice and guidelines, the Prudential Committee summarized the task ahead. "You are," it instructed, "to aim at nothing short of covering those Islands with fruitful fields, and pleasant dwellings, and schools and churches; of raising up the whole people to an educated state of Christian civilization."[82]

This was more than a religious enterprise designed to convert a few pagans. It was, instead, an attempt to re-create a seventeenth-century New England Christian commonwealth in the middle of the Pacific Ocean. "We know of no Mission," the press reported, "that has hitherto left this country, which has excited such general interest and prompted so many prayers as that to the Sandwich Islands."[83]

7.   THE STRUGGLE FOR STABILITY

Clergy and laymen alike rejoiced at the departure of the Sandwich Islands Mission. After almost a decade of trying to encourage public support for foreign missions the ABCFM appeared to have been successful by the fall of 1819. But news from the islands would not reach the board's offices in Boston for several months, and the excitement sparked by the mission's departure could not last without something to sustain public interest. What remedies did the Prudential Committee have to offer? To their dismay, committee members quickly discovered that despite the enthusiasm surrounding the Sandwich Islands Mission, little had changed from the struggles of the previous decade. Societies still had to be formed, and foreign missions would not yet promote themselves.

The ABCFM fell back on techniques that were, by 1819, quite routine. In December the *Christian Spectator* published an article that described the Sandwich Islands and emphasized their future usefulness in dispensing the gospel "to other idolatrous lands." Clearly this mission represented just the beginning of the board's activities. That the natives anxiously awaited the arrival of missionaries no one doubted, and the journal optimistically predicted success.[1] At home, meanwhile, pastors once again turned to the theme of Christian unity and republican virtue. In an attack on festive and frivolous conduct, Lyman Beecher pressed the necessity of hard work and Christian kindness to preserve American values. "The happiness of domestic life," he warned, "depends on substantial realities of care and labour." He who looked "down with disdain on the laboring classes of society, is a man of weak intellect, or of a bad heart."[2]

Foreign missions remained central to clerical hopes for a new Christian commonwealth; and pastors used the network of foreign mission societies to preserve public interest in the missionary cause. In January 1820 Bostonians heard Sereno Edwards Dwight argue that foreign missions would create a holy kingdom on earth. Before its arrival, however, the gospel must be preached to all nations and the "ignorance, bigotry and superstition of Catholic countries" destroyed.[3] This was clearly a Protestant crusade. A catalog of heathen horrors highlighted Dwight's sermon, supported by statistics on the "millions of mankind" who were without "civilization." In what was becoming a set-piece of missionary rhetoric, Dwight warned his listeners that "the Heathen when left to themselves have no tendency to reformation, and only grow worse instead of growing better."[4] The gospel could remedy these evils, but only missionaries could carry the message overseas. Dwight urged the audience to assist in bringing the kingdom of God to earth. The heathen and the Bible must be brought together and support given to missionaries who would learn native languages and translate the Bible.[5]

Money continued to be a primary concern of board officers. With expenses for 1820 estimated at $190 per day, a steady flow of donations was essential to the permanency of their operations. At the same time continued economic instability plagued New England. Many societies donated clothing instead of money, and this presented a problem for the ABCFM. Jeremiah Evarts insisted that money "must be our main reliance." Too often donations of clothing replaced donations of money.[6] In a public appeal the Prudential Committee warned that the "experiment" of foreign missions was approaching a crisis. To allow it to fail would dash the hopes of "many thousands" and condemn the heathen to darkness. Donations must increase to keep pace with the board's expanded operations. Who else would do the work?[7]

The Reverend David Perry emphasized the same theme at the Foreign Mission School's annual exhibition in 1820. Perry insisted that charity must be reduced to a system. Something should be set aside each week for foreign missions, and "youth and children be early trained to systematic charity." Public benevolence was most efficient when it was systematic, and efficiency promised success.[8]

Elsewhere in New England promoters of foreign missions attempted to make the old appeals and methods bear fruit once more. The foreign mission society in Northampton, Massachusetts, announced that members had donated the produce from several acres of rich meadowland to the cause. After selling the goods the society would forward the proceeds to the ABCFM in Boston. Students at Andover Theological Seminary explored the "Influence of Heathen Religions on Moral and Intellectual Character," presumably as preparation for missionary activity. Joseph Harvey complained from Cornwall that ministers in the area were upset because their donations had not been acknowledged in the *Religious Intelligencer*.[9] Such were the concerns of those who supported foreign missions in the spring of 1820. There was nothing here designed to attract new support, and little except habit to induce present contributors to continue past assistance. Promoters of foreign missions seemed to be in danger of becoming leaders without a following.

The ABCFM tried to shake New Englanders from this lethargy with a new series of appeals in the spring and summer of 1820. Publication of the *Memoirs of the Rev. Samuel J. Mills* assisted their efforts. The book circulated widely among the reading public and probably reached those persons most able to afford substantial donations. The board's officers then took two steps designed to promote their cause. They first adopted the *Missionary Herald*, formerly the *Panoplist*, as their official publication. Hereafter this journal devoted its pages almost exclusively to missionary news and information, becoming a useful propaganda organ for the board.[10]

The Prudential Committee also appealed to all foreign missionary societies. Noting that contributors had not increased in proportion to the board's activities, it insisted that donations to foreign missions were insurance for the future. Patrons could not take their money with them, but by contributing to the ABCFM they could lay "up in store a good foundation against the time that is to come." The committee further cautioned local societies that without constant reminders donors would seize on "every adverse change, to withhold or diminish their benefactions."[11] Samuel Worcester concluded with a few caveats to agents of the board throughout New England. Admitting that a decline in donations should be expected in times of economic instability, he argued that "countervailing influences and efforts became the more necessary" during such crises. Without the wasteful burdens of war, prosperity would soon return. Agents and societies must be ready to capitalize on any improvement to speed the flow of contributions.[12]

For the duration of the year this theme of economic crisis, both for New England and the ABCFM, dominated public discussion of foreign missions. In September the *Panoplist* published a lengthy analysis of the problem. Since the journal was by now the house organ of the ABCFM, the editor's conclusions can be taken as an accurate index of official thinking. He found three reasons for the decreased aid to foreign missions. First, a general scarcity of money prevailed in society. This partly explained the increase in donations of clothing that Jeremiah Evarts had observed several months earlier. Many people had also withdrawn from their local foreign mission society to join another benevolent institution. With increasing competition among the variety of charitable organizations, frequently the most recent or most successful attracted patrons from its competitors. Finally, the editor complained about a noticeable decline in missionary spirit. Undoubtedly the conflicting claims of benevolent societies were in part responsible, for they directed attention away from a single specific objective. In their growing support for these other institutions patrons of the ABCFM demonstrated that they were no longer primarily concerned about foreign missions. The board's apparent lack of success, after nearly a decade of effort, drove many to find causes that held promise of quicker rewards.[13]

A correspondent from Vermont tentatively advanced a solution to the board's ills. In a letter to the treasurer he urged the ABCFM to "induce the Congregational Churches of New England to form themselves into auxiliary societies."[14] Since the board published the letter in the *Panoplist*, its officers must have thought highly of the proposal. But this suggestion merely repeated previous efforts. An extensive network of societies had been organized during the previous decade, and by 1820 it was apparent that societies alone could not provide the necessary monies to fund the board's operations. Something else was needed. With a major mission on its way to the Sandwich Islands, and with other missions planted elsewhere around the world, this was not the time to fall back on optimistic predictions and hopes for future successes. The ABCFM faced a dilemma from which there appeared to be no easy escape. There was a lull in public excitement. Enthusiasm for outfitting the Sandwich Islands Mission had worn off; and it was still too early to hear any news of its arrival in the islands. Promoters of the cause cast about in search of continued financial support.

One pastor suggested that his parishioners give to foreign missions an amount equal to that normally spent in celebrating the Fourth of July. Here was a pleasant mix of piety and patriotism, but few followed his advice.[15] The *Boston Recorder*, the city's leading religious newspaper, fell back on exhortation to raise money, editorializing that only the formation of new societies could solve the crisis. Through these organizations thousands of dollars could be collected that would otherwise be lost to "the cause of benevolence." The editor suggested that readers scrimp and save on food, clothing, or household furniture in order to donate something to foreign missions.[16] The paper continued to print glowing tales of success among the Sandwich Island natives in this country, but could not yet report the fate of the missionaries to those islands.[17]

Early the next year Connecticut clergymen unveiled a new technique to promote foreign missions—a missionary catechism for children to use in schools or at home. The catechism outlined the "wretchedness of the heathen, together with the efforts which had been made, and which yet remain to be made to relieve them."[18] Through a carefully constructed series of questions it propagandized the cause of foreign missions and emphasized that the gospel made heathen peoples "happier in life" by showing them the evils of their present religion. To interest women and children in the crusade it stressed the importance of female missionaries in the education of heathen children and insisted that all heathens be taught the arts of "civilization." The authors then defined a civilized society, arguing against geographic mobility and social disorder while advancing the virtues of agriculture, hard work, and education.[19] The catechism explicitly set forth the clergy's prescription for a virtuous republic (religion, education, hard work, and agrarian individualism) in an instruction manual for the good society. In so doing, the authors not only delineated the path of righteousness but also criticized New England's deviation from that path.

In Boston, meanwhile, the Prudential Committee turned to its own organ of publicity and propaganda: the *Missionary Herald*. Joseph Harvey suggested that all documents and news of ABCFM activities be reserved exclusively for the *Herald*. Too often people read the same information first in the *Boston Recorder* or in New Haven's *Religious Intelligencer*. This deprived the *Herald* of its interest and impact and made subscriptions more an act of charity than a necessity. Harvey warned that people must be induced to take the *Herald*, concluding, "If you can keep the official papers of the Board from these literary pilferers, who are filling their own pockets at the expense of the cause of religion, untill the Herald has announced them to the world, its triumph will be complete."[20] Two months later Harvey again wrote Jeremiah Evarts and urged him to secure a copyright. Only this could stop the "leeches" from profiting from the board's labors.[21] But the committee moved slowly. Several months passed before the *Missionary*

Herald became indispensable for persons interested in the latest missionary news or information. The other journals still published the same information, but now had to copy it from the *Herald*. It was a small advance.

Despite its attention to publicity the board suffered declining financial support. Throughout the winter and into the spring of 1821 most religious publications boosted foreign missions, but with unimpressive results. An editorial in the *Boston Recorder* castigated the growing use of luxuries and blamed hedonistic selfishness for the decline in contributions. As if to illustrate how many small donations could produce a mighty flow, the editor asked for contributions equal only to 1 percent of one's income. It was "chilling," he complained, to note how wealthy persons who professed godliness could only seem to "drag out a single dollar," and that only after considerable persuasion.[22] The equation of benevolence with piety found constant expression throughout New England. "It is invariably the case," the *Recorder* explained, "that there is the most real religion where there is the most universal benevolence." Those parishes that do the most to spread the gospel excite the greatest interest in religion among their inhabitants.[23] These anxious remarks illustrated the limits of the appeal for foreign missions. Without successes to report, proponents struggled to keep their cause before the public.

In April 1821 the board's fortunes suddenly improved. Officers received news from their mission to the Sandwich Islands and quickly reported its successes in the *Missionary Herald*. Hiram Bingham wrote that the mission had arrived safely and established a permanent settlement. He reported that a great change had occurred in the islands while the mission company was at sea. King Kamehameha had died, and his death had sparked a religious revolution. Bingham happily announced that "the Idols and Moreahs of these Islands are burned with fire, the priesthood of superstition is abolished, & the religious taboos are at an end."[24] This news electrified New Englanders. Sandwich Island missionaries now appeared to face few problems in their efforts to evangelize the heathen. The future of foreign missions seemed brighter than at any time since their departure.

Meanwhile, few bright spots appeared to lighten the financial problems of the ABCFM. Local farmers donated proceeds from the sale of crops, and writers urged everyone to set aside a portion of their income for foreign missions.[25] But news from the Sandwich Islands had not yet registered its impact, and subscriptions from local foreign missionary societies continued to decline.[26] To add to the board's woes, its guiding spirit over the past decade died in 1821. The death of Samuel Worcester deprived the board of its most untiring and zealous supporter. He had been primarily responsible both for the departure of the early missionaries and for the network of societies that labored to support their activities.

Almost all attention, however, centered on the news from the missionaries in the Sandwich Islands. The *Boston Recorder* published extracts from their correspondence, and throughout April nearly every issue contained news about the islands' natives and exotic customs. Each issue of the *Missionary Herald* reproduced long segments of the missionaries' journal. These proved good propaganda and stimulated the flow of donations. Here was the success that organizers had so long awaited; it was greater than anyone could have predicted. Not only had the missionaries received permission to land, their arrival had coincided with the destruction of the native religion. "The case is so new, and so unparalleled in the history of the world," the missionaries exclaimed, "that we know not what to say. *When hath a nation changed its gods?*"[27]

To forestall complacency and convince readers that the burning of idols did not mean the triumph of Christianity, the ABCFM reminded New Englanders that this was just the beginning. Jeremiah Evarts, editor of the *Missionary Herald* and board treasurer, warned that now was the time for greater efforts and larger donations. Sandwich Island missionaries still faced trials, terrors, and the spectre of death. "Though the missionaries have met with unexpected facilities, and the arm of the Lord has been made bare for them," the editor cautioned that "still they may be called to trials as unexpected. This should not be forgotten a single day."[28]

Throughout the remainder of the year board officials, assisted by their network of societies, worked diligently to retain public interest in the Sandwich Islands Mission. With communication now established to the missionaries, officials found their task relatively easy. Each ship that arrived from the mid-Pacific brought news, letters, and even artifacts from the mission stations. In June the pages of the *Recorder* announced that "TWO HEATHEN GODS" could be seen on display at a Boston bookstore. The editor urged everyone to view the strange and curious sight, since the idols represented visible evidence of what the missionaries had "conquered."[29] Two months later a front-page article urged the ABCFM to send another mission company to the same islands to profit from recent successes there. This was the time, the author charged, to support foreign missions.[30] The *Recorder* also published a list of supplies needed by the missionaries and asked all readers to search their homes for useful items.[31]

During the autumn months board officials remained preoccupied with the problem of fund-raising. In a series of letters to Jeremiah Evarts, the board's new corresponding secretary, Joseph Harvey suggested a reconsideration of collection methods. He told Evarts that the use of agents appeared to be growing unpopular. If a different method was not used "the tone of public feeling will decline." The major cause of public ill-feeling toward traveling agents seemed to be their increasing numbers. Societies of all descriptions and purposes had agents knocking on doors across New England in search of funds, and New Englanders were becoming weary of solicitors. Harvey recommended the appointment of a permanent agent, one who would be an officer and member of the ABCFM.[32] Such a person would have far greater authority and command more respect than would representatives of competing societies.

Three weeks later Harvey again raised the issue in another letter to Evarts. Rejecting a suggestion that a man with a horse and wagon tour each county for donations, Harvey reminded Evarts that "people in this region are tired of the solicitations of travelling Agents." But his main objection lay with the possible damage such a person would do to the network of foreign mission societies. People would probably give to the agent and these fledgling institutions would quickly dissipate. Harvey wanted to inject a note of subtlety into the board's solicitations. Agents should lead the churches and people to adopt their own measures for encouraging contributions. In a moment of candor, the supervisor of the Foreign Mission School revealed the genius behind his plan: "This will avoid the odium of a solicitation, it will save the expense of employing an Agent with a horse and waggon, and will not be likely to supercede our collections for the County Society. . . . The consequence has been, that collections have been made in several towns, and their example will stimulate others, and thus in the result we hope to move the whole mass and still have it a matter of their own contrivance."[33] In counties with strong religious structures and many societies, this scheme promised enormous rewards. Each society could give money separately through what appeared to be self-induced enthusiasm, thereby greatly augmenting the board's financial resources.[34]

With the new successes of foreign mission, opponents again criticized the endeavor. In November the *Religious Inquirer* launched an attack on both foreign missions and the network of societies. In an outburst of sarcastic amazement, the editor, a Unitarian, marveled that people still fell prey to the demands of foreign mission societies. "We had concluded," he wrote, "that clerical ingenuity had become exhausted in the numerous societies already formed for getting money, and that the people would have been suffered to rest." But this had not happened. Instead, the editor continued, people continued to give and the cause appeared to prosper.[35]

Coincident with his caricature of the board's persistent fund-raising, the editor objected to the whole purpose of foreign missions. He lashed out at missionaries of the ABCFM who, he insisted, held out false hopes to the heathen. In an ill-disguised attack on Calvinism, the paper noted that the heathen "are not able to avail themselves of any blessing in the gospel, and when, the more light they have will only sink them deeper into hell." Since the elect will be saved and the nonelect damned, natives of the Pacific islands were better off with their own system of religious magic than with a new system that would seem equally magical.[36] In its criticism of the board's efforts, however, the *Religious Inquirer* stood almost alone; and its attack was as much against Trinitarians as against foreign missions. Most New Englanders either rejoiced at the news from Hawaii or ignored the venture entirely.

Unitarian criticism did not deter officers of the ABCFM, and they pressed forward to enlarge their activities, ignoring charges that the rich only donated to their cause to purchase "a pardon of sins." The *Religious Inquirer* still fulminated against the network of societies organized to channel money to the board, labeling the system "Popery in all its deformity." But few seemed to care why people gave, so long as they continued to give. The persistent coincidence of Unitarian attacks with Trinitarian successes only indicated the influence of foreign missions at home.[37] As the board entered what was to be the most successful year in its short history the Unitarian assault grew frantic— and at times perceptive. In February 1822 the *Religious Inquirer* railed: "Why, a few Missionaries, sent from a nation of about two hundred years standing, about ten thousand miles distant, and the existence of which is scarcely known to the Hindoos, are to *persuade* them that their religion, government, laws, manners, and those of their ancestors, for almost five thousand years, are absurd superstitions—that they had better renounce them and embrace Christianity. Was there ever so chimerical a scheme as this entered the heart of man?" [38]

The ABCFM ignored these attacks and worked to enlarge and strengthen its system. In the face of demands from a growing array of charitable organizations, the board continued to increase its financial resources. Promoters exhibited an incredible ability to surpass even the most insistent appeals of the past. An article in the *Christian Spectator* highlighted this skill. The anonymous contributor argued that the present time was the greatest period of benevolence and good deeds in the history of Christianity. Bubbling with optimism, he predicted that each generation would be more pious and zealous than the last. [39] Board officials agreed. Jeremiah Evarts insisted that people would not tire of giving, for they had "no excuse for being weary in well-doing, till they have done all the good in their power." [40] Events substantiated his estimations.

In its annual report for 1821 the Prudential Committee was exultant. News from the Sandwich Islands had opened a new phase in the development of the ABCFM. Contributions had jumped almost ten thousand dollars over those for the previous year. Although part of this increase undoubtedly mirrored improved domestic economic conditions, much of it also reflected the new successes in Hawaii. Each new victory over heathenism stimulated more donations to the board. The Prudential Committee realized this and was always alert to publicize anything favorable to its cause. If receipts could be increased this much in six or seven months, what could be done in a year? [41]

During the spring of 1822 the ABCFM built enthusiasm for the departure of another mission company. Notices again appeared describing Sandwich Islands youths living in New England. New appeals for greater support accompanied records of donations to the board. In May, the Reverend Sylvester Burt told an attentive audience at the Cornwall school, "A vast moral machine is, indeed, in operation. The design of its movements is infinitely grand—nothing less than the conversion of the world is intended." Burt noted the enormous effort necessary to keep the machine operating and urged all listeners to donate as much as possible to the cause. The title of his sermon conveyed his theme: *The Importance of True Charity.* [42]

Reports of progress at the Sandwich Islands appeared not only in religious publications but also in local newspapers throughout New England. All hinted that much more would be accomplished if additional missionaries could be sent into the field. In June the *Boston Recorder* published passages from a letter of one of the Sandwich Islands missionaries. The selection and timing were not accidental. "Are we then to give up the hope of seeing additional laborers and adequate supplies sent to our aid, unless other important plans of the Board be neglected? . . . I will not only deny myself 'the use of sugar,' but of *bread* also, rather than that any of the plans of the Board should be embarrassed, and the conversion of the world retarded."[43] From Cornwall, Herman Daggett, principal of the Foreign Mission School, had written the year before that a reinforcement should be sent to the Sandwich Islands without delay. Daggett had questioned Evarts about the Prudential Committee's intentions and reminded him that New Englanders remained excited about prospects at the islands. He urged the board to take advantage of this popular support and to give preference to this mission over all others.[44]

In the summer of 1822 the ABCFM responded. The Prudential Committee inserted a report in the *Missionary Herald* that reiterated the value of a mission station on these mid-Pacific isles. The station served seamen and natives in the area, and it was strategically located with respect to further diffusion of missionary labors. Most important, the committee reported, "It is central; and from it heralds of salvation may go to the tribes and nations in the north-western and western parts of America, in the north-eastern and eastern parts of Asia, and on the numerous islands of the Pacific."[45] Manifest Destiny, missionary labors, and Christian evangelism proved a devastating combination. Support for the ABCFM increased, and the Prudential Committee organized a reinforcement to sail in November for the Sandwich Islands.[46]

Since the departure of the first missionaries to these islands three years earlier, many persons had offered themselves for assignment to the Sandwich Islands Mission. Confronted by a surplus of applicants, the ABCFM selected a bachelor, six married couples, a former slave, three natives of Hawaii, and one native of the Society Islands to reinforce the earlier detachment. Of these new missionaries, William Richards was probably best known to the Prudential Committee. His brother James was one of the board's missionaries to Ceylon, and William had long expressed hopes of becoming a foreign missionary himself. Born in Plainfield, a small farming community in a secluded region of western Massachusetts, William followed his brother to the Reverend Moses Hallock's school in Plainfield and then to Williams College. He proved an excellent student and reflected his father's love for learning and religion. In 1808 a revival swept through western Massachusetts and the youth professed religion. He joined the church three years later. Entering Williams College in 1815, he belonged by his senior year to the Mills Theological Society and the Society of Brethren. In 1819 Richards entered Andover Theological Seminary, where he remained a member of the same society, renamed the Society of Inquiry. Like so many missionaries in the first company, William Richards married only weeks before his departure.[47]

James Ely, a second member of the reinforcement, had also been interested in foreign missionary work for several years prior to his departure for the Sandwich Islands. In 1817 he applied for admission to the Foreign Mission School at Cornwall. Skilled as a cooper, but without any financial resources, Ely admitted at once that he wanted to go to the Sandwich Islands. For the next five years the school employed him to collect money and clothing throughout New England.[48] The youth from Lyme, Connecticut, asked to be included in the first company to the islands, but officials at the Cornwall school thought him too inexperienced for the task and recommended that he remain at the school for a few more years.[49] Less than a year later they changed their minds and found him fully qualified for missionary work. Ely's pleas for service overseas, however, remained frustrated. His future mother-in-law was "utterly opposed" to her daughter's leaving the country, so the young couple waited two more years before embarking for the Sandwich Islands in November 1822.[50]

The other members of the mission company had also been close to the ABCFM's activities or influence for a number of years. Charles Stewart, graduate of Princeton Theological Seminary, had committed himself to foreign missions several years before his acceptance for the Sandwich Islands reinforcement. Like so many of these early missionaries, Stewart was in debt, owing at least $1,000.[51] One of his close friends from the seminary, Artemas Bishop, joined the company. Bishop was also in debt. Prior to their departure both men became agents for the ABCFM to collect enough money to pay off their indebtedness. Inclined to corpulence, the amiable Bishop labored for several months during the summer of 1822 in pursuit of funds. By November he had successfully recovered his debts. Just before embarking he chose a wife, Elizabeth Edwards, a girlhood friend of Lucy G. Thurston. The missionary spirit seemed to follow the paths of friendship.[52]

Three other men completed the reinforcement. Born in Wethersfield, Connecticut, Joseph Goodrich joined the local church during the revivals of 1814. He was educated at Yale and offered himself to the board in 1821. Abraham Blatchley filled the need for a physician. Although he lacked a college education and at thirty-five was older than his colleagues, Blatchley had attended two lecture courses at the medical school in New Haven. Following this brief venture into medical training, he conducted a practice for a few years in his hometown of East Guilford, Connecticut.[53] The last member of the company, Levi Chamberlain, served as superintendent of secular affairs for the mission. For six years prior to his departure Chamberlain had owned a successful dry goods business in Boston. In 1818 he joined the Park Street Church and soon after decided to become a missionary. He sold his prosperous business in 1821 and entered Andover Academy. At the same time he accepted a position in the Treasury Department of the ABCFM and tendered his services as a missionary teacher. As an inducement for employment, he proposed to turn over all his financial resources (about $3,500) and will all his remaining property to the ABCFM. Early in 1822 the board appointed him to the mission.[54]

This completed the board's second detachment to the Sandwich Islands, with one exception. Betsey Stockton, a mulatto and former slave, accompanied the mission as a teacher. Raised as a slave in the family of the Reverend Ashbel Green, president of Princeton, she gained her freedom in 1818. Deciding to remain with the Greens as a domestic, she received an education and joined the Presbyterian Church. For several years the young girl "appropriated a part of every week to the instruction of coloured children" and acquired an urge to become a missionary in Africa. Forestalled by opposition from her friends, she welcomed the chance to accompany the Reverend and Mrs. Charles Stewart to the Sandwich Islands in 1822, and the ABCFM accepted her offer of services. In an age when foreign missions was just beginning, her presence as a teacher at the Sandwich Islands Mission was quite extraordinary.[55]

Much like members of the first company to these islands, the hopes of these missionaries reflected both the accomplishments of the Second Great Awakening and the publicity given foreign missions in New

England. Joseph Goodrich mirrored the sentiments of his colleagues in a letter to Jedidiah Morse in 1821. Goodrich concluded that he had "had a desire to go on a foreign mission ever since the first publication of the 'Narrative of the Sandwich Island youth.' "[56] Artemas Bishop was even more specific about his plans and volunteered particularly for the Sandwich Island Mission. Expressing a deep religious commitment and disclaiming any notion that he expected pleasures or material rewards, Bishop denied that the success of the first company had influenced his decision.[57] Both Ely and Richards also expressed early desires to go to the Sandwich Islands. They reached their decisions under different influences, but both men reflected the impact of foreign missions on New England during the preceding decade. Publicity given to Sandwich Islands natives in the region and the activity of the ABCFM in foreign missions had clearly exerted their influence.[58]

Throughout the autumn months the new missionaries and agents of the board scoured New England in search of funds. They reported considerable success. At the ordination of William Richards and Artemas Bishop, the Reverend Samuel Miller of Princeton Theological Seminary recalled the virtues of foreign missions and urged greater donations to the cause. After issuing the usual pleas to save the heathen and reporting the catalog of heathen evils, Miller emphasized the importance of foreign missions and reminded his audience that they assisted religion at home. "All experience demonstrates," he concluded, "that we are never so likely to receive an ample blessing at home as when we open our hearts, and send help to our brethren abroad."[59]

Organization of the new company of missionaries provoked another venemous attack from the *Religious Inquirer*. In March 1822 the editor charged that only derelicts became foreign missionaries. "Those who can find no employment at home," he wrote, "are thought fit vessels to convey the glad tidings of life and immortality to the Heathen."[60] As the departure date approached, the criticism became more specific. In October the editor expressed numerous objections to the ABCFM and its activities. The missionaries were too young and inexperienced. They had fallen prey to sectarian prejudices and preached, not "that religion contained in the Bible," but "Calvinistic dogma." These youths, moreover, had volunteered in a moment of excitement and were neither competent preachers nor learned ministers. "Those who are sent out," the editor warned, "appear not to be called of God, but chosen of men."[61]

At issue here was not really the validity of foreign missions, but, as the editor noted in his criticism, sectarian prejudices. Unitarians protested any extension of Calvinist influence and used foreign missions as a pretext to keep alive domestic religious controversy. But, once again, the criticism aroused little interest. Unitarians agreed with the editor, and Calvinists ignored him. That the criticism might be valid meant little. Too many people had succumbed to the argument that foreign missions aided domestic piety and ignored the suggestion that material contributions might not reflect religious commitment. The editor argued in vain that the "Missionary Scheme" drew too much money away from domestic charity. "Learned competency" did not seem too important to the ABCFM so long as its emissaries established a foothold in the Pacific.[62]

By November the reinforcement was ready to sail, and the brig *Thames* pulled away from its New Haven pier on November 19, 1822. Local newspapers extensively publicized the departure, emphasizing the global importance of the mission. If this company successfully reinforced the mission already at the Sandwich Islands the gospel would have a permanent station in the Pacific. From these islands Bibles and missionaries could accompany the sandalwood to the pagodas of China. Owhyhee, the *Boston Recorder* predicted, would become a "radiating point of religion." At the same time, the missionaries would provide instruction in agricultural techniques, improve the lot of Sandwich Islands natives, and make Hawaii an international showplace; it would be an example of what missionary labors could accomplish. It would, of course, be unique—but only for a short while. Soon this system would spread throughout all heathen lands.[63]

As 1822 drew to a close, promoters and patrons of foreign missions were more enthusiastic than ever before about the future of their cause. There was good reason for their optimism. The treasury of the ABCFM had never been so full. Receipts for 1822 far surpassed those of any previous year, climbing to a record $60,087.87—more than ten thousand dollars above the highest previous figure.[64]

The Reverend Joel Hawes expressed clerical reaction to these accomplishments in the title of his year-end sermon: "What Hath God Wrought!" Briefly tracing the rapid rise and apparent success of foreign missions, Hawes noted that thirty years ago the "Christian world was asleep on this subject." How quickly circumstances had changed. Now missionaries were beginning to spread over the globe. Not only had they extended religion abroad, their accomplishments had aroused considerable interest in the United States. Accordingly, "exertions to promote religion at home have been multiplied."[65]

Hawes concluded his survey with a warning. "To be indifferent then, or to stand still, and refuse to act," he cautioned, "is rebellion. To possess wealth, and talents, and influence, and not employ them in advancing the cause of Christ, is disobedience which God will punish."[66] Foreign missions had become the new orthodoxy. The reasons for giving, like the reasons for church attendance, became less important than the giving itself. Promoters of the cause did not pretend that contributors were pure of spirit, although they might argue that donations reflected a certain purity. But purity, or piety, mattered little so long as people remained convinced that the missionaries were dedicated to the cause of God and Calvinistic religion.

The most crucial year in the board's brief history now dawned. By 1823 the ABCFM had greatly expanded its operations. Expenses had risen, and it became imperative that contributions keep pace with this expansion. In December 1822 one of the board's agents suggested the organization of additional societies to promote its activities. Writing from Connecticut, Horatio Bardwell urged that these new societies be designed to support "individual schools at our missionary stations." New societies were needed so as not to "impede" the operations of existing county societies. Bardwell also hinted that in return for a town's support, one of these schools might bear its name. Not only would the religion and customs of New England be exported, but the place names as well. The Prudential Committee raised no objections and agents began to assemble the new organizations. At the same time the ABCFM adopted a plan to organize an even greater array of auxiliaries and foreign mission associations throughout New England. The final struggle for stability among the directors of foreign missions took place in 1823.[67] Officials hoped that permanence would follow stability.

Promotion of the extended system began early in 1823. Speaking before the Boston Foreign Mission Society in January, the Reverend James Sabine linked the recent advances in foreign missions to the coming millennium. Only continuous efforts, he insisted, could preserve these "beneficial effects" both at home and abroad. As if to support Sabine's argument, that same month the *Christian Spectator* noted that "Hundreds of publications" now devoted much of their effort to the promotion of missionary work.[68] The ABCFM meanwhile, issued a series of statements outlining how the money was spent.[69] In doing so board officials tried to discredit opposition charges that a few men personally benefited from the frequent solicitations for foreign missions.

During the winter the Prudential Committee faced another problem. The Foreign Mission School in Cornwall needed more money. With the expansion of foreign missionary activities during the preceding half-dozen years the school had also increased its operations. As new students came to Cornwall school officials confronted a growing number of problems, usually related to student behavior. At the same time the board decided that Sandwich Islanders should remain in their native land and attend the new missionary schools. This would enhance the usefulness of the mission and save money. Enrollment at Cornwall, consequently, fell; and Herman Daggett wrote the Prudential Committee to request help in securing more "promising youths from different Indian tribes to the West & South." Without such an increase the survival of the school seemed precarious. The ABCFM quickly dispatched agents in search of students and money. As these men collected funds, they also urged donors to subscribe to the *Missionary Herald*. In this manner they raised money for the board; in doing so, they sold one of its publications and perhaps acquired a lifetime contributor to foreign missions.[70]

Throughout the year pastors preached the necessity of maintaining religious institutions to preserve a Christian society. Yet, with the first blush of organization over, they also warned of dangers that lurked among the shadows of religious benevolence. A few ministers, perhaps in response to Unitarian criticism, urged donors to consider their motives and to recognize that financial support for religion was not religion. An increasing tendency to substitute "evangelical charities" for "vital religion" seemed particularly dangerous. Ebenezer Porter reminded students at Andover Theological Seminary that there were too many people who promoted "the cause of missions on the general assumption that religion is a *good* thing, is friendly to the interests of philanthropy, and civilization, and social order."[71]

But these warnings remained unheeded in most households across New England, and the *Missionary Herald* continued to enumerate donations in its pages each month. Another exhortation remained more popular: that religious institutions were essential to a Christian society. Participation in their activities could only be beneficial.[72] The Reverend Nathaniel Taylor bluntly summarized these benefits in his 1823 election sermon at Hartford, concluding that "change, innovation, revolution in a community, where religious institutions exert their proper influence, are hopeless."[73] In a time of social turbulence such panaceas were most appealing.

But while ministers argued about the motives and piety of contributors, officials of the ABCFM in Boston worried about more material problems. The need for money and difficulties at the Foreign Mission School still plagued the Prudential Committee. In the face of persistent disciplinary problems and deteriorating community relations, the board proposed moving the school to another location. In an elaborate defense, Joseph Harvey objected. He cautioned against the evil influences found in more populous communities. The youths, he insisted, "should be removed as much as possible from the society of vicious and unprincipled persons." This could hardly be done to any extent in a populous place. Citing increased expenses, sacrifice of existing property, and an animus against change, Harvey convinced ABCFM officials to keep the school in Cornwall.[74]

After deciding the fate of the Foreign Mission School the Prudential Committee turned to solve its financial headaches. At the September meeting of the Boston Foreign Mission Society officers discussed the question of fund-raising in detail. The *Missionary Herald* published an account of these proceedings, thereby carrying the message to all societies and associations. Officials of the Boston society argued that women presented the most fruitful source for solicitation. Emphasizing the need for personal contact with each individual, they instructed societies to employ a collector for every five persons. Personal appeals would be more difficult to resist, and closeness between donor and collector was likely to elicit substantial and annual contributions. Extension of this system throughout New England could produce "a thousand, or ten thousand collectors." More people than ever before soon became personally involved in the operations of the American Board of Commissioners for Foreign Missions.[75]

To systematize further the collection of funds, Boston officials recommended the establishment of still more auxiliary societies across New England. Every town and district should have at least one. To increase annual contributions officials urged all societies to arrange their anniversaries so that "a delegation from the Prudential Committee, or from the Board, may attend half a score of them, or even a greater number, in the course of a single month."[76] Board members also tried to enlarge circulation of the *Missionary Herald*. Since this publication was the "primary instrument of promoting a spirit of practical benevolence," an increase in subscribers would undoubtedly mean an increase in donations.[77]

From these preliminary soundings, in November the board launched a full-scale effort to achieve a permanent and effective system. The *Missionary Herald* outlined the plan to be adopted. The board cited a need for greater discipline, so that in an emergency it would be possible "to bring the whole effective force into the field." At present, it complained, too little calculation is made to future needs. People give when they want, or can, and future planning is ignored. To correct these deficiencies and to create a systematic organization that could swell the treasury on a given signal from Boston, the Prudential Committee proposed a general plan.

Two kinds of societies would be formed; one large, one small. The large societies were designed for cities, large towns, or counties. They would be "immediately auxiliary" to the ABCFM and would be designated "Auxiliary Societies." Smaller societies, on the other hand, were to be used in towns, parishes, or school districts. To be known as "Associations," they would be subsidiaries of the larger auxiliaries. This network would provide both a system for raising money and a web of communication radiating from Boston. As a final touch, every small society should have two component parts: a ladies' and a gentlemen's society. Sex segregation would be preserved and in "most places, greater funds will be secured, and in the manner least objectionable."[78]

To induce a rapid reorganization of existing societies along these lines, the board included forms for constitutions—one a model for an auxiliary society, another for an association. Local officials only had to fill in a few blanks and their constitution was complete. This further centralized the process and gave uniformity to the scheme.[79]

Guidelines for subscriptions provided the final and perhaps most ingenious touch. Donations were to be for one year. Every year, therefore, an army of collectors would descend on the New England countryside in pursuit of funds. The board hoped to reap several benefits from this annual harvest. It would give collectors a sense of responsibility and keep them active. Activity meant publicity for the ABCFM, and few would be able to escape this incessant activity. Board officials expected that greater publicity would increase individual donations, and they thought donors would give more if they gave each year, rather than for a longer period. Through careful organization of local societies and an extensive network of collectors, the Prudential Committee hoped to enlist 750,000 persons in the foreign missionary movement.[80]

The plan was not entirely new, but it was more ambitious than any tried to date. Officials had found themselves trapped between decreasing contributions and increasing expenses. They acted promptly and with careful planning. If the scheme worked, the ABCFM could conduct its operations in a meticulously orchestrated manner. If it did not work, then the entire enterprise was in grave difficulty.[81]

The increased emphasis on the importance of organization and local societies to mobilize public opinion and monies also made clear the motives behind the clergy's earlier attack on Jeffersonian societies. Ministers did not condemn all societies, but each one must be evaluated in light of its goals. Those that subverted "all true principles" in religion, morality or politics should be condemned. Nathaniel Emmons's earlier evaluations of Jeffersonian societies remained the criteria for acceptance. "They have," he noted, "zealously affected the populace, but not well."[82]

More important was the impact of these benevolent societies. Ostensibly designed to augment religious principles and assist the work of pastors and churches, they really effected a revolutionary shift in the function of both church and clergy. The various societies and local auxiliaries usurped much of the church's former role and influence in confronting social problems. At times they even replaced the church entirely. Increased lay leadership in these societies, moreover, pushed local ministers from the forefront of social leadership. Superintendency of community morals and republican virtues belonged more and more to nonecclesiastical personnel. Pastors still warned of evils and sought to realize their ideal of a Christian commonwealth, but actual leadership fell to the new societies. Certainly the clergy remained active in these organizations, but popular identification and credit went to the society and not to the church. Another barrier had arisen between the people and their religion.

8.   ACHIEVING PERMANENCE

Directors of foreign missions now believed they were on the threshold of permanence. Further to explain and publicize their motives they issued yet another outline of their proposed system. The new directive indicated the sweep of this activity. Agents were to visit every neighborhood in search of donations and were to facilitate regular contributions and prompt action. The board also used an array of sermons, public addresses, and monthly concerts. All had proved effective in creating excitement for foreign missions in previous years. "Especially the attention is aroused," it noted, "when these services are performed by a stranger, who visits a place for this express purpose."[1] Enjoining agents and patrons to work toward a well-oiled system of societies, the board urged laymen as well as clergy to lead the campaign. Prominent local businessmen should accompany agents in their respective towns. Their introductions, endorsements, and personal solicitations would "have the best effects."[2]

Not content with one circular, the ABCFM inserted additional items in all its publications. Nothing escaped its attention. Urging the creation of a vast missionary apparatus to embrace preachers, teachers, families, the press, tracts, historical works, and native colleges, a section on "Hints for Promoting Systematic Exertions" in the board's 1824 summary of missionary activities succinctly indicated the design. Promoters expressed dismay that they needed "external forces" to prevent the missionary spirit from continually "running down." Associations did not solve the problem, but provided a collective discipline unavailable to individual donors.[3] The *Missionary Herald* quickly added its voice to the new call, urging all readers to give regularly and systematically even if the amounts were not large.[4]

Throughout the year board members carefully constructed and extended their system. Concentrating at first on wealthy patrons in Boston, they worked to embrace all New England. Not everyone saw the urgency of the appeal and often needed reminders that their ardor had dimmed. Account books usually told the story, and agents grimly pointed to the evidence. Writing from Ashfield, Massachusetts, John Richards outlined the method. He listed annual contributions during a meeting of the Auxiliary Foreign Mission Society of Franklin County. No one disputed the figures, which showed a steady decline from $213 in 1813 to $93 in 1822. Richards then told ABCFM officers, "This state of things presents a favourable opening for me and my object. They see the inefficiency of their system and are convinced something new is needed."[5] Agents repeated this procedure elsewhere across New England.

Even Unitarians responded—not with donations, but with a detailed explanation of their views toward foreign missions. Long criticized for not participating in the venture, they now explained this failure. Expressing a distaste for religious conformity, Unitarians argued that the heathen were safe *"as far as respects the future world,"* even though they were without Christianity. This argument contradicted the fundamental Trinitarian rationale for foreign missions. Unitarians not only rejected the basis for foreign missions, they also opposed the manner in which the ABCFM conducted those missions. They lamented the waste of excitement, money, and life on foreign peoples, while at the same time admitted the benevolent design of missionary operations.[6] William Bentley's earlier charge of "sectarian prejudices" continued to lie at the heart of the Unitarian complaint, and their attack seemed to be directed as much against Calvinism as against foreign missions.[7]

By the end of the year a few rewards from the board's efforts had appeared. Local societies and associations reported a new excitement for foreign missions. Those communities that had not yet formed societies began to do so, and existing societies extended their influence.[8] The call for system and efficiency seemed to be having the desired effects. But progress toward financial stability was slow in 1824, and the ABCFM looked to 1825 to achieve the long-awaited permanence.

As if to keynote this final drive, in January the Reverend Warren Fay addressed the Boston Foreign Mission Society on *The Obligation of Christians to the Heathen World*. Praising all benevolent activity, Fay argued that foreign missions aimed "at the greatest and noblest results,—the conversion and salvation of the world."[9] Foreign missions not only carried the gospel to heathen lands; they also conveyed the essential virtues and blessings of American civilization. "And would not these blessings," Fay asked, "be equally valuable to ignorant and degraded Pagans?" Christianity would bring the Bible, social order, and civil government to peoples "enveloped in mental and moral darkness."[10] Listing several objections to foreign missions and then carefully refuting each one in turn, Fay sprinkled his sermon with stories of missionary successes and admonitions for the future. He concluded with an impassioned plea for support. "Angels in Heaven are looking down with interest to see what you do this evening to bring Pagans to repentance, and swell their joys; and are waiting the results. *Jesus Christ himself is here, sitting over against the Treasury*, waiting to approve a generous, a noble, a holy offering, to spread the savior of His name among the Heathen."[11]

New Englanders gradually responded. Fay's arguments had not been new, but mere repetition seemed to build support, however slowly. Some persons still opposed the enterprise, but board officials found themselves increasingly able to ignore their criticism. Promoters of the undertaking set out to procure greater donations, and pastors forecast a general revival of religious principles. Lyman Beecher wrote from Connecticut that for the first time in six or seven years he was "at ease in respect to the general course of events which concern the Church in Connecticut." Voluntarism found acceptance, and Beecher rejoiced that "the rock remains, not a fragment broken off nor its base shaken."[12]

Pastors throughout the region noticed a change in the religious atmosphere. Efforts at Christian benevolence were "working out for us an abundant reward of national happiness." Missionaries and missionaries-to-be roamed the region, and officials of the ABCFM had difficulty persuading these young men to remain in Boston to work in the board's offices.[13] Even Unitarians commented with some favor on the growing number of benevolent associations. During the summer the *Christian Examiner* published an article that outlined the work of these societies and extended a smattering of qualified praise. The author concluded that men should work toward doing good, whatever their principles and motives.[14] Their endeavors would open the path for the reconstruction of an orderly, Christian commonwealth. The Reverend Joshua Bates summarized the influence of Christianity toward this goal in his sermon before the ABCFM at its annual meeting. Positing a causal relationship between Christianity and social order, Bates surveyed the globe and found "nothing like civil liberty, united with social order in security," in any non-Christian country.[15] This was the message of American foreign missions.

The board issued a progress report in September that outlined the advantages of reorganization and cited impressive statistical evidence of success. An extensive network of societies had been constructed, with every one under direct supervision. Since each association embraced only one parish, the resident minister served as its watchman. The board had now established a clear line of responsibility and communication from its Boston offices to all points in the New England countryside.[16]

Elsewhere in its report the ABCFM suggested numerous techniques that could be used to increase donations. Contributions should be solicited "immediately after the anniversaries of the Associations" so as to capitalize on any excitement stirred up at the anniversary celebration. Each ceremony should be designed to create some new feeling for foreign missions. The board recommended that local pastors excite an interest, delegations from the regional auxiliary be present, and tales of missionary trials and successes be read. Leaving nothing to chance the ABCFM provided suggestions for a model anniversary meeting. Officers argued that "five or six addresses—*short*, comprehensive, abounding in fact and animated illustration—will, with the Report, and the prayers, and select pieces of music, and a collection at the close, send the people home abundantly repaid for their attendance."[17] Following this celebration each society should publish an annual report, to include a report of the meeting, the sermon delivered, a financial report and list of donations, and brief abstracts of any addresses. These reports would effectively publicize both increasing contributions and the extension of this system throughout New England.[18] At the same time they would stimulate other societies to greater efforts. Mutual excitement would mean larger contributions. By December many towns had formed societies, and donations to the ABCFM rose.[19]

By 1826 the ABCFM seemed assured of success. An "age of exciting beginnings" had given way to one of "organized administration."[20] But promoters of foreign missions never relaxed their drive for support. The Reverend Warren Fay, speaking before the Auxiliary Foreign Mission Society of Essex County in April 1826, recited the catalog of missionary achievements. He noted particularly the influence of foreign missions on domestic religion and found the enterprise a "life-giving, a redeeming spirit in many languishing, declining churches."[21] Other speakers before the society emphasized the same theme and argued that extensive contributions to foreign missions would increase, not reduce, America's resources. At the conclusion of the proceedings Lyman Beecher extended the argument in an interesting and unusual fashion. Beecher insisted that "instead of hermetical sealing, to preserve our income within the nation, we need safety valves to let out our superfluous abundance. And national improvements, and missionary efforts to evangelize the world, are the merciful provisions of providence for this end."[22] Here lay the power and potential of American foreign missions. The Christian religion, led by American wealth and energy, would conquer the world.

American foreign missions had achieved prominence and success; and each new achievement stimulated other benefits. In April 1826 the *North American Review*, under the guise of a book review, published a lengthy article on the American mission at the Sandwich Islands. Noting the missionaries' accomplishments, the author predicted greater success for the future, "when the children of the schools shall go out into society, with minds properly stored, and habits rightly trained."[23] That same month Levi Chamberlain wrote from Honolulu to praise the board's new efforts to reorganize societies. Observing that success of the new scheme seemed imminent, Chamberlain added, "Missionaries abroad are encouraged when they see the Churches at home associating themselves for the purpose of furnishing the means for carrying forward the missionary enterprise."[24] Efforts to rebuild a Christian commonwealth seemed to promise success.

As the education and training of heathen children would determine the fate of foreign missions abroad, so would the proper training of American youth decide the fate of support for foreign missions at home. Now that the yearning for immediate success had been partially gratified, pastors urged local societies to form juvenile associations. "We are engaged," one society reported, "in a work which will require many years to accomplish. Who will carry it on when we are dead?" It was the duty of every parent to "train up his children for the church and its service."[25]

Promoters of foreign missions overlooked no opportunity to advance their cause. Officers of the Rutland County Foreign Missionary Society in Vermont suggested that parents let their children "cast into the treasury of the Lord, with their own hands" a portion of the family's contribution to foreign missions.[26] Meanwhile, in Massachusetts

Horatio Bardwell recommended that societies reverse the process and use children to get greater donations from parents. With calculated bluntness, Bardwell reminded his audience "how easy it is to obtain access to a parent, through the medium of a beloved child."[27]

For the rest of the year pastors spoke of the intimate connection between civilization, Christianity, foreign missions, and support for domestic religious institutions. Not only would local churches profit from their parishioners' support for foreign missions, churches in surrounding communities would also benefit. The example of one could influence the other, advance domestic religion, and strengthen community ties. Discord and divisiveness would cease as all persons labored in the cause of foreign missions.[28] A few months later, at the September meeting of the ABCFM the Reverend Edward D. Griffin elaborated the relationship between Christianity and civilization. "What nation since the commencement of the Christian era," he asked, "ever arose from savage to civilized without Christianity?" Only Christianity could save the heathen. At the same time, Griffin noted, these efforts increased religious convictions at home.[29]

By December the ABCFM had achieved permanence. Increased contributions heralded financial stability. The Prudential Committee would always need funds, but the danger of collapse disappeared. To crown their success board officials announced a proposed union with the United Foreign Missionary Society. Union would avoid duplication of effort, ease all financial strain, and increase efficiency. Just how strong the board had grown became evident the following year, when trouble erupted at the Foreign Mission School in Cornwall.[30]

For eight years the Foreign Mission School had educated foreign youth, trained missionary candidates, and attracted praise and attention. In 1825 a marriage between Harriet Gold, daughter of one of Cornwall's most prominent citizens, and Elias Boudinot, a Cherokee at the school, shattered this placid atmosphere. Violent opposition to the marriage surfaced immediately, and the uproar forced the ABCFM to reconsider the school's future. Two years elapsed before board officials made their decision, and the controversy grew more heated. Indians as well as whites protested the marriage, and all parties petitioned the ABCFM to act. The Prudential Committee, slow to understand the problem, moved cautiously. Jeremiah Evarts wrote the Reverend Calvin Chapin in July 1825 to ask advice. "Can it be pretended, at this age of the world," Evarts asked, "that a small variance of complexion is to present an unsuperable barrier to matrimonial connexions?"[31] Domestic controversy once again enveloped the board.

After evaluating the problem for more than a year, the ABCFM in 1826 announced that the school would be discontinued. Believing that their objectives could better be accomplished elsewhere, officials decided that heathen youth should remain in their native lands, to be taught by missionaries from the ABCFM. They also noted that the largest single group of students came from the Sandwich Islands, where a fully established mission had begun religious and literary instruction. Few could quarrel with the force of these arguments; certainly the school did duplicate other efforts of the board. More to the point, however, was the argument that "there are serious difficulties in conducting an institution, composed of young men brought from the wilderness, or from distant pagan countries, and formed into a little community by themselves, while they are more or less exposed to various influences from the surrounding population."[32] The proposed marriage clearly illustrated these difficulties.

At the same time, board officials did not ignore the cause of these conflicts. In their report for 1826 they bluntly admitted the existence of red/white racial problems. Local residents treated Indians, and all foreign youth, as inferiors. Blaming this racism on a combination of "inquisitive curiosity," mixed with "Christian benevolence" and "established prejudices," the board argued that these attitudes disrupted school activities. Young men could not study so long as they were *"mere shows*, a feeling which is too accurate an index of their real situation."[33] The school would be disbanded.

Public announcement came the following January. An article in the *Missionary Herald* reprinted pertinent sections of the board's annual report for the preceding year and listed the reasons for the board's action. The author praised the school's usefulness and indicated its important role in prompting the mission to the Sandwich Islands. Designed to aid foreign missions, the Foreign Mission School had outlived its usefulness. Few missions could now avail themselves of its aid and local difficulties curtailed its domestic influence. A noble experiment, the school closed in 1827.[34]

Yet, despite turbulence and ill feeling at Cornwall, operations of the ABCFM did not suffer. The issue was closed, and officials quickly turned to preserve and extend advances made the previous year. The Prudential Committee's "Address to the Christian Public" in February reiterated the standard litany of foreign missions and again urged support of board activities. Local auxiliaries picked up the message, recommending systematic contributions. Pastors recalled the trials of missionary work and repeated arguments perfected during the previous decade.[35] In November the Reverend C. J. Tenney confidently announced, "We, my brethren, can indulge no doubt, that the God of Israel has distinguished and exalted our nation, and especially New-England."[36]

But officers of the ABCFM did not relax their efforts. Believing that too much money could not be collected, they pursued all promising donors. In his instructions to a New York committee chairman, Jeremiah Evarts admonished that any special effort to raise more money should be "confined to the wealthy and the prosperous, to those who are able to engage a handsome donation." This would prevent interference with efforts of local associations and avoid duplication of more systematic solicitations.[37]

These efforts came under yet another attack in 1828, with publication of *The Black Book; or a Continuation of Travels in the United States*, an account of the wanderings and observations of Mrs. Anne Royall.[38] In a flood of sarcastic and critical comment Royall attacked the operations and motives of the benevolent empire. Chastising the men and women who supported these societies as "silly" and "unprincipled," she labeled the scheme a clerical attempt to gain "universal power."[39] She reserved the brunt of her criticism, however, for missionaries. Their training, she argued, consisted of a few lessons in theological school where they were taught to regard "all other sects as heretics" and to "model their countenance into that of demons." These "young vipers" then went out into society "to make a long face, and a long prayer, and (more to the point) a long *purse*."[40]

Royall condemned these men as intolerant bigots and argued that the benevolent empire sought money ("wrung from ignorance and poverty") to instill a distrust of nonconformity throughout the world. These "pirates" were everywhere she complained. Travelers and residents alike could not escape their ministrations. Money was their aim, and their pursuit knew no bounds. At length she concluded that one bright spot remained, namely, many failed to pay attention to all this preaching. "While the preacher is running on about money, the old people go to sleep, and the young ones ogle each other."[41]

These were strong charges, and it is difficult to measure their impact;

but in 1828 the Prudential Committee moved to dispel any notion that the board had sufficient funds. At the same time the committee reiterated the advantages of its system and the careful preparation given to missionaries.[42] The *Missionary Herald* carried an address from the committee to refute the unfounded rumor that "there is no occasion, at the present time, for even the common exertions to raise funds."[43] Emphasizing the need for constant liberality, it warned all readers about the dangers of any relaxation in their efforts. Anyone who withheld even the smallest donation would do irreparable injury to the cause of foreign missions. The board set its goals high and insisted that no one could be satisfied until all auxiliaries doubled their contributions for the previous year; or until every professing Christian became a contributor.[44] With their enterprise firmly established, board officials watched carefully for backsliders and moved quickly to prevent even the smallest defection.

During the year the ABCFM issued other notices reminding patrons of the need for continued and systematic giving. Too many persons, it noted, donated to the "first object that is presented," with no regard for other causes throughout the year.[45] Patrons should give the same amount (or more) to each cause every year. At the same time, local societies should create an interest in missions among themselves. Then the board could curtail its use of agents. This would save money as well as release more men for missionary duty abroad.[46] While the board issued press releases, pastors preached their message. Active, liberal Christians were needed to meet the crisis of heathenism. Journals once again resorted to tales of horror and exaggeration to excite the public, lest donors become complacent with the board's continued success. "Infidelity," announced the *Christian Spectator*, "is stealing over the world like a poisonous vapor." Only the "moral discipline of benevolent action" could defeat its design.[47]

But this discipline remained strong. Perhaps afraid that any relaxation would lead to decline, the ABCFM still refused to slow its pace. Although 15,000 copies of the *Missionary Herald* had circulated in 1828, officers urged all friends of missions to enlarge the journal's circulation. Insisting that the *Herald* should reign preeminent among all religious publications, they sought domination as well as success.[48] By the close of 1828 they had achieved the latter, if not the former. Contributions jumped almost fourteen thousand dollars in one year, and for the first time topped $100,000.[49] Over 150 associations and auxiliaries blanketed New England. Agents visited each society at least once a year to solicit contributions. Occasionally a society's annual contribution declined from that of the previous year; but the cause of the decrease was usually clear—a business recession hitting the county, a leading contributor moving out of town. Competition among the many benevolent causes then current also alarmed directors of foreign missions and often diminished donations to the board.[50]

This proliferation of associations received a critical evaluation in the Unitarian press. William Ellery Channing noted the work of these groups in 1829 and admitted that, while some were evil, most of them exhibited a high degree of competency and organization. He who ignored these associations could not understand society. They were a "mighty engine" that could act for good or evil. Made viable by the transportation revolution, associations spurred the growth of nationalism and unity. "Through these means," Channing noted, "men of one mind, through the whole country, easily understand one another, and easily act together."[51]

But dangers lurked here too, and Channing expressed the Unitarians' fear that individual responsibility would disappear in the face of group action and conformity. To Channing and his fellow Unitarians, individualism and self-determination were the repositories of virtue. "There is no moral worth," he warned, "in being swept away by a crowd, even towards the best objects. We must act from an inward spring." Promoters of benevolence could argue that individual conscience drove people to contribute money, but Channing and others knew better. They had watched the careful construction and orchestration of the societies for years and knew that claims of spontaneity were largely delusions. Summarizing his objection to foreign missions, Channing argued, "The great obstruction to Christianity among foreign nations, is, its inoperativeness among the nations which profess it. We offer others a religion, which, in their apprehension, has done the givers no great good."[52] To Lyman Beecher's claim that these associations represented "the best hearts, the most willing hands, and the most vigorous enterprise," Channing would admit only qualified agreement.[53]

Amid pleas for even greater systematic efforts in the collection of funds and continuing admonitions to save the heathen, advocates of foreign missions eagerly looked forward to the 1830s. They had elevated the art of missionary propaganda to new heights of rhetoric and effectiveness, and through this propaganda they had made foreign missions a popular movement. Future generations "would look upon us of the nineteenth century," insisted one speaker, "as the most enviable of the whole race, who have lived from Adam downward."[54]

Blind to how the use of statistics to measure Christian progress had changed American Christianity, these men pushed ahead in their pursuit of an "evangelical majority."[55] To relieve their insecurity and preserve their notion of America as a Christian nation, they had steadfastly simplified the difference between right and wrong. To overcome their crisis at home the clergy had sought a new frontier overseas. This, too, altered the nature of Protestant Christianity. In their search for a new Christian community among all Americans, pastors accommodated their attitudes and arguments to the new economic individualism. For three decades they had gathered support for their vision. The clergy told people not only what to support, but how and when to participate. Arguing that all men had the same nature and should embrace Christianity, they insisted at the same time that purity and freedom "from every foreign mixture or adulteration" remained essential to their cause.[56] This had been done and would continue to be done through interference in "the more sordid interests of men." Through their "superior intelligence," and with support from their country's commercial wealth, American foreign missionaries attempted to change the world. They sought to create a global community modeled after the New England example. "Our design," admitted one pastor, "is radically to affect the temporal and external interests of the whole race of man."[57]

9. FIGHTING THE WAY TO EMPIRE

The appearance of destitution, degradation, and barbarism, among the chattering, and almost naked savages, whose heads and feet, and much of their sunburnt swarthy skins, were bare, was appalling. Some of our number, with gushing tears, turned away from the spectacle. Others with firmer nerve continued their gaze, but were ready to exclaim, "Can these be human beings! . . . Can such beings be civilized? Can they be Christianized?"[1]

The American missionaries at the Sandwich Islands yearned to fulfill two goals. Confronted by what seemed to them the grossest degradation, vice, and ignorance, they hoped to apply religious principles to extend God's kingdom. At the same time they sought to realize their earthly ideal of the Christian commonwealth. Like their Puritan forebears, the missionaries were certain that the appearance of a new Zion to the west would revive true religious principles at home. Their assumptions, hopes, and fears emerged at the first moment of contact with the Sandwich Islands natives. Tales of vice and misery were undoubtedly embellished on occasion to produce greater excitement back home, but in most instances their initial reactions reflected clear perceptions of the task before them.

Yet behind this crusade lay an even broader purpose—an unspoken conviction that religious principles and republican virtues from the New England past remained the guideposts to civilization and progress. The missionaries tried to illustrate the vitality of these principles by demonstration at the Sandwich Islands. Two decades earlier Nathaniel Emmons had warned: "The world is in arms and opposed to our national prosperity and existence. We must, therefore, like the Israelites, fight our way to empire, in opposition to the power, and policy, and disorganizing principles of the most formidable nations on earth."[2] At a time when political strife, economic change, and religious turbulence seemed to be eroding these principles at home, the Sandwich Islands missionaries sought to demonstrate the timelessness of those principles by example abroad. Directors of the ABCFM in Boston, as well as the missionaries, shared the conviction that piety alone controlled the contentious spirit and led to peace and brotherhood. If the natives of a poor, exploited, and backward Pacific island could embrace these tenets of Christian progress and rise to glory, the world would take notice of the change. Americans would be forced to admit the virtues of piety and stability. The divisive spirit of the age could be checked, and the Bible returned to its rightful place as the complete guide to Christian living.[3]

But the conditions that greeted the missionaries upon their arrival in the islands signaled that the task would be difficult. More important were the missionaries' perceptions of their circumstances and the contrast they presented to their ideal of a pious and harmonious republic. No prior training could have prepared them to expect these conditions. Continual references to pagans and heathenism in the abstract could not substitute for the actual confrontation. Yet this training did provide these men and women with a resource and weapon to advance their cause. Theological training and the work at the Foreign Mission School instilled a sense of empathy. Here the generalized passages in the Bible proved their usefulness, developing not only a sense of mission but an awareness that conditions might well be more decadent than had been imagined. Their brief training also gave them principles and conviction. God had commanded that the world be evangelized, and since God did not demand the impossible, surely he would show the way. (Had not the Hawaiians overturned their gods prior to the missionaries' arrival?) Theological principles and biblical command also instilled a sense of guilt. Why had foreign missions been so long delayed? This guilt drove the men toward completion of their mission and energized those at home to support their efforts.[4]

The missionaries' first records of native customs and beliefs illustrated their perceptions of native society as well as the task before them. All saw the recent abandonment of traditional gods and religious customs as a hopeful sign. But experience soon proved that this religious revolution was pervasive primarily in public behavior. Elisha Loomis reported that he found "relics of superstition" in all the people's actions and thoughts and predicted a long battle before they were removed.[5] In their early reports the missionaries graphically described the conditions that lay before them. These narratives, which emphasized the poor housing, slovenly native dress and appearance, and lack of religion, also conveyed, of course, an implied standard of civilization.[6] These people must be given the gospel and with it all the attributes of Christian civilization.

Saving souls meant preaching the gospel, but to the missionaries it also implied much more than that. The tenets of the Bible alone were not enough, for Christianity itself did not transpose heathenism to civilization. To instill Christian principles without altering the very character of native society would ultimately result in the failure of the mission. Seeking to create a Christian *civilization*, the Sandwich Islands missionaries tried to alter every institution within their range. Hiram Bingham, leader of the mission, noted their purpose: "Their uncouth and disgusting manners were to be corrected, their modes of dress and living to be improved, their grossness, destitution, and wretchedness, if possible, removed; and taste, refinement, and comfort, substituted."[7]

To accomplish this transformation these men and women struggled to overcome centuries of native tradition as well as the growing opposition of traders and commercial interests in the islands. Missionary labors did not seek to restrict or punish commercial activity, so long as it was conducted in a Christian manner and did not contribute to instability in their Hawaiian affairs. Because their goal was to create a Christian nation and not merely to distribute Bibles or preach to throngs of curious natives, the missionaries' activities involved matters of trade and state as well as conscience. They did not maliciously seek to meddle; their sense of duty and mission impelled them to exert their influence on all aspects of native society.

Ship captains and British missionaries who visited the islands during the early years of the mission—when efforts at reform were still just beginning—outlined the difficulties confronting the venture. The crucial geographic location of Hawaii, and its role as a supply station for traders in furs and sandalwood as well as whalers, attracted persons whose income depended upon a friendly government. Without cheap labor to harvest sandalwood, and native women to satisfy the sexual appetites of restless sailors their difficulties would multiply. To preserve these perquisites of wealth, traders attacked all who spoke of change.

At the same time the behavior of Europeans and Americans at the islands encouraged natives to oppose or disregard missionary endeavors. After all, these captains and sailors were men of the world and apparently men of wealth. They could read and write and possessed fine weaponry. Domination hinted at superiority, and this encouraged imitation. Only if the missionaries could demonstrate alternative paths to power could they successfully challenge the traders' influence; and had it not been for the sailors' callous and haughty attitude toward the Sandwich Islanders, even the best missionary efforts might have been in vain.[8]

Despite the obstacles before them the newly arrived New Englanders remained optimistic and looked on the venture as a challenge and an opportunity. Right principles must triumph over moral depravity and licentiousness. In his later defense of the mission, Hiram Bingham summarized the views of the little band: "Rarely has a missionary a more favorable opportunity to exert an influence on a whole nation, than was here afforded in the circle of the highest chiefs of these islands, balancing, as they were, between idolatry, atheism, and the service of the true God."[9]

Secure in the knowledge that they carried with them the only true religion and convinced that the principles of their religion must pervade all the institutions of society before that society could be called Christian, these warriors of the Messiah at once began to build a new Zion in the mid-Pacific. The instructions of the ABCFM warned them to avoid all interference with "local and political interests of the people," while at the same time to promote the virtues of a Christian republic.[10] Despite later criticism from those who opposed their efforts, the missionaries did not believe their instructions to be contradictory. They were to instruct the people in biblical truths and principles. If successful, the laws of the kingdom would soon reflect these principles. This would be, not a theocracy, but a Christian republic. America would take notice.

The methodology of the Sandwich Islands Mission illustrates both the principles and the perceptivity of the missionaries. At the very outset of the mission Samuel Worcester carefully instructed them to take care to learn the habits and views of the king, "that you may conciliate & secure his favours, without existing jealousies or subjecting yourselves or the Mission to embarrassment." Close attention to the habits and customs of the rulers and people would enable the missionaries to "become all things to them."[11] To fulfill their goals the missionaries first attempted to gain the confidence of the chiefs. All authority in the islands emanated from the top, and without support from influential chiefs there was little chance of success.

This course of action was not something improvised on the spur of the moment, but stemmed from long discussions in the Society of Inquiry at Andover Theological Seminary. Discussants had concluded that missionary stations must obtain access to the nobility if they were to have much influence among the common people.[12] Local lines of authority reinforced this conviction, and experience in the field proved its viability.

Hiram Bingham's sturdy defense of the Hawaiian Mission, although biased and defensive, clearly indicates how the missionaries sought to use royal influence among the native population. Immediately after their arrival the first missionaries sought to gain influence with the rulers. They set about to learn their language and habits, as well as the "best means of access to their minds and hearts." Led by Bingham, the little band concentrated on converting a few local kings to their cause, catering to their "capacities and most urgent wants."[13]

Believing that good rulers meant good government and that a good government would promulgate wise and Christian legislation, the missionaries eagerly bowed to the demands of King Kamehameha II (Liholiho) and first began instruction among the chiefs. The king hoped that by learning the white man's magic of reading and writing he would be able to deal more shrewdly with traders. At the same time, it was unthinkable that the common people should learn the *palapala* before their superiors. From the vantage point of the missionaries, all efforts to influence the mass of natives would be fruitless without the attention and encouragement of the chiefs. Without such support missionaries would be unable to offset the material advantages and influences of traders and sailors.[14]

Yet, even by January 1821 the missionaries had thoroughly identified their cause with the future welfare of the Sandwich Islanders. They argued that constant attention to the king and chiefs was essential to promote their own comfort and security, as well as the "good of the nation."[15] A natural outgrowth of their views on Christianity and government, this assumption reflected their perception of the task ahead. For the next three years letters from the islands told a story of efforts to implement this design.

Whether confined to private correspondence with the ABCFM or recorded in journals to be published in the American press, the remarks of the missionaries reflected their efforts to convert the chiefs. No one reported much success, although all hailed each small advance. By 1822 few successes were evident. Bingham wrote the board that the king still awaited the arrival of a house the board had promised him.[16] Material rewards remained the path to influence in royal circles. Until a breakthrough could be achieved here, progress in education and religion remained blocked.

In February 1823 the *Missionary Herald* explained to readers and contributors the difficulties of the missionaries and urged that no one despair for the lack of success to date.

> Surely we ought not to despise the day of small things, even if we could do no more, for many years, than we have been allowed to attempt to-day,—to teach the king and queen a little manuscript catechism in the vernacular tongue. It was not, indeed, to be expected, that the dissipated rulers of this land would heartily embrace the glorious Gospel, with all its divine claims upon the heart, as soon as it should be proposed to them. Should the king, however, as an individual, be brought to obey the Gospel, who can estimate the benefits, which might be expected to flow from his influence, to present and future generations![17]

Typical of most missionary utterances in its all-consuming optimism, this plea nonetheless clearly revealed the methods of the Sandwich Islands missionaries. Subsequent issues of the *Herald* pursued the same theme: that once the chiefs were converted the people would follow their lead. By the end of the year the young missionaries had assumed full stewardship for the native population—at least that was their perception.[18]

Progress among the chiefs, however, was less encouraging. Convinced that the native population anxiously awaited religious and educational instruction, the missionaries pressed their demands on the king and chiefs. But in many sectors they met hostility or indifference.[19] The death of King Liholiho while on a visit to London in 1824 brought a sudden improvement in missionary fortunes. Although he had been generally friendly to the missionaries, Liholiho had never completely embraced their cause. He had sought some education to secure trading advantages and had occasionally exhibited some fascination with Christianity. But he had never placed himself thoroughly under missionary teaching. His periodic drinking and revelry impaired further progress.

The death of Liholiho in 1824 opened a new era for the Sandwich Islands Mission. All the leading chiefs were now favorable to the mission. Liholiho's underage stepbrother, later King Kamehameha III, succeeded to power. Kaahumanu, a friend and ally of the mission, was his co-ruler and exercised regental authority for several years. Led by Hiram Bingham, meanwhile, the missionaries educated the young monarch. Henceforth missionary influence steadily increased and its connection to political authority solidified. With stability and the promise of future success at hand, the missionaries purposively set out to realize their goals.[20] Hawaii was to become a Christian nation, an idealized version of American society. Guided by missionaries, and with the political support of the regent and chiefs, Sandwich Islands natives began to receive instruction in the "arts of civilization."[21]

The effort to Christianize native society in the Sandwich Islands, as elsewhere, involved much more than preaching the gospel and winning converts to Calvinist doctrines. Individual souls could not be saved so long as society and the institutions of government remained hostile to Christian principles. Missionary efforts, therefore, embraced education and politics as well as religion. Improvement in all these areas would lead the islands toward the ideal of a Christian republic.

As in New England, education remained the basis for all future progress. Aside from any literary or mental advantages inherent in the process, it was essential to the distribution of Bibles and the inculcation of Christianity. Through educational primers the missionaries could instill the lessons of duty, destiny, and Christian obligation. That these efforts began with the very rulers and lawmakers of the islands enhanced their influence. From the summer of 1820 all the missionaries and their wives had busily engaged in the instruction of native youth. Bingham himself taught the king and higher chiefs. Progress was slow, but the natives appeared eager to learn. Undoubtedly much of this interest can be traced to the novelty of what they were hearing. Observers expected few permanent results from adults, but hoped for greater progress among the children.[22]

As both chiefs and people gained pleasure and advantage from the new learning, the permanence and importance of the mission company increased. In January 1822 the first printed documents in Hawaiian came off the missionary press. Mass production of primers and lessons became possible, further expanding the power and influence of the missionaries. In New England pastors praised these efforts while telling their congregations "of kings and queens sitting down patiently to learn the alphabet, and obtain the rudiments of an education."[23] Local clergy urged greater support of the venture at the very time that

Sandwich Islands missionaries were writing in search of money, books, and slates for heathen children. Combining the usual cataclysmic expectations of future progress with the spectre of immediate decay, Hiram Bingham asked the board for more slates, predicting that 20,000 natives would be able to read and write within three years.[24] Such promises spurred New Englanders to form societies for the education of heathen children, as well as earmark donations for this purpose.

Missionary control of education and language proved crucial for the realization of their goals. These men had a monopoly as well as a captive audience. Hiram Bingham later summarized the importance and influence that this control carried with it: "to us it was a consolation ... to have ourselves the exclusive privilege of furnishing them with reading matter, and putting into their hands, and bringing into contact with their minds, such books only as were designed to have a salutary tendency, or were, on the whole, favorable to the service of God."[25] As well as reading and writing, this introduction also emphasized morals, religion, sacred music, geography and biblical history. All sought to instill Christian principles. By November 1824 the fascination of the new learning had swept the islands and the chiefs supported its propagation, calling it the *mea maitai* (the good thing).[26]

Education furthered the mission's goals as much by its novelty as by its usefulness. To the natives the art of writing was evidence of the white man's magic; to be let in on its secrets increased one's power and influence. "More than once," noted the English missionary William Ellis, "we have been asked whether the knowledge of it was not given to man by God himself."[27] Possessed with the ability to read and write, Sandwich Islands chiefs would now presumably be equal to the white traders. But instruction of the common people promised more revolutionary effects, for they would be placed on an equal footing with their rulers. The introduction of mass education, New England style, therefore marked the first step in the eradication of traditional native culture. Yet this was but the beginning of the missionaries' efforts to model native society along the lines of their New England upbringing. They thought they were bringing with them the best of all possible worlds and could only view its impact as beneficial.

Mass education was also the first step toward the creation of a Christian commonwealth. Preaching the gospel remained central to their ideal, but religious institutions could be guaranteed support and influence only if the laws and lawmakers of the kingdom reinforced

Christian principles. Led by Hiram Bingham, therefore, the missionaries exerted pressure on the chiefs and king to inculcate these principles in the islands' political institutions. They tried to create stable social and political institutions to ensure the steady progress of missionary work.[28] At the same time they sought legal codification of their religious and social ideals.

This mixing of politics, education, and religion was not novel to Sandwich Islanders, for tradition granted absolute power to chiefs and king in all these areas. The introduction of missionary influence, therefore, found ready channels for implementation. It did, however, eventually destroy traditional sources of authority.

What course did the missionaries pursue? Their instructions remained their guide; and these instructions, traditionally cited to show how the missionaries transgressed them, bear scrutiny. They appear ambiguous, or at any rate the official interpretation of them left considerable latitude for independent action. The mission's goal was to promote Christianity, and its members were to restrain themselves "entirely from all interference and intermeddling with the political affairs & party concerns of the nation or people."[29]

These were the instructions of the ABCFM in Boston. Once in Hawaii, however, members of the mission company interpreted them in a slightly different context. Remembering the command to Christianize the islands, as well as their religious training and social assumptions, and believing that only a thorough reformation of native society could achieve these goals, they perceived their role to be something greater than that of advisers. In a meeting in September 1826 they clarified this new position, asserting, "The choice of rulers & magistrates the levying & collecting of taxes, the apportioning out of the lands the buying & selling of chiefs & people either with foreigners or with each other and the manner of administering the government of the islands, together with the customs and usages of the country *that are not in direct varience* [sic] *with the spirit and precepts of the Gospel* are things with which we are not to interfere and over which we are not to attempt to exercise control."[30] The missionaries would interfere in affairs of state if they thought these affairs were not being conducted in a Christian manner. The mission company, moreover, did not see this intervention as contravening its earlier instructions, for it always held its goal to be the promulgation of Christianity and Christian principles in all areas of human activity.

At the same meeting the missionaries further elaborated their assumptions and actions. Disclaiming all intention to interfere in affairs that did not affect their role as missionaries, they agreed not to give advice on these matters except when requested, *"when they do not interfere with the Gospel or the progress of civilization."*[31]

Here lay the key to the future course of missionary activity. The Sandwich Islands missionaries would freely offer advice and actively seek to direct Hawaiian affairs to achieve their ideal of a Christian commonwealth. From the moment of their arrival they sought to curry favor and influence with the king and chiefs. They would continue to do this, while at the same time take their message to the people through education and religion. In areas where these failed to conquer heathen superstition and practice, they would assert their influence to legislate morality. This stewardship was not assumed with a malevolent view of native traditions or a desire merely to effect change, but with an optimistic assumption that what they saw as a dark and heathen land could become a beacon to the world. The power of example, not a lust for land or office, drove the missionaries toward their goal. Convinced that they were right and held the keys to the kingdom, they cast aside all criticism as a reflection of greed and self-interest.

Laws passed after the arrival of the first mission company reflected these assumptions and advice. One of the earliest missionary efforts was to translate the Ten Commandments and present a copy to the chiefs. Admonishing them that this was the law of God, they implied that the chiefs would do well to use the Commandments as a guide for their own decrees.[32] The most controversial issue evolved from a discussion on the evils of polygamy and prostitution. The latter brought the missionaries into conflict with traders and ship captains, unleashing a barrage of antimissionary criticism and encouraging furtive acts to undermine missionary influence. In the midst of the conflict sat the chiefs, dependent on foreign vessels for luxuries and capital, but intrigued by missionary "magic" and advice.

The strategic geographic position of the Sandwich Islands astride the mid-Pacific trade routes had brought kings and chiefs considerable wealth. To procure these material advantages local rulers had deliberately ignored the rampant prostitution and erosion of native culture. After months at sea sailors demanded women and relaxation. These they found at the islands. Missionary ideals and objectives, however, could not tolerate such licentiousness and decay, and the missionaries looked upon such practices as barriers to the progress of Christianity.[33]

A bitter struggle between the conflicting parties lasted more than four years. By November 1824 the mission's leaders had induced the king to consider a ban on female visitations to ships in Honolulu harbor. Violent opposition quickly surfaced, and throughout the following year sailors rioted and hostility toward the mission grew. By October 1825 the ban on these visitations had become effective. Few girls now boarded the vessels, and many informal liaisons between native girls and visiting sailors either became permanent or ended altogether.[34]

Other native customs upset the missionaries and were viewed as anathemas to Christian society. Bingham and his colleagues, therefore, counseled the chiefs to end certain practices—ranging from dancing the hula on the Sabbath to gambling and intemperance. After the accession of Kaahumanu as regent in 1824 they found their advice accepted. The chiefs issued decrees against gambling and Sabbath activity. Following her conversion to missionary principles, Kaahumanu also decreed that all persons "shall learn the *palapala*" when schools were established.[35]

These laws also provoked virulent hostility from merchant and shipping interests, who wished to exploit the islands in their own manner. This was the same class of persons that the New England clergy blamed for the growing materialism and economic individualism in the United States. It was also the same class that had generously supported foreign missions from New England for more than a decade. On their home ground the clergy had been unable to surmount economic self-interest to reform society and had sought accommodation. But in the Sandwich Islands they had their missionaries, who in turn had the ear and trust of the regent and were in charge of educating the king. The different circumstances in Hawaii produced a settlement more favorable to religious interests.[36]

The missionaries made no effort to conceal their purposes; quite the opposite. They thought their scheme so important that they made clear its outlines from the beginning. Yet by 1826 there was a concern about possible unnecessary interference in civil, commercial, and political affairs. Meeting at Kailua in September, the missionaries pondered the problem and resolved that their activities remained consistent with their instructions. They determined that as Christian teachers their duty impelled them to offer advice on the "arts and institutions and usages of civilized life and society." This meant the continued use of persuasion and influence to "discountenance every vice, and encourage every virtue." The missionaries remained determined to produce an "entire change" at the islands.[37]

That same year the mission issued a circular highlighting its progress and influence. Emphasizing the instruction of the chiefs in the Decalogue, the circular announced the mission's objectives: "justice, honesty, integrity, punctuality, truth, purity, good order, union, and peace."[38] The missionaries sought a stable, Christian republic modeled on a yet-to-be-realized ideal. At the same time they made it clear that they did not want land or riches, insisting that "we seek not theirs but them."[39] It was this concern that impelled the mission company to pay close attention to the laws passed and customs practiced. To fulfill their dream they needed organization, and that organization must be carried out in a Christian spirit. The chiefs, in essence, codified the Christian advice of the missionaries and enacted it into law. The first clause of the islands' Constitution indicated their success: "no law shall be enacted which is at variance with the word of the Lord Jehovah, or at variance with the general spirit of his word. All laws of the island shall be in consistency with the general spirit of God's law."[40]

Yet the main purpose of the missionaries' presence was, of course, to Christianize the natives. Even Hiram Bingham, traditionally considered the most meddlesome and politically oriented of the missionaries, admitted that the passing of strict laws against sin "can never outstrip the advances of evangelical light." Unless the Christian religion captured the minds and hearts of the natives, Bingham concluded, no radical reformation could be expected.[41]

It was in their religious teachings that the missionaries effected their most revolutionary change. For centuries natives had lived in fear of the king's laws and taboos. Now the missionaries told them of a higher, more powerful force with even more threatening taboos. Hiram Bingham laid down the outlines of this new doctrine in a sermon in 1821. The word of God, Bingham instructed his native audience, is the paramount authority. Fear of God must prevail, for it is "the only means adequate" to guarantee the peace, order, and prosperity of the nation.[42] This doctrine shattered native traditions and promised a revolutionary shift in political as well as religious practice. It indicates, perhaps better than any other action or utterance, how all-encompassing missionary influence could be on native societies. Christianization meant not only adopting new religious doctrines and practices, but an unsettling of traditional authority. With this power in their hands it is not surprising that bewildered or intrigued chiefs turned to the missionaries for political advice.

The missionaries proceeded cautiously with their religious instruction. Aware that Hawaiians would be suspicious of all new religious teachings, they tried to win native confidence before imposing new institutions and doctrines on them. Missionaries also faced the hostility of native priests, whose influence remained strong despite the overthrow of traditional religion and taboos. Abruptness or impatience would frighten, not convert. Early instruction, therefore, mixed the new with the familiar and emphasized the reading and interpreting of the *Memoir of Henry Obookiah*. Although not explicitly doctrinal, the memoir embodied the traits and virtues the missionaries wished to implant.[43]

Natives attended the strange religious ceremonies largely out of curiosity. Many thought the missionaries capable of praying people to death and stayed away out of fear. Once in attendance, however, they found the Christian doctrines and missionary preaching quite familiar. Warnings about sins and the word of God seemed understandable to a people long used to a variety of taboos. This tradition made the introduction of Christianity at once easy and difficult. The restrictions on behavior, although different in emphasis, paralleled the old taboos. Yet mere obedience to these admonitions did not indicate acceptance or understanding of Christian doctrine, only a desire to avoid the penalties of transgression. Until the mid-1820s, moreover, the language barrier added to the missionaries' difficulties. Natives secretly retained many of their old idols, while at the same time explored the new ones introduced by the mission company.[44]

The missionaries achieved their first significant breakthrough in October 1822, when Hiram Bingham began to preach in Hawaiian. This enlarged the mission church and excited the natives. Yet by 1824 only four Hawaiian names were on the membership roster of the church, and all had come from New England on the brig *Thaddeus*.[45] Natives had clustered in large numbers at each service, but few had displayed the strict piety that the missionaries demanded. The lack of native church members, consequently, reflects the strict criteria of the mission as much as native reluctance to accept the new doctrines.

Careful attention to the chiefs during the next two years reaped greater dividends, and the accession of Kaahumanu in 1824 quickened

missionary progress in religion as it did elsewhere. Yet evidence remained strong that the missionaries and their doctrines were primarily
objects of fascination. Natives frequently referred to them as the
"King's Curiousities."[46] But with the support of Kaahumanu and
Kapiolani, two of the more influential princesses, attendance at religious meetings grew and missionaries professed to see greater evidence
of piety. Fears remained among some natives that they might be prayed
to death, but public support from the chiefs gradually diminished its
import. By 1825 almost a dozen chiefs had presented themselves for
examination and professed a desire to be baptized.[47]

Although a few of the chiefs earnestly accepted Christian doctrine
and missionary preaching, others merely hoped to partake of whatever
powers it possessed to augment their earthly authority. In this respect
Kapiolani proved a stalwart friend to the mission. During a visit in 1825
to the Kilauea volcano she defied the wrath of the god Pele and
publicly proclaimed her belief that "Jehovah is my God." While the
natives breathlessly awaited her imminent destruction for this defiance
of an ancient taboo, she declared that "the gods of Hawaii are vain."[48]
When Pele did not respond to this denunciation, Sandwich Islanders
looked in awe at the missionaries' god. To them his power had been
verified, and they turned in increasing numbers to embrace Christianity.
They accepted the new religion, however, in much the same terms that
they had the old; that is, they memorized and obeyed its precepts for
fear of retaliation. The chiefs' public attendance at religious services
reinforced native commitment, although again more from fear of earthly authority than true understanding. Fright and enlightenment proceeded hand-in-hand; whatever god was stronger would triumph.[49]

The missionaries generally recognized the reasons for their success
and remained cautious when accepting new church members. To explain this to supporters of foreign missions, the *Missionary Herald*
published an explanation from William Richards that went to the heart
of the matter. Richards noted that while many at the Lahaina station
were pious, only two had been admitted to the church. But this did not
indicate failure: "It may be a matter of serious inquiry with our
patrons, why the church should remain so small while the number of
praying persons is so large. But it should be remarked, that the outward
form of Christianity is so very popular here, that the only way in which
we can distinguish the good from the bad is to wait a long season, that
their fruit may appear."[50]

Determination of true piety had also been a problem in New England, so readers could readily understand the problem. Progress at the Sandwich Islands would be slow, despite some encouraging outward appearances and a few significant examples of conversion. Missionaries struggled to make progress among influential adults, but rested their hopes for the future on the children then in school. If the new generation could be trained in Christian principles, the future would be secure.[51]

By 1830 the Sandwich Islands missionaries could look back on a decade of trials mixed with success. They had encountered many obstacles in pursuit of their objectives—some expected, others unexpected. Prepared for the worst, they found sufficient evils of heathenism to sustain their fears. Yet they encountered less opposition than expected from the native population and suffered more from internal dissent and the attacks of traders and ship captains.

In all their reports and letters written for publication, the missionaries carefully avoided mention of internal problems. Even the most discriminating and critical reader could not penetrate the image of Christian progress overcoming heathen debauchery. Yet the emergence of controversy within the ranks of the mission should not have been surprising, for in many instances these men and women had but the slightest acquaintance with one another before embarking for the Sandwich Islands. Although their youthful zeal and piety might sustain them on the long ocean voyage, the appearance of new trials and hardships in Hawaii tested the mettle of even the strongest. It would be only human to quarrel on occasion.

There was a human side to these men, for they were not greedy power-seekers or incipient land barons, but Christian missionaries. The dedication and pious zeal so apparent when they were in New England remained strong in Hawaii. In a candid letter to the ABCFM, the Reverend William Ellis evaluated their strengths and weaknesses and thereby provided an insight into the activities of the mission company. He was critical of Bishop for his lack of prudence, although admitting that his wife's actions were so beneficial that they softened his frequent indiscretions. Stewart, Richards, and Thurston all received commendation for their character and effort. Characterizing Elisha Loomis as only a printer, Ellis nonetheless praised him along with the Blatchleys. He reserved some of his sharpest criticism for James and Louisa Ely, remarking that "Mr. Ely is unsocial" and "has a disagreeable disposition." "His wife," Ellis noted, "is like him; probably makes him more difficult than he otherwise would be."[52]

It was in Ellis' evaluation of Hiram Bingham that he revealed some smoldering tensions within the mission company. Hinting that Ely and Blatchley were strongly opposed to Bingham, Ellis also indicated that Asa Thurston was less than happy with Bingham's conduct of the mission. Part of this animosity stemmed from the Vermonter's assumption of full authority for the mission company, an authority that Thurston technically shared. The abrasiveness of Bingham's actions, however, appears to have been more substantial in fomenting opposition; and Ellis noted that "Mr. Bingham is much less popular among those who went out in the reinforcement, than among the first missionaries. They have the impression that he assumes too much."[53]

From the outset Bingham's self-righteousness and imperious attitude alienated many in the mission. He seemed determined to lead the Sandwich Islanders, and the missionaries as well, to the new Zion on his own terms. Friction developed during the voyage on the *Thaddeus*, but the difficulties with the Holmans diverted attention and energy from all other internal factionalism. Bingham's leadership in the disciplining, and eventual expulsion, of the couple from the mission found strong support among the other members of the company. Holman had asserted his independence, broken the rules of the little band, and complained endlessly about the conditions of missionary labor. Writing to support the Holmans' ouster, Daniel Chamberlain concluded that they had volunteered in the hope of acquiring money and property, intending to stay but a short time. Bingham's judgment was swift and harsh. All must conform or return home. There was no room for independence of thought or action.[54]

Aside from internal conflicts, the ABCFM had to avoid acute embarrassment from the backsliding of George P. Tamoree. Trained at the Foreign Mission School and used to publicize the susceptibility of the heathen to Christianity, Tamoree had accompanied the first company of missionaries to the islands. Soon after his arrival, however, Tamoree led an insurrection. Thereupon the board carefully disassociated itself from any responsibility for his actions, arguing that it never regarded him as pious and brought him along solely because his father wanted to see him again. Board spokesmen candidly admitted his usefulness in gaining influence for the missionaries, since his father was "one of the principal rulers of the islands." But under no circumstances was he to be considered a missionary, nor was the board "in any degree responsible for his conduct."[55]

Criticism from traders and ship captains, however, presented the most formidable obstacle to missionary success. Most of their comments, both favorable and unfavorable, found expression in the press. Some represented mere pique at changing conditions; others were blatantly nationalistic, and a few struck sharp blows at personalities within the mission. But among critics the theme remained constant: missionaries were destroying the native economy and usurping the authority of island chiefs. Ship captains particularly assailed the actions of Hiram Bingham. Bingham, they insisted, showed a greater interest in ruling than in preaching. He meddled in commercial and political affairs and was an "unenlightened enthusiast" who seemed oblivious to true native interests.[56] Otto von Kotzebue, a Russian explorer, charged that Bingham masked his real designs in a cloak of religion. His real intentions, Kotzebue insisted, were often dishonest, and to get them he had forced the natives "to an almost endless routine of prayers."[57]

Other visitors levied similar charges at Bingham and through a variety of publications tried to discredit both his work and that of the mission. By 1826 Bingham's critics had become so numerous and vocal that they threatened to draw up a petition asking the king to expel him from the islands. The most scathing attack on the mission, not surprisingly, came from the *Westminster Review*, published in London. British vessels had long enjoyed privileges at the islands, but now found their influence eroded by the growing importance of American commerce and missionaries. The *Review* attacked the mission's "uncalled-for interference" in nonreligious matters and lashed out at the growing missionary influence. "It is greatly to be feared, indeed, that these (we doubt not, well-intentioned) men are creating much mischief among these simple-minded islanders. They have so little judgment, and are so little acquainted with the human heart, as to let their zeal out-run discretion on many occasions and in many shapes; and this we knew to be the case before now. But certainly we were not prepared for such amazing absurdity as the attempt to force the darkest and most dreary parts of puritan discipline upon these poor people."[58]

Criticism of missionary activities, moreover, was not confined to Englishmen, Russians, or visiting ship captains. John Coffin Jones, Jr., first American commercial agent at the islands, attacked the missionaries as "blood suckers of the community." He assailed the mission for telling the Hawaiians that white traders cheated them and for trying to Christianize the people, expressing the hope that "Providence would put a whip in every honest hand to lash such rascals naked through the world."[59]

Jones's remarks revealed the rationale behind much of the criticism. Religion and commerce had collided head-on. The self-interest of each sought to shape the island and their people in contradictory ways. Each charged the other with exploiting the natives for selfish purposes, and both were correct. Merchants and missionaries alike believed their interests to be paramount and thought the activities of the other undermined progress. So long as each group held firm to its assumptions and objectives, reconciliation remained impossible. The missionaries, of course, had not come to compromise.

Religious societies and the religious press in New England supported the missionaries. A foreign mission society in Worcester, Massachusetts, adopted a resolution condemning the attacks and praising the missionaries' "Christian fortitude." Attacking the British and Foreign Bible Society as well as British publications critical of American missionaries, the society railed against "ultra Monarchists and ultra Churchmen."[60] Republican virtues must triumph, and the *Boston Recorder* emphasized the national importance of acquiring influence and advantage at the Sandwich Islands.[61] Missionaries would be most useful in both instances.

The men and women at the islands did not shrink from these assaults either and used a number of devices to increase patronage at home. Along with the board's judicious publication of letters and journals, the mission printed its own propaganda emphasizing progress in orthography and translation as well as conversion and piety. The *Memoirs of Keopuolani* highlighted this effort. Keopuolani was the wife of King Kamehameha I and an early friend to the mission. The book included a few examples of native writing to demonstrate educational progress, but was published primarily to indicate missionary benevolence and progress to the American people.[62] Throughout the memoir the author reminded readers that here was a former heathen, to whom blood sacrifices had been offered, who had become a Christian. Only Christian benevolence had made such a transformation possible. Supporters of foreign missions should remember that their patronage "furnished a part of that light."[63]

In their letters the missionaries cited encouraging prospects at all the mission stations. Admitting that much remained to be done, they pleaded for greater financial support and more missionaries. A beginning had been made, now more laborers must advance the work. Referring to criticism of these efforts, the missionaries complained only "against those illiberal and unmanly charges, by which the mission is made accountable for the daily blunders, the childish actions, the long established customs, and even the inherent depravity of the people; and all, forsooth, because we attempt to make them better."[64]

But the people *had* changed, and the mission had made substantial progress in its effort to create a Christian commonwealth in the mid-Pacific. Schools were well-attended, and religious convictions were less frequently affected for advantage. Missionary influence had awakened a new interest in self-preservation among island chiefs, an interest their laws and decrees reflected. The novelty of missionary customs still fascinated the natives, and much of the change undoubtedly remained superficial. But the success of the missionaries encouraged emulation—in religion, education, and dress.[65]

The missionaries' influence with the chiefs led to success, and greater success followed their influence. Natives sought earthly blessing and security. They wished to know how to proceed in all circumstances, so as to avoid erroneous conduct and punishment or loss of favor. Sandwich Islanders, consequently, queried members of the mission company on every conceivable point, seeking advice and direction. Fear of sin replaced fear of supernatural forces. The consequences of this fear located the missionaries as ruling authorities themselves, an addition to native political institutions.[66] In their attempts to establish a stable Christian commonwealth these men had unwittingly created a theocracy, in practice if not in theory.

What had these men and women accomplished after a decade of labor at the Sandwich Islands? To argue that they willfully attempted to destroy a native culture is, of course, correct. That was their intention from the beginning. Christianization of the islanders meant, to the missionaries, effecting revolutionary changes in traditions, customs, and practices. It never occurred to members of the mission company that what seemed to promote stability and piety in New England might not effect the same results in Hawaii.

The introduction of Christianity, moreover, did not mean the acceptance of Christian principles. Native taboos, although superficially similar to Puritan prohibitions, were in at least one respect quite different. Missionary warnings about sinful transgressions of God's law concerned the hope of rewards after death. The taboos of native chiefs, on the other hand, carried the fear of death itself. When natives understood the new prohibitions in the context of their own traditions, therefore, they did so from an earthly, not heavenly, perspective.[67]

Ultimately the youth and training of the missionaries determined their attitudes and actions. All had undergone a conversion and deepening of religious conviction in the years immediately before sailing for the Sandwich Islands. The clergy among them had a thorough theological education in Calvinist doctrines, while the others subscribed to those principles. They were young and had the zeal and dedication of youthful converts. Convinced that they had only recently been wretched sinners themselves, they believed religion explained the condition of the heathen. Only Christian salvation could rescue them from idolatry and superstition. Before his arrival at the Sandwich Islands, Hiram Bingham indicated the remedy to be applied: "Inasmuch as the natural disposition of our race is to indulge the sordid, sinful passions, it may be affirmed that no man is better than his principles, and no nation is better than its religion."[68] Coming as they did from an area undergoing the turbulence of change and transition, the missionaries remained convinced that Christianity had immense social usefulness.[69] The empire they sought to establish was the kingdom of God; that it was also American seemed only providential.

APPENDIX: A NOTE ON SOURCES

The *American Quarterly Register* is an indispensable source of information for all aspects of New England life in the late eighteenth and early nineteenth centuries. The data on ministerial terms of office can be found in a number of compilations. All include information on birth and birthplace, collegiate education (and sometimes theological training), settlement and dismissal dates, date of death, and frequently a column of several brief remarks. A series of notes and comments on the respective churches and ministers usually follows each listing of clergymen. My statistics on permanency have been compiled from the following lists, all in the *American Quarterly Register* unless otherwise noted.

Vermont

Anderson, James. "Survey of the Congregational Churches in the County of Bennington, Vt. from Their Organization Down to the Present Time," 15 (November 1842): 131-36.

Glines, Jeremiah. "Complete List of the Congregational Ministers and Churches in Essex Co., Vt. from the First Settlement to the Present Time," 13 (May 1841): 448-51.

Kingsley, Phinehas. "A Brief Survey of the Congregational Churches and Ministry in the County of Franklin, Vt., from Its First Settlement to the Present Time," 12 (May 1840): 352-57.

Lamb, Dana and Merrill, Thomas. "Complete List of the Congregational Ministers and Churches in Addison County, Vt., from the First Settlement to the Present Time," 12 (August 1839): 52-63.

Steele, Joseph. "Complete List of the Congregational Ministers and Churches in Rutland County, Vt., from the First Settlement to the Present Time," 14 (August 1841): 34-42.

Walker, Charles. "Complete List of the Congregational Ministers and Churches in Windham County, Vt., from the First Settlement to the Present Time," 13 (August 1840): 29-34.

Worcester, Leonard. "List of Congregational Churches and Ministers in Caledonia County, Vt. from Its First Settlement to July 31, 1840," 13 (February 1841): 280-84.

Massachusetts

Edwards, Bela Bates. "Complete List of the Congregational and Presbyterian Ministers in Massachusetts, from the Settlement of the Colonies of Plymouth and Massachusetts Bay to the Present Time," 7 (August 1834): 28-30. (List for Suffolk County.)

_____. "Complete List of the Congregational Ministers in the Old County of Hampshire, Ms. (Including the Present Counties of Hampshire, Franklin, and Hampden), from the First Settlement to the Present Time," 10 (February 1838): 260-76; (May 1838): 379-407.

Felt, Joseph. "A List of the Congregational and Presbyterian Ministers, Who Have Been Settled in the County of Essex, Mass., from Its First Settlement to the Year 1834," 7 (February 1835): 246-61.

Field, David D. "Churches and Ministers of Berkshire County," 7 (August 1834): 31-38.

Folger, Paul. "Ecclesiastical Statistics of the First Congregational Church and Society in Nantucket," 15 (May 1843): 498-500.

Gannett, Allen. "A Complete List of the Congregational Ministers of Duke's County, Mass., from the First Settlement to the Present Time: With Accompanying Notes, and Some Account of the Missionaries to the Indians on Martha's Vineyard," 15 (May 1843): 492-98.

Longley, Jonathan. "Complete List of the Congregational Ministers in the County of Bristol, Ms., from Its Settlement to the Present Time," 12 (November 1839): 135-49.

Noyes, Thomas. "Complete List of the Congregational Ministers, in the County of Norfolk, Mass., from the Settlement of the County to the Present Time," 8 (August 1835): 42-58.

_____. "Complete List of the Congregational Ministers, in the County of Plymouth, Mass., from the Settlement of the County to the Present Time," 8 (November 1835): 144-59.

_____. "Complete List of the Congregational Ministers, in the County of Worcester, Mass., from Its Settlement to the Present Time," 10 (August 1837): 47-62; (November 1837): 126-45.

Pratt, Enoch. "Complete List of the Congregational Ministers in the County of Barnstable, Ms., from the Settlement of the County to 1842," 15 (August 1842): 58-72.

Sewall, Samuel. "A Brief Survey of the Congregational Churches and Ministers in the County of Middlesex, and in Chelsea in the County of Suffolk, Ms., from the First Settlement to the Present Day," 11 (August 1838): 45-55; (November 1838): 174-97; (February 1839): 248-79; (May 1839): 376-402. Sewall published a number of appendixes to the above lists: see 12 (February 1840): 234-50; 13 (August 1840): 37-57; 14 (February 1842): 251-64; (May 1842): 393-411.

Connecticut

"Complete List of the Congregational Ministers of Connecticut, from the Settlement of the Colony to the Present Time," 4 (May 1832): 307-22.

Rhode Island

Shepard, Thomas, "A Brief History of the Congregational Churches and Ministers in the State of Rhode Island, from Its Earliest Settlement to the Present Time," 12 (February 1840): 261-73.

Maine

Gillett, Eliphalet, "Complete List of the Congregational Ministers, Pastors of Churches, in the State of Maine, from the Settlement of the Country to the Present Time," 13 (November 1840): 144-62; (February 1841): 253-69; 14 (February 1842): 269-84.

New Hampshire

Farmer, John, "A List of the Congregational and Presbyterian Ministers in the State of New Hampshire, from the First Settlement of the State to the Year 1831," 6 (May 1834): 234-48.

Hazen, Henry, "Ministry and Churches of New Hampshire, Congregational and Presbyterian," *Congregational Quarterly* 17 (1875): 545-74; 18 (1876): 283-314, 592-600.

NOTES

ABBREVIATIONS

AAS – American Antiquarian Society, Worcester, Mass.
ABC – American Board of Commissioners for Foreign Missions, Archives at
    Houghton Library, Harvard University, Cambridge, Mass.
AN – Andover-Newton Theological Seminary Library, Newton Centre, Mass.
CL – Congregational Library, Boston, Mass.

Introduction

1. For reference to this upsurge in extrainstitutional development, see John Higham, *From Boundlessness to Consolidation: The Transformation of American Culture, 1848-1860* (Ann Arbor, Mich., 1969), passim. Higham is concerned with attempting a reinterpretation of the post-Jacksonian period, but his remarks also raise pertinent questions about both the evolution of Jacksonian society and the response to this "boundlessness."

2. Lyman Beecher, *A Reformation of Morals Practicable and Indispensable: A Sermon Delivered at New-Haven on the Evening of October 27, 1812* (New Haven, Conn., 1813), p. 16.

3. Numerous studies of the New England town in the seventeenth and eighteenth centuries have demonstrated the close correlation and interaction of religious and secular institutions. Although frequently more concerned with demographic, political, and economic change, the new local history has, nonetheless, indicated the changing nature of religion in the social structure of eighteenth-century America. Few of these studies, unfortunately, have carried this analysis into the nineteenth century. I have found the following studies especially useful and provocative: Michael Zuckerman, *Peaceable Kingdoms: New England Towns in the Eighteenth Century* (New York, 1970); Charles S. Grant, *Democracy in the Connecticut Frontier Town of Kent* (New York, 1961); Richard L. Bushman, *From Puritan to Yankee: Character and the Social Order in Connecticut, 1690-1765* (New York, 1970); and Kenneth A. Lockridge, *A New England Town: The First Hundred Years* (New York, 1970). Only one study that examines town growth from the eighteenth through the nineteenth centuries has come to my attention: John B. Armstrong, *Factory under the Elms: A History of Harrisville, New Hampshire, 1774-1969* (Cambridge, Mass., 1969). A perceptive overview of the evolution of these institutions is in James Henretta, "The Morphology of New England Society in the Colonial Period," *Journal of Interdisciplinary History* 2 (Autumn 1971): 379-98.

4. For a broader statement of the problem see Lefferts A. Loetscher, "The Problem of Christian Unity in Early Nineteenth Century America," *Church History* 32 (March 1963): 3-16.

5. The role of youth in the myriad reform movements of the nineteenth century has been sadly neglected. For an overview see Lois W. Banner, "Religion and Reform in the Early Republic: The Role of Youth," *American Quarterly* 23 (December 1971): 677-95.

6. Nathaniel Emmons, "God Never Forsakes His People," in *The Works of Nathaniel Emmons*, ed. Jacob Ide, 6 vols. (Boston, 1842), 2:179.

7. This positive side of mission work and reform has been too long neglected. One article supporting my conclusions came to my attention too late for inclusion throughout the work; see Lois Banner, "Religious Benevolence as Social Control: A Critique of an Interpretation," *Journal of American History* 60 (June 1973): 23-41.

Chapter One

1. Joseph S. Clark, *A Historical Sketch of the Congregational Churches in Massachusetts from 1620 to 1850* (Boston, 1858), p. 224. See also L. K. Mathews, *The Expansion of New England*, reprint ed. (New York, 1962), p. 267; Lyman Beecher, *A Reformation of Morals*, p. 18; Donald G. Mathews, "The Second Great Awakening as an Organizing Process, 1790-1830: An Hypothesis," *American Quarterly* 21 (Spring 1969): 27. For a perceptive treatment of mobility as a central concept in American social history, see Rowland Berthoff, "The American Social Order: A Conservative Hypothesis," *American Historical Review* 65 (April 1960): 495-514.

2. For some perceptive comments on their impact see especially Orville Dewey, *Letters of an English Traveller to His Friend in England, on the "Revivals of Religion," in America* (Boston, 1828), pp. 1-2. Historians have commented on the dominance of the revival technique, but often failed to look beneath the "intellectual" crust to discover its impact on all echelons of society. The best treatments are in Perry Miller, *The Life of the Mind in America from the Revolution to the Civil War* (New York, 1965), p. 7; and Charles Keller, *The Second Great Awakening in Connecticut* (New Haven, Conn., 1942), p. 3. An insightful analysis of the First Great Awakening, and one that is equally applicable to the Second, is in William McLoughlin, *New England Dissent, 1630-1833: The Baptists and the Separation of Church and State*, 2 vols. (Cambridge, Mass., 1972), 1: 329-39. I have been guided here by many of his hypotheses.

3. This spirit is captured intact in Harriet Beecher Stowe, *Oldtown Folks* (Cambridge, Mass., 1966), p. 475. Its power and impact are measured in Daniel W. Howe, *The Unitarian Conscience: Harvard Moral Philosophy, 1805-1861* (Cambridge, Mass., 1970), pp. 160-61; Sidney E. Mead, *Nathaniel William Taylor, 1786-1858: A Connecticut Liberal* (Chicago, 1942), p. 47; David Ludlum, *Social Ferment in Vermont, 1791-1850* (New York, 1939), pp. 42-43. Alan Heimert, in *Religion and the American Mind; From the Great Awakening to the Revolution* (Cambridge, Mass., 1966), p. 534, argues that revivals threatened the Standing Order and were an expression of "social discontent and political aspiration." After 1800, however, this discontent came as much from the Standing Order as from dissenting sects. For other estimates of the impact of these revivals, see Sanford Fleming, *Children and Puritanism: The Place of Children in the Life and Thought of the New England Churches, 1620-1847* (New Haven, Conn., 1933), p. 16; George Leon Walker, *Some Aspects of the Religious Life of New England with Special Reference to Congregationalists* (New York, 1897), p. 153.

4. McLoughlin, *New England Dissent*, 1:330, 335. An overview of the organizing process is in Mathews, "The Second Great Awakening." This response was not

status-induced. For arguments on the dangers of this approach, see Robert W. Doherty, "Status Anxiety and American Reform: Some Alternatives," *American Quarterly* 19 (Summer 1967): 329-37.

5. Noah Worcester, *Impartial Inquiries Respecting the Progress of the Baptist Denomination* (Worcester, Mass., 1794), pp. 9-10.

6. Ibid., p. 11. Worcester's admonition is, of course, a concise summary of the principles of stewardship.

7. Ibid., p. 15.

8. Letter to Asahel Hooker, November 24, 1812, in Lyman Beecher, *Autobiography*, 2 vols. (New York, 1864), 1:258.

9. Richard D. Pierce, ed., *The Records of the First Church in Boston, 1630-1868*, Publications of the Colonial Society of Massachusetts 40 (Boston, 1961): 591 (italics added).

10. Ebenezer Porter, *The Duty of Christians to Pray for the Missionary Cause: A Sermon Preached in Boston, November 1, 1827, before the Society for Propagating the Gospel among the Indians and Others in North America* (Andover, Mass., 1827), p. 8. For commentary on this general lack of enthusiasm see Mary H. Mitchell, *The Great Awakening and Other Revivals in the Religious Life of Connecticut* (New Haven, Conn., 1934), p. 32; Bennet Tyler, *New England Revivals as They Existed at the Close of the Eighteenth and the Beginning of the Nineteenth Centuries* (Boston, 1846), pp. viii-ix.

11. William Tudor, *Letters on the Eastern States* (Boston, 1821), p. 76.

12. Emerson Davis, *The Half Century; or a History of the Changes That Have Taken Place, and Events That Have Transpired, Chiefly in the United States, between 1800 and 1850* (Boston, 1851), p. 273. See also Josiah Holland, *History of Western Massachusetts*, 2 vols. (Springfield, 1855), 1:316.

13. Stowe, *Oldtown Folks*, p. 254.

14. Tyler, *New England Revivals*, p. 161. The beneficial effect of revivals in stabilizing churches is discussed in Tyler, p. vii; Timothy Dwight, *Travels in New England and New York*, 4 vols. (London, 1821), 4:301; and the Reverend William F. P. Noble, *1776-1876. A Century of Gospel Work: A History of the Growth of Evangelical Religion in the United States* (Philadelphia, 1876), p. 259.

15. For some remarks on these revivals and their causes see Daniel Dow, *A Reminiscence of Past Events: A Semi-Centennial Sermon, Preached in Thompson, (Conn.), April 22, 1846* (New Haven, Conn., 1846), pp. 28-30. Of major importance in these revivals is their growth. There was no elaborate scheme perpetrated by the clergy. The Awakening began at different times in different places. This accounts for its persistence over three decades and for its constant reappearance throughout the region.

16. Letter to his parents, January 5, 1808, in the Reverend Asa Cummings, comp., *Memoir, Select Thoughts and Sermons of the Late Rev. Edward Payson, D.D. Pastor of the Second Church in Portland*, 3 vols. (Philadelphia, 1859), 1:144.

17. Letter to his mother, March 28, 1808, in ibid., p. 150.

18. The Reverend Luther Hart, "A View of the Religious Declension in New England, and of Its Causes, during the Latter Half of the Eighteenth Century," *Quarterly Christian Spectator* 5, series 3 (June 1833): 227. Indications of rising Baptist strength among the young are in John Peak, *Memoir of the Elder John Peak* (Boston, 1832), p. 122. An account of one youth's shift to the Baptist denomination is in Peter Young, *A Brief Account of the Life and Experience, Call to the Ministry, Travels, and Afflictions of Peter Young, Preacher of the Gospel* (Portsmouth, N.H., 1817), p. 8.

19. *Religious Inquirer* (March 2, 1822): 66. For examples of the prevalence of revivals during these seasons, see Tyler, *New England Revivals*, passim; *Records of the Congregational Church in Colebrook* [Conn.] (Hartford, Conn., 1822), p. 9; and Joshua Bradley, *Accounts of Religious Revivals in Many Parts of the United States from 1815 to 1818* (Albany, N.Y., 1818), passim.

20. Letter IV, June 11, 1827, in Dewey, *Letters*, p. 53.

21. The Reverend Dana Lamb and the Reverend Thomas Merrill, "Complete List of the Congregational Ministers and Churches in Addison County, Vt.," *American Quarterly Register* 12 (August 1839): 63; Walker, *Some Aspects of the Religious Life of New England*, p. 146; the Reverend Samuel L. Gerould, *A Brief History of the Congregational Church in Hollis, N.H.* (Bristol, N.H., 1893), p. 22. This tendency toward diminishing returns has been noted during the First Great Awakening, and it seems likely to apply to the Second as well. See Gerald Moran, "Conditions of Religious Conversion in the First Society of Norwich, Connecticut, 1718-1744," *Journal of Social History* 5 (Spring 1972): 331-43; James Walsh, "The Great Awakening in the First Congregational Church of Woodbury, Connecticut," *William & Mary Quarterly*, 3d series, 28 (October 1971): 543-62.

22. Beecher to the Reverend Asahel Hooker, February 24, 1812, in Beecher, *Autobiography*, 1:243. See also pp. 253-55 for his letter to Hooker, July 28, 1812. On the character of these revivals see Samuel Worcester, *The Life and Labors of Rev. Samuel Worcester, D.D.*, 2 vols. (Boston, 1852), 2:165. Use of these various devices is noted in Tyler, *New England Revivals*, passim; and Bradley, *Accounts of Religious Revivals*, passim.

23. Worcester, *Impartial Inquiries*, p. 15.

24. (April 1816): 15; (June 1, 1816): 16. See also Dwight, *Travels*, 4:387-88.

25. Bennet Tyler, *Memoir of the Life and Character of the Reverend Asahel Nettleton* (Boston, 1856), pp. 159, 174-75; Walker, *Some Aspects of the Religious Life of New England*, p. 147. For Nettleton's views on revivals see his letter to the Reverend J. Frost, April 18, 1827, in George H. Birney, Jr., "The Life and Times of Asahel Nettleton, 1783-1844" (Ph.D. diss., Hartford Theological Seminary), pp. 315-17.

26. Davis, *The Half-Century*, pp. 355-56; Miller, *Life of the Mind*, p. 30. The Puritan view of eloquence and the function of the sermon is delineated in Perry Miller, *The New England Mind: The Seventeenth Century* (Cambridge, Mass., 1939), pp. 296, 307.

27. (New York, 1828). Finney's flamboyant methods and their impressive results have captivated historians. This is unfortunate, for the real locus of controversy and institutional change remained in the older settled regions. See McLoughlin, *New England Dissent*, vol. 2.

28. *Letters of the Reverend Dr. Beecher and Reverend Mr. Nettleton on the "New Measures" in Conducting Revivals of Religion* (New York, 1828), p. iv.

29. Letter from Nettleton to the Reverend M. Aikin, January 13, 1827, in ibid., pp. 11-12.

30. Ibid., p. 13. Finney's youthful radicalism is not uncommon. See Kenneth Keniston, *Young Radicals: Notes on Committed Youth* (New York, 1968), for a perceptive study of the phenomenon.

31. Letter from Beecher to the Reverend Nathan Bermon, December 15, 1827, in *Letters of Beecher and Nettleton*, p. 80.

32. Ibid., p. 84. The impact of this morbid fear on young children is depicted in Joseph F. Kett, "Growing up in Rural New England, 1800-1840," in *Anonymous Americans: Explorations in Nineteenth-Century Social History*, ed. Tamara K. Hareven (Englewood Cliffs, N.J., 1971), p. 5.

33. Letter VI, September 13, 1827, in Dewey, *Letters*, p. 128.

34. Cummings, *Memoir*, 1:263.

35. Joel Hawes, *To Commend Truth to the Conscience the Object of a Faithful Minister: A Sermon, Delivered March 9th, 1825, at the Installation of the Reverend Leonard Bacon, as Pastor of the First Congregational Church and Society in New-Haven* (New Haven, Conn., 1825), p. 7. Hawes delivered this same sermon a number of times in the next few months.

36. Joseph R. Anthony, *Life in New Bedford a Hundred Years Ago* (New Bedford, Mass., 1940), p. 8. This is quoted from his diary entry for February 9, 1823.

37. An excellent portrait of this process at work in one community can be found in William McLoughlin, "The Relevance of Congregational Christianity: Barrington Congregational Church, 1717-1967," *Rhode Island History* 29 (Summer-Fall 1970): 71. A more general view is in Mathews, "The Second Great Awakening," p. 33.

38. *The Diary of William Bentley, D.D.*, 4 vols. (Salem, Mass., 1911), 3:545.

39. Beecher, *A Reformation of Morals*, p. 16.

40. Beecher, *Autobiography*, 2:32-33. Some analyses of the organizing process are in Mathews, "The Second Great Awakening," p. 28; Clifford S. Griffin, "Religious Benevolence as Social Control, 1815-1860," *Mississippi Valley Historical Review* 44 (December 1957): 423. For a comparison with other efforts to achieve social stability, also in part elitist, see David Rothman, *The Discovery of the Asylum: Social Order and Disorder in the New Republic* (Boston, 1971), p. 217; Raymond Mohl, *Poverty in New York, 1783-1825* (New York, 1971), passim.

41. Evarts B. Greene, "A Puritan Counter-Reformation," American Antiquarian Society *Proceedings* 42 n.s. (1932): 23; *Proceedings of the Missionary Jubilee, held at Williams College, August 5, 1856* (Boston, 1856), p. 22; Clifford Griffin, *Their Brothers' Keepers* (New Brunswick, N.J., 1960), p. xi.

42. *Panoplist* 14 (May 1818): 212-13.

43. Beecher, *A Reformation of Morals*, pp. 19-20. A discussion of the "reflex" actions of Congregationalists can be found in Daniel Calhoun, *Professional Lives in America* (Cambridge, Mass., 1965), p. 107. For another view see the speculations of Rowland Berthoff in *An Unsettled People: Social Order and Disorder in American History* (New York, 1971), p. 234.

44. Clark, *A Historical Sketch of the Congregational Churches in Massachusetts*, p. 236.

45. William Sprague, *The Life of Jedidiah Morse, D.D.* (New York, 1874), p. 112.

46. Morse to Green, December 24, 1805, in ibid., p. 92.

47. Woods to Morse, October 21, 1806, in ibid., p. 97; Dr. John H. Church to John Norris, September 15, 1807, in the Reverend Leonard Woods, *History of the Andover Theological Seminary* (Boston, 1885), p. 501. For a discussion of these influences see William W. Sweet, *Religion in the Development of American Culture, 1765-1840*, reprint ed. (Gloucester, Mass., 1963), pp. 179-80; William W. Sweet, "The Rise of Theological Schools in America," *Church History* 6 (September 1937): 260-73 passim.

48. *An Address of the General Association of Connecticut, to the Congregational Ministers and Churches of the State, on the Importance of United Endeavors to Revive Gospel Discipline* (Litchfield, Conn., 1808), p. 13. For the general problem of ministerial education, see Mary W. Gambrell, *Ministerial Training in Eighteenth Century New England* (New York, 1937), pp. 52-53, 55, 125.

49. "Thoughts on the Importance of a Theological Institution," *Panoplist* 3 (1808): 308.

50. For their donations see Joshua Coffin, *A Sketch of the History of Newbury, Newburyport, and West Newbury, from 1635 to 1845* (Boston, 1845), p. 275. Brief sketches of these men are in Milton H. Thomas, ed., *Elias Boudinot's "Journey to Boston" in 1809* (Princeton, N.J., 1955), p. 69 n. Capsule biographies of Brown and Bartlet are in Benjamin Labaree, *Patriots and Partisans: The Merchants of Newburyport, 1764-1815* (Cambridge, Mass., 1962), pp. 207-8. The Norris family later donated several thousand dollars more to the Andover coffers.

51. Woods, *Andover*, pp. 237-38; Jerry W. Brown, *The Rise of Biblical Criticism in America, 1800-1870; The New England Scholars* (Middletown, Conn., 1969), p. 46.

52. The development of Andover is discussed in Woods, *Andover*, pp. 115-35, 187. For a discussion of student expenses see Timothy Dwight, *A Sermon, Preached at the Opening of the Theological Institution in Andover; and at the Ordination of Rev. Eliphalet Pearson, LL.D. September 28, 1808* (Boston, 1808), pp. 10-11. Examples of student riots during these years are given in Donald Cole, *Jacksonian Democracy in New Hampshire, 1800-1851* (Cambridge, Mass., 1970), p. 36.

53. *Diary*, 4:12-14. For his other criticisms see his *Diary*, 3:386, 412, 431. These were the years when the Trinitarian-Unitarian struggle became especially heated.

54. Tudor, *Letters*, p. 102; Adam Hodgson, *Remarks during a Journey through North America in the Years 1819, 1820, and 1821* (New York, 1823), p. 72; Worcester to Burder, January 3, 1811, in *First Ten Reports of the American Board of Commissioners for Foreign Missions* (Boston, 1834), p. 18. Worcester was corresponding secretary for the board.

55. Descriptions of early organizing efforts are in Griffin, *Their Brothers' Keepers*, chapt. 2; *Contributions to the Ecclesiastical History of Essex County, Mass.* (Boston, 1865), p. 254; Clarence Shedd, *Two Centuries of Student Christian Movements: Their Origin and Intercollegiate Life* (New York, 1934), pp. 38-39. The most perceptive analysis of the problems inherent in home missions is in Bertram Wyatt-Brown, "The Antimission Movement in the Jacksonian South: A Study in Regional Folk Culture," *Journal of Southern History* 36 (November 1970): 501-29. Wyatt-Brown notes that Westerners would not tolerate the notion that they should be served permanently by circuit riders or missionaries. He also indicates the class and sectional hostilities such efforts aroused.

56. "On Contributions for the Spread of the Gospel," *Christian Spectator* 1 (April 1819): 212. For comments on the Boston societies see Thomas, *Elias Boudinot's "Journey,"* pp. 80-81. A superb statement of the new inclinations is in Richard Birdsall, "The Second Great Awakening and the New England Social Order," *Church History* 39 (September 1970): 359. For a more general commentary see Kenneth S. Latourette, *A History of the Expansion of Christianity*, 7 vols. (New York, 1945), 4:429.

57. Perry Miller argued that revivals and missions had the same effects in that they both were aimed more toward those at home in the churches than the heathen overseas. This is generally true, but Miller failed to mark the evolution from revivals to foreign missions and treated the two as one. See *Life of the Mind*, p. 10. Similar expressions of this relationship are in Clark, *A Historical Sketch of the Congregational Churches in Massachusetts*, pp. 236-37; Samuel Worcester, "Origins of American Foreign Missions," *American Theological Review* 2 (November 1860): 715-16.

58. For Indian missions see R. Pierce Beaver, "Methods in American Missions to the Indians in the Seventeenth and Eighteenth Centuries: Calvinist Models for Protestant Foreign Missions," *Journal of Presbyterian History* 47 (June 1969): 148. British influences are noted in Louis B. Wright and Mary I. Fry, *Puritans in the South Seas* (New York, 1936), p. 270; William E. Strong, *The Story of the American Board* (Boston, 1910). Links between social turbulence and foreign missions are briefly analyzed in Oliver Elsbree, "The Rise of the Missionary Spirit in New England, 1790-1815," *New England Quarterly* 1 (July 1928): 296-97.

59. *A Collection of Letters Relative to Foreign Missions* (Andover, Mass., 1810), p. 7.

60. Ibid., pp. 15-16; see also pp. 3, 17.

61. Bits and pieces on its origin can be found in several places. See Worcester, *Life and Labors*, 2:54, 57; Oliver Elsbree, *The Rise of the Missionary Spirit in America, 1790-1815* (Williamsport, Pa., 1928), pp. 65-66, 95; Peter G. Mode, *The Frontier Spirit in American Christianity* (New York, 1923), p. 24; "Jeremiah Evarts, Esq.," *American Quarterly Register* 4 (November 1831): 74-75.

62. An example of this promotional material is in the review of George Burder's *Village Sermons* in the *Panoplist* 3 (September 1807): 185.

63. Samuel Austin to George Burder, March 1, 1805, in Worcester, *Life and Labors*, 2:52-53. Burder was secretary of the LMS.

64. Gardiner Spring, *Memoirs of the Rev. Samuel J. Mills, Late Missionary to the South Western Section of the United States, and Agent of the American Colonization Society, Deputed to Explore the Coast of Africa* (New York, 1820), pp. 10, 18. The most complete history of this society is Richard D. Pierce, "A History of the Society of Inquiry in the Andover Theological Seminary, 1811-1920, together with Some Account of Missions in America before 1810 and a Brief History of the *Brethren*, 1808-1873" (B.D. thesis, Andover Theological Seminary, 1938).

65. Early Records, The Brethren Papers, AN; Worcester, *Life and Labors*, 2:84-85.

66. Mills to Hall, December 20, 1809, in Spring, *Memoirs of the Rev. Samuel J. Mills*, p. 50. Hall later became a missionary to Asia.

67. Pierce, "A History of the Society of Inquiry," p. 26. For brief biographical sketches of the society's members see *Memoirs of American Missionaries, Formerly Connected with the Society of Inquiry Respecting Missions, in the Andover Theological Seminary* (Boston, 1833). See also Theodore Bacon, *Leonard Bacon: A Statesman in the Church* (New Haven, Conn., 1931), p. 55. Among the members were many men later prominent in American foreign missions: Hiram Bingham, Asa Thurston, Adoniram Judson, Samuel Newell, Samuel Nott, Luther Rice, Gordon Hall, and James Richards.

68. *Panoplist* 4 n.s. (April 1812): 504-5. For the formation of the Princeton society see the letter to the secretary of the Society of Inquiry at Andover, February 16, 1814, in *Memoirs of American Missionaries*, pp. 20-21.

69. From a "Paper Presented June 27, 1810, at the General Association of Massachusetts at Their Annual Meeting at Bradford," in John O. Choules and Thomas Smith, *The Origins and History of Missions*, 2 vols. (Boston, 1832), 2:236. For background on these youths see Elsbree, *Rise of the Missionary Spirit*, p. 111; American Board of Commissioners for Foreign Missions, *One-Hundredth Anniversary of the Haystack Prayer Meeting* (Boston, 1907), p. 4. The most complete history of the founding of the ABCFM is Joseph Tracy, *History of the American Board of Commissioners for Foreign Missions* (New York, 1842). My concern here is with the organization of the Board, not its history.

70. *A Collection of Letters Relative to Foreign Missions* (Andover, Mass., 1810), pp. 147-48. Notice of Mrs. Norris's bequest is in the *Panoplist* 4 n.s. (September 1811): 184. The Board apparently hoped that publication of all donations would encourage others to give. Public piety became recognized as indicative of good character. For general comments on the timing of the Board's organization, see Francis Wayland, *A Memoir of the Life and Labors of the Rev. Adoniram Judson, D.D.*, 2 vols. (Boston, 1853), 1:44; Elsbree, *Rise of the Missionary Spirit*, p. 110.

71. Worcester to Burder, January 3, 1811, in the *Panoplist* 4 n.s. (September 1811): 180.

72. Worcester to Judson, September 18, 1811, in ibid., p. 179. See also Earl R. MacCormac, "The Transition from Voluntary Missionary Society to the Church as a Missionary Organization among the American Congregationalists, Presbyterians, and Methodists" (Ph.D. diss., Yale University, 1961), p. 24. For parallel developments in Great Britain see Johannes Van Den Berg, *Constrained by Jesus' Love: An Inquiry into the Motives of the Missionary Awakening in Great Britain in the Period between 1698 and 1815* (Kempen, 1956). Unlike MacCormac, Van Den Berg sees a parallel development in missionary activity in the two countries, not a period of dependence for the United States until 1812. He is correct only in the sense of origins, for there was an early dependency in the conduct and location of missions. The primary variant in the two efforts is that American missions promoted stability for American interests, whereas British activities were frequently a destabilizing influence within the Empire.

73. *Diary*, 4:98-99. The contradiction in Bentley's position should be obvious, for Massachusetts still had a religious establishment, and Unitarians were beginning to benefit handsomely from its legal perquisites.

74. Edward Starr, *A History of Cornwall, Connecticut* (New Haven, Conn., 1926), p. 138. Starr includes among his opposition a former vice president and a secretary of the navy, as well as other prominent Massachusetts citizens. Unfortunately he mentions no names, although B. N. Crowninshield apparently was the hostile secretary of the navy. See Bentley's *Diary*, 4:98-99.

75. See ABCFM, *Instructions of the Prudential Committee of the American Board of Commissioners for Foreign Missions to the Sandwich Islands Mission* (Lahainaluna, 1838), pp. 5-7, for a copy of the Act of Incorporation. Control rested with the wealthy, since no member of the Prudential Committee received compensation for his services; see Worcester to Joseph Harvey, February 26, 1819, ABC 12.1, v.2, No. 20. See also the Reverend Rufus Anderson, *Memorial Volume of the First Fifty Years of the American Board of Commissioners for Foreign Missions* (Boston, 1861), p. 145.

76. A good study of the early Puritans and the missionary ideal is Peter Carroll, *Puritanism and the Wilderness* (New York, 1969); see especially pp. 3-4, 62, 66. Changes in American society toward this "moral" approach are noted in Mohl, *Poverty in New York*, pp. 117-18. For other comments on the need to combat heathenism see Joseph Tuckerman, *A Letter on the Principles of the Missionary Enterprise* (Boston, 1826), p. 18. Tuckerman was a Unitarian. See also Hollis Read, *The Hand of God in History* (Philadelphia, 1870), p. 124; "On Contributions for the Spread of the Gospel," *Christian Spectator* 1 (April 1819): 212; Paul Varg, *Missionaries, Chinese and Diplomats: The American Protestant Missionary Movement in China, 1890-1952* (Princeton, N.J., 1956), p. 3.

77. Sereno Edwards Dwight, *Thy Kingdom Come: A Sermon, Delivered in the Old South Church, Boston, before the Foreign Mission Society of Boston and the Vicinity, January 3, 1820* (Boston, 1820), p. 28.

Chapter Two

1. Clarence Danhoff, *Changes in Agriculture: The Northern United States, 1820-1870* (Cambridge, Mass., 1969), p. 254; James Morris, *A Statistical Account of Several Towns in the County of Litchfield* (New Haven, Conn., 1815), p. 91.
2. J. M. Sturtevant, Jr., ed., *Julian M. Sturtevant: An Autobiography* (New York, 1896), p. 38; Chard Smith, *Yankees and God* (New York, 1954), p. 300. Conditions in Maine are in Eliashib Adams, *A Successful Life: Autobiography of Eliashib Adams* (Bangor, Maine, 1871), pp. 45-46.
3. Percy W. Bidwell, "Rural Economy in New England at the Beginning of the Nineteenth Century," *Connecticut Academy of Arts and Sciences Transactions* 20 (1916): 245; Percy W. Bidwell, "The Agricultural Revolution in New England," *American Historical Review* 26 (July 1921): 684; Danhoff, *Changes in Agriculture*, p. 3. For another view of the problem see Jarvis Morse, *The Rise of Liberalism in Connecticut, 1828-1850* (New Haven, Conn., 1933), p. 3. Morse argues that farm self-sufficiency ended only with the advent of commercial agriculture and thereby overlooks the impact of worldly change on everyday farm life.
4. Harold F. Wilson, *The Hill Country of Northern New England: Its Social and Economic History, 1790-1930* (New York, 1936), p. 22; Nell M. Kull, *History of Dover, Vermont: Two Hundred Years in a Hill Town* (Brattleboro, Vt., 1961), p. 141; Lewis D. Stillwell, *Migration from Vermont* (Montpelier, Vt., 1948), pp. 128-29.
5. S. G. Goodrich, *Recollections of a Lifetime*, 2 vols. (New York, 1856), 2: 78.
6. *Connecticut Courant*, September 6, 1815.
7. Ibid., April 16, 1816. See also Jedidiah Morse, *The American Universal Geography* (Charlestown, Mass., 1819), pp. 334-35; Henry B. Fearon, *Sketches of America* (London, 1819), p. 103.
8. Lyman Beecher, *The Means of National Prosperity: A Sermon Delivered at Litchfield, on the Day of the Anniversary Thanksgiving, December 2, 1819* (Hartford, Conn., 1820), p. 5.
9. Margaret Pabst, *Agricultural Trends in the Connecticut Valley Region of Massachusetts, 1800-1900*, Smith College Studies in History, v. 26, numbers 1-4 (October 1940-July 1941), pp. 35-38; Donald Marti, "In Praise of Farming: An Aspect of the Movement for Agricultural Improvement in the Northeast, 1815-1840," *New York History* 51 (July 1970): 353.
10. Pabst, *Agricultural Trends*, p. 107; Davis, *The Half-Century*, p. 283.
11. *Columbian Centinel*, April 16, 1815; Richard J. Purcell, *Connecticut in Transition, 1775-1818* (Washington, D.C., 1918), pp. 79, 110. The Reverend William Bentley was much less sanguine about prospects for profit through speculation in Merinos. See his *Diary*, 4:319 (entry for March 7, 1815).
12. Beecher, *The Means of National Prosperity*, pp. 6-7.
13. H. S. Tanner, *A Description of the Canals and Railroads of the United States* (New York, 1840), p. 43.
14. Edward C. Kirkland, *Men, Cities, and Transportation*, 2 vols. (Cambridge, Mass., 1948), 1: 38; Starr, *History of Cornwall*, p. 62; Dwight, *Travels*, 2:365-88 passim, 4:139-40; Emily Vanderpoel, comp., *Chronicles of a Pioneer School* (Cambridge, Mass., 1903), p. 20.
15. Danhoff, *Changes in Agriculture*, p. 4; Berthoff, *An Unsettled People*, pp. 227-28. Although Berthoff generally slights New England during these years, his emphasis on mobility and disorder is quite applicable.

16. Danhoff, *Changes in Agriculture*, pp. 51, 109; Jane Mesick, *The English Traveller in America, 1785-1835* (New York, 1922), p. 154. William Tudor in his *Letters on the Eastern States*, pp. 234-35, observed the tendency of many farmers toward complete abandonment. They emigrated westward instead of using greater skills or new methods of farming.

17. Bidwell, "Rural Economy," p. 353; John Krout and Dixon Ryan Fox, *The Completion of Independence, 1790-1830* (New York, 1944), p. 107.

18. Albert L. Demaree, *The American Agricultural Press, 1819-1860* (New York, 1941), pp. 323 n, 324 n.

19. Anne Royall, *Sketches of History, Life, and Manners in the United States. By a Traveller* (New Haven, Conn., 1826), p. 340; Margaret E. Martin, *Merchants and Trade of the Connecticut River Valley, 1750-1820*, Smith College Studies in History, v. 24, numbers 1-4 (October 1938-July 1939), p. 198. See also Rolla M. Tryon, *Household Manufactures in the United States, 1640-1860* (Chicago, 1917), pp. 170, 182-84. Per capita value in these counties in Massachusetts was $6.60, compared to $3.05 in the coastal and island counties. In Connecticut the trend was similar, with inland regions having a per capita value of $9.25, and those on Long Island Sound but $8.14. More revealing is that Barnstable and Nantucket counties, on the Massachusetts coast, had per capita values of $0.94 and $0.44 respectively in 1810. On the other hand, Hampshire County, in western Massachusetts, sported a per capita value of $7.87. See also Tench Coxe, *A Series of Tables of the Several Branches of American Manufacturing* (Philadelphia, 1813), p. 28.

20. P. 8.

21. Josiah Temple, *History of North Brookfield* (North Brookfield, Conn., 1887), p. 268; John W. Barber, *Connecticut Historical Collections* (New Haven, Conn., 1836), pp. 362-64; Harvey Wish, *Society and Thought in Early America* (New York, 1950), p. 266.

22. Mesick, *The English Traveller*, p. 169; Victor S. Clark, *History of Manufactures in the United States, 1607-1860* (New York, 1929), pp. 438-39; Caroline Ware, *The Early New England Cotton Manufacture: A Study in Industrial Beginnings* (New York, 1966), p. 37 n; Bruce C. Hawthorne, "Industrialism and the Foreign Missionary Movement in New England, with Special Reference to Massachusetts" (Ph.D. diss., Boston University, 1953), p. 92; Alain White, *History of the Town of Litchfield, Connecticut, 1720-1920* (Litchfield, Conn., 1920), p. 128; Morse, *American Universal Geography*, p. 235; American State Papers, *Finance*, 4:398-409 passim.

23. Robert F. Balivet, "The Vermont Sheep Industry: 1811-1880," *Vermont History* 33 (January 1965): 244; Zadock Thompson, *History of Vermont, Natural, Civil, and Statistical* (Burlington, Vt., 1842), p. 214; John Bristed, *The Resources of the United States of America* (New York, 1818), p. 62. Also see Harold F. Wilson, "The Rise and Decline of the Sheep Industry in Northern New England," *Agricultural History* 9 (January 1935): 12-40.

24. William A. Robinson, *Jeffersonian Democracy in New England* (New Haven, Conn., 1916), p. 100; Ronald F. Banks, *Maine Becomes a State: The Movement to Separate Maine from Massachusetts, 1785-1820* (Middletown, Conn., 1970), p. 57. For the problems of unemployment see Peak, *Memoir*, p. 115; and *Memoir of the Life of Eliza S. M. Quincy* (Boston, 1861), pp. 112-13. An indication of the growing selfishness is in *New England Blockaded in 1814: The Journal of Henry Edward Napier* (Salem, Mass., 1939), p. 18.

25. Brother Joseph Brennan, *Social Conditions in Industrial Rhode Island: 1820-1860* (Washington, D.C., 1940), p. 10. See also Frances R. Morse, ed.,

Henry and Mary Lee: Letters and Journals, with Other Family Letters, 1802-1860
(Boston, 1926), p. 184 (entry for May 21, 1813).
26. Mary W. Tileston, ed., *Memorials of Mary Wilder White* (Boston, 1903), p.
326 (from a letter written in Concord, Mass., August 29, 1808). The town of
Newbury voted to petition for relief on January 31, 1813. See Coffin, *A Sketch
of the History of Newbury*, p. 278, for petitions to the legislature, and the
Connecticut Courant, December 19, 1815, for lamentations on the effect of peace
on American manufacturing, as well as for lobbying efforts to rectify this distress.
See also the Reverend David L. Parmelee's Address, in Litchfield County Foreign
Mission Society, *Semi-Centennial, Celebrated at Litchfield, October 16, 1861*
(Hartford, Conn., 1861), p. 14.
27. January 4, 1815. See also Harold F. Wilson, "Population Trends in
North-Western New England, 1790-1930," *New England Quarterly* 7 (June
1934): 283.
28. *Connecticut Courant*, May 21, 1816; *Pittsfield Sun*, September 1, 1819.
29. Daniel Henshaw's Address in Auxiliary Foreign Mission Society of Worcester North Vicinity, *Report of the Executive Committee: With an Account of
the Proceedings, at Their Third Annual Meeting in Winchendon, October 19, 1826*
(Concord, N.H., 1826), p. 14. For Stowe's portrait of the influence of the Bible
on New England life see *Oldtown Folks*, p. 355. For other shifts see Martin,
Merchants and Trade, p. 191; Purcell, *Connecticut in Transition*, pp. 67-68. This
shifting was of course as much social, religious, and political as it was economic;
and struggles for control of banking facilities often mirrored this. See also H. W.
Bellows, "Influence of the Trading Spirit upon the Social and Moral Life of
America," *American Review: A Whig Journal of Politics, Literature, Art and
Science* 1 (January 1845): 95. For the impact of this exaggerated individualism
on the family see Arthur W. Calhoun, *A Social History of the American Family*, 2
vols. (Cleveland, Ohio, 1918), 2:52, 132. A number of sources indicate the
magnitude of this change. Among the more poignant are the Reverend Timothy
Gillett, *The Past and the Present in the Secular and Religious History of the
Congregational Church Society of Branford: A Semicentennial Discourse Delivered July 7, 1858* (New Haven, Conn., 1858), pp. 22, 25; John Bernard, *Retro-
spections of America, 1798-1811* (New York, 1887), p. 333; Charles S. Phelps,
Rural Life in Litchfield County (Norfolk, Conn., 1917), p. 24.
30. Timothy Flint, *Recollections of the Last Ten Years*, reprint ed. (New
York, 1932), pp. 369-70. These remarks were contained in a letter written in
September 1825. The *Connecticut Courant*, December 12, 1815, editorialized on
the new instability in society.
31. Washington Irving, "Rip Van Winkle," p. 34; Douglas T. Miller, *The Birth
of Modern America, 1820-1850* (New York, 1970), p. xii; Berthoff, *An Unsettled
People*, p. 206. For changes in population see Bidwell, "Rural Economy," p. 251,
and his article on "Population Growth in Southern New England, 1810-1860,"
American Statistical Association, *Quarterly Publication* 15 (1916-17), n.s., no.
120, pp. 813, 815. In 1810 throughout this region, 67 percent of the people lived
in villages with a population of less than 3,000.
32. Almost all serious analyses of New England life during these years cite the
increased westward emigration. The most comprehensive account is Stewart
Holbrook's *The Yankee Exodus* (New York, 1950). A more provocative and
analytical view is Kenneth Lockridge, "Land, Population and the Evolution of
New England Society, 1630-1790," *Past and Present* 39 (April 1968): 62-80.
John Palmer, an Englishman traveling through the region in 1817, quickly
perceived the same trend. See his *Journal of Travels in the United States of North*

America, and in Lower Canada (London, 1818), p. 202. Other works that cite a variety of statistics and effects are Bidwell, "Rural Economy," pp. 387-88; "Population Growth," p. 814; Stilwell, *Migration from Vermont*, pp. 125-28; Phelps, *Rural Life*, p. 109. The Reverend A. G. Hibbard quotes a letter in his *History of Goshen, Connecticut* (Hartford, Conn., 1897), pp. 364-65 that indicates the inequalities in the exchange of goods with the West. Geographic dispersal throughout the New England region was a problem from the time of the earliest settlement, as Peter Carroll notes in *Puritanism and the Wilderness*, p. 128.

33. Yasukichi Yasuba, *Birth Rates of the White Population in the United States, 1800-1860: An Economic Study*, Johns Hopkins University Studies in Historical and Political Science 79, no. 2 (1961), pp. 51-52, 70.

34. Morris, *Statistical Account*, p. 105.

35. *Statistical View of the Population of the United States, from 1790 to 1830 Inclusive* (Washington, D.C., 1835), p. 36; Wilson, in his essay on "Population Trends," pp. 276-77 provides several convenient maps depicting population trends in northern New England.

36. *Statistical View*, pp. 20-22; Wilson, "Population Trends," pp. 276-77, 280.

37. For the statistical evidence from which these conclusions are drawn, see the United States Census Reports for the decades 1800-1830. Chester, New Hampshire, personifies this trend. Chester's population, 2,046 in 1800, dropped to 2,030 in 1810, but rose to 2,262 in 1820 before declining to 2,028 in 1830.

38. *Statistical View*, pp. 24-26; Bidwell, "Population Growth," pp. 838-39. David H. Fischer, *The Revolution of American Conservatism* (New York, 1965), p. 215, highlights the differing growth rates for the various counties. The number of new towns recognized by the Massachusetts legislature remained relatively stable from 1798 to 1824, then declined to almost zero until the 1840s. See P. M. G. Harris, "The Social Origins of American Leaders: The Demographic Foundations," *Perspectives in American History* 3 (1969): 236.

39. *Statistical View*, pp. 32-34; *A Statistical Account*, p. 95. For other evaluations of this emigration see the *Hampshire Gazette* editorial of January 22, 1834, quoted in Pabst, *Agricultural Trends*, p. 26. White's *History of Litchfield*, p. 206, indicates the changing population figures for that community and notes its steady decline in the rankings of most populous Connecticut towns. Fred Somkin, *The Unquiet Eagle* (Ithaca, N.Y., 1967), p. 14, depicts the joyous celebration of fecundity in America. The awful despair is an obvious response when the reverse occurs. The disappearance of farms from the hillsides is noted in Herbert C. Parsons, *A Puritan Outpost: A History of the Town and People of Northfield, Massachusetts* (New York, 1937), p. 219.

40. Increase Tarbox, ed., *Diary of Thomas Robbins, D.D.*, 2 vols. (Boston, 1896), 1:114. More representative, but equally venomous, are the remarks of the Reverend Nathaniel Emmons. See Ide, *Works of Emmons*, 2:200, 214. Emmons feared a loss of religion and virtue should Jefferson be elected and attacked all who opposed existing religious institutions as "aggravatedly criminal."

41. Tarbox, *Diary*, 1:118.

42. Letter of February 13, 1808; Tileston, *Memorials of Mary W. White*, pp. 322-23.

43. Paul Goodman, *The Democratic-Republicans of Massachusetts* (Cambridge, Mass., 1964), pp. 128, 131; Edmund Potter, "Sectionalism in Massachusetts, 1804-1814" (M.A. thesis, University of Texas, 1938), p. 1.

44. By a Federal Republican (Hartford, Conn., 1817). See also John J. Reardon, "Religious and Other Factors in the Defeat of the 'Standing Order' in Connecticut, 1800-1818," *Historical Magazine of the Protestant Episcopal Church*

30 (June 1961):106. See also Goodrich, *Recollections,* 1:115, 117; Elsbree, *The Rise of the Missionary Spirit,* p. 87. Also see the entry for February 1809 in Charles Warren, ed., *Jacobin and Junto: Or Early American Politics as Viewed in the Diary of Dr. Nathaniel Ames, 1758-1822* (Cambridge, Mass., 1931), p. 228. The best study of events in Massachusetts is James M. Banner, Jr., *To the Hartford Convention: The Federalists and the Origins of Party Politics in Massachusetts, 1789-1815* (New York, 1969), p. 169.

45. Historians have made various estimates of these changes. Some of the more perceptive are Richard Birdsall, *Berkshire County: A Cultural History* (New Haven, Conn., 1959), p. 15; Charles Foster, *An Errand of Mercy: The Evangelical United Front, 1790-1837* (Chapel Hill, N.C., 1960), p. 10; and Cole, *Jacksonian Democracy in New Hampshire,* p. 29. The new divisiveness also revived remembrances of the religious divisions that followed the First Great Awakening. Many feared a repetition. The best analysis of disestablishment is McLoughlin, *New England Dissent;* see especially volume 2.

46. For a provocative and perceptive treatment of insecurity and politics, see Richard Buel, Jr., *Securing the Revolution: Ideology in American Politics, 1789-1815* (Ithaca, N.Y., 1972); and Banner, *To the Hartford Convention,* pp. 169-71.

Chapter Three

1. Dwight, *Travels,* 4:418. The decline of clerical power and the erosion of communal unity are noted in Calhoun, *Professional Lives in America,* pp. 93, 110.

2. Lamb and Merrill, "Complete List of the Congregational Ministers and Churches in Addison County, Vt.," pp. 52, 355. For some general comments on this problem see John R. Bodo, *The Protestant Clergy and Public Issues, 1812-1848* (Princeton, N.J., 1954), p. 13; and McLoughlin, *New England Dissent,* 2:791.

3. The Reverend Phinehas Kingsley, "A Brief Survey of the Congregational Churches and Ministry in the County of Franklin, Vt., from the First Settlement to the Present Time," *American Quarterly Register* 12 (May 1840): 352-53, 355, 357. The Reverend David Haskel noted that 97 towns in Vermont had no stated preacher of the gospel for any denomination. Moreover, 154 towns were without a Congregational or Presbyterian pastor. See *A Sermon Delivered in Randolph, at the Annual Meeting of the Vermont Juvenile Missionary Society, October 13, 1819* (Middlebury, Vt., 1819), pp. 14-15.

4. John Farmer, "A List of Congregational and Presbyterian Ministers in the State of New Hampshire, from the First Settlement of the State to the Year 1831," *American Quarterly Register* 6 (May 1834): 234-48; Henry A. Hazen, "Ministry and Churches of New Hampshire, Congregational and Presbyterian," *Congregational Quarterly* 17 (October 1875): 545-74. Both Farmer and Hazen differentiate between those installed and those merely ordained. Hazen also indicates ministers that were neither and is the more comprehensive of the two. For other, more dubious statistics on religion in the New England states, see Dwight, *Travels,* 4:411, 456-57. Information on the other states was gleaned from the sources noted in the Appendix. See also the letter from the Reverend Edward Payson to his parents, June 14, 1805, in Cummings, *Memoir,* 1:28.

5. Dwight, *Travels,* 1:176-77. See also the Reverend Theophilus Packard, *A History of the Churches and Ministers, and of Franklin Association, in Franklin County, Mass.* (Boston, 1854), p. 17; and McLoughlin, *New England Dissent,* 2:978 n.

6. Joseph Lyman, *A Sermon, Preached before the Convention of the Clergy of Massachusetts, in Boston, May 29, 1806* (Boston, 1806), p. 23. Lyman was pastor of the church in Hatfield, Mass.

7. E. C. Bridgman, "2nd Report of the Committee on Foreign Missions to the Society of Inquiry, Sept. 8, 1829," p. 13. Society of Inquiry, Student Dissertations, vol. 18, AN.

8. George Stewart, Jr., *A History of Religious Education in Connecticut*, reprint ed. (New York, 1969), pp. 170-71.

9. The Reverend James Anderson, "Survey of the Congregational Churches in the County of Bennington, Vt., from Their Organization Down to the Present Time," *American Quarterly Register* 15 (November 1842): 134. In 1812 Manchester, Vt., found it necessary to dismiss the Reverend Abel Farley, its first ordained pastor, for lack of adequate support.

10. The Reverend Jonathan Longley, "Complete List of the Congregational Ministers in the County of Bristol, Ms., from Its First Settlement to the Present Time," *American Quarterly Register* 12 (November 1839): 148. See also Haskel, *A Sermon*, pp. 14-15. These divisions between church and society often split parishes because religious and theological views frequently varied widely within a church. State law required all members of the community to support the Congregational church, and those who did so became members of that church. For one reason or another, however, they might not be Congregationalists. These differing religious opinions quite frequently pitted them against the Congregational society that ran church affairs, usually without regard for other church members' opinions. Such divisions became increasingly common in nineteenth-century New England.

11. Longley, "Complete List of the Congregational Ministers in the County of Bristol, Ms.," pp. 146, 141. For Maine see Jonathan Greenleaf, *Sketches of the Ecclesiastical History of the State of Maine* (Portsmouth, N.H., 1821), pp. 122-23.

12. *Statistical View*, pp. 193-210, passim. This is the statistical compilation for New Hampshire in the 1830 Census and is invaluable for social developments in this period.

13. For a perceptive analysis of this problem in an earlier time, see David D. Hall, *The Faithful Shepherd: A History of the New England Ministry in the Seventeenth Century* (Chapel Hill, N.C., 1972), pp. 132, 190.

14. (New York, 1827). See also Donald M. Scott, "Watchmen on the Walls of Zion: Evangelicals and American Society, 1800-1860," (Ph.D. diss., University of Wisconsin, 1968), pp. 2, 92. The best discussion of these professional changes is in David F. Allmendinger, Jr., "The Strangeness of the American Education Society: Indigent Students and the New Charity, 1815-1840," *History of Education Quarterly* 11 (Spring 1971): 3-22.

15. Allmendinger, "The Strangeness," passim.

16. Scott, "Watchmen," p. 113; The Reverend Rufus Anderson, *Memorial Volume*, p. 198.

17. Cummings, *Memoir*, 1:25-26.

18. The Reverend Eliphalet Pearson, *A Sermon Delivered in Boston before the American Society for Educating Pious Youth for the Gospel Ministry, Oct. 26, 1815* (Andover, Mass., 1815), pp. 7-8.

19. Arthur L. Perry, *Williamstown and Williams College: A History* (Norwood, Mass., 1899), p. 229. For a careful consideration of these problems see the Reverend Myron Dudley, "Historical Sketch of Newington, N.H., 1713-1810," *New England Historic and Genealogical Register* 58 (July 1904): 247-54.

20. My analysis of this data had two purposes. It would provide some indication of any changes in the lengths of the terms of the clergy. The appearance of significantly shorter terms would indicate a distinct shift in settlement patterns. Then other information could be used to seek explanations for these alterations. Second, any appearance of a downturn in the length of ministerial terms might also signify problems or shifts within the church or even the community structure. Out of all this emerged a picture of the changing nature of the clerical structure and its relationship to other groups and elements in early nineteenth-century New England society. See the Appendix for a complete list of the sources for these data. Daniel Calhoun, in *Professional Lives*, used a small portion of this material in his analysis of permanency in New Hampshire and Rhode Island, but it has been largely neglected. My study of the problem grew out of an effort to test his conclusions in the other New England states throughout the early decades of the nineteenth century. The emphasis is on the Congregationalists, not because the data were readily available, but because they later took the lead in organizing the vast panorama of benevolent societies.

21. For sources of these data see the section on Vermont in the Appendix. The graphs were first figured on an annual basis. These figures were then grouped into ten-year running averages and expressed in five-year increments. No real differences distinguished the annual or five-year plots, but the latter smoothed out some of the erratic behavior of the single-year graphs and made it easier to see the trends.

22. The sources for the data on Maine are in the Appendix.

23. In 1809, for example, the average was only 9, but the residence of one pastor for 31 years elevated this markedly. Without this individual, the average would drop to 6. This same pattern persists for every year and is particularly prevalent during the 1820s.

24. To cite just a few examples, in 1800 nine pastors began their terms; in 1815 twenty-three did so, and in 1830 twenty-nine settled in a new pulpit. See the section on Massachusetts in the Appendix for the many sources of these data.

25. In 1798, for example, only four pastors ended their stay in a pulpit, but eleven did so in 1797, and seventeen in 1799. The graph dipped sharply in 1798, but the average for the other two years remained constant. The turbulence of individual years from 1730 to 1740 is not reflected in the graphs until the running averages for 1740 to 1765. This is natural when you use a ten-year running average. For example, the point at 1740 includes data from 1731 to 1740 inclusive.

26. For the sources of these data see the section on Connecticut in the Appendix. See Calhoun, *Professional Lives*, pp. 116-25 passim for data and conclusions on New Hampshire and Rhode Island. The situation in Rhode Island was unique, since Congregationalists there were in the minority.

27. See the discussion below on church divisions as a contributory cause of impermanency. See also *The History of New Ipswich, from Its First Grant in 1736 to the Present Time* (Boston, 1852), p. 175.

28. The Reverend Samuel Sewall, "A Brief Survey of the Congregational Churches and Ministers in the County of Middlesex, and in Chelsea in the County of Suffolk, Ms.," *American Quarterly Register* 11 (November 1838): 189.

29. Ibid. (February 1839): 264. For the role of distance, convenience, and the hazards of nature in these disputes see Dudley, "Historical Sketch," p. 252. See also Anderson, "Survey of the Congregational Churches in the County of Bennington," p. 135, for the problems of locating a meetinghouse.

30. Ibid. (May 1839): 385.

31. The Reverend Thomas Noyes, "Complete List of the Congregational Ministers, in the County of Worcester, Mass.," *American Quarterly Register* 10 (August 1837): 51-52, 56-57; (November 1837): 143. The towns were Athol, Berlin, Fitchburg, Gardner, Grafton, Hardwick, and West Boylston.

32. Anderson, "Survey of the Congregational Churches in the County of Bennington," pp. 135-36.

33. Cummings, *Memoir*, 1:125. The quotation is contained in a letter to his parents, August 31, 1807.

34. This became increasingly widespread as Republicans challenged Federalists throughout New England. See Bela B. Edwards, "Complete List of the Congregational Ministers in the Old County of Hampshire, Ms. (including the Present Counties of Hampshire, Franklin, and Hampden)," *American Quarterly Register* 10 (May 1838): 394. Some ministers requested a dismission to avoid local political squabbling. See "Records of the First Church of Rockingham, Vermont," *New England Historic and Genealogical Register* 54 (October 1900): 435.

35. Samuel Manning, *Some Friendly Remarks upon the Present State of the Congregational Churches in New England, Originally Written in a Letter to a Friend* (Walpole, N.H., 1806), pp. 13-14. For a commentary on the impact of this insecurity see Scott, "Watchmen," p. 45. The impact of emigration is in Calhoun, *Professional Lives*, p. 161.

36. Letter to his parents, February 9, 1806, in Cummings, *Memoir*, 1:33.

37. For a sensitive treatment of these problems in the seventeenth century, see Hall, *The Faithful Shepherd*, pp. 186-87.

38. The Reverend George Carrington, "The Causes and Effects of Frequent Dissolutions of the Pastoral Relation," *Literary and Theological Review* 5 (September 1838): 350-51.

39. See ibid., pp 349-71, passim for a perceptive contemporary analysis of these problems; especially pp. 363-64. By the mid-1830s these ills, along with a thirst for "respectability," had even overtaken the Baptists. See James D. Knowles, "Removals of Ministers," *Christian Review* 1 (September 1836): 393-403, for a Baptist condemnation of frequent removals. Knowles's language is a striking parallel to that of Nathaniel Emmons three decades earlier.

Chapter Four

1. Flint, *Recollections*, pp. 375-76.

2. For the origins of these ideals see Hall, *The Faithful Shepherd*, passim. A sensitive reconsideration of early nineteenth-century reform is in Bernard Wishy, *The Child and the Republic: The Dawn of Modern American Child Nurture* (Philadelphia, 1968). See especially pp. 4-5 for a concise summary of Wishy's views.

3. A discussion of this problem in the early eighteenth century is in J. M. Bumsted, "A Caution to Erring Christians: Ecclesiastical Disorder on Cape Cod, 1717 to 1738," *William & Mary Quarterly*, 3d series, 28 (July 1971): 413-38. See also Ludlum, *Social Ferment*, p. 37; Griffin, *Their Brothers' Keepers*, p. x.

4. J. Hammond Trumbull, ed., *The Memorial History of Hartford County, Ct., 1633-1884*, 2 vols. (Boston, 1886), 1:575. This is just one of the small indexes of change in New England society.

5. Bidwell, "Agricultural Revolution," p. 702; Vernon Stauffer, *New England and the Bavarian Illuminati* (New York, 1918), pp. 26, 96. For comments on this network see Francis J. Grund, *The Americans in Their Moral, Social, and Political Relations*, 2 vols., (London, 1837), 1:272.

6. "Survey of [New England] Churches," *Panoplist* 2 (September 1806): 171.

7. Ibid., 2 (April 1807): 503-4.

8. The Andover Association, *A Serious Call to Family Religion: With Some Helps in Performing Its Duties* (Cambridge, Mass., 1802), p. 5.

9. Ray Potter, *Memoir of the Life and Religious Experience of Ray Potter* (Providence, R.I., 1829), p. 19. See also Isaac Holmes, *Account of the United States of America, Derived from Actual Observation during a Residence of Four Years* (London, 1823), pp. 396-97.

10. *Pittsfield Sun*, October 13, 1819. For some perceptive speculations on changes in the family during these years, see Berthoff, *An Unsettled People*, p. 205. The problems of one town are detailed in James F. Hunnewell, *A Century of Town Life: A History of Charlestown, Massachusetts, 1775-1887* (Boston, 1888), pp. 26, 27 n.

11. Benjamin Wood, *Labourers Needed in the House of Christ* (Worcester, Mass., 1812), p. 8.

12. Dwight, *Travels*, 4:392. See also pp. 355 n, 366-67, 378. Dwight's analysis came under attack from those outside the religious establishment. See the Reverend Freeborn Garrettson, *A Letter to the Rev. Lyman Beecher, containing Strictures and Animadversions on a Pamphlet Entitled An Address of the Charitable Society for the Education of Indigent Pious Young Men for the Ministry of the Gospel* (New York, 1816). Garrettson, a Methodist, defended the religiosity of itinerating clergymen and urged Beecher to transcend local and denominational prejudices. These very problems, of course, were the heart of the controversy.

13. *Religious Intelligencer* (March 26, 1818): 641.

14. Emil Oberholzer, *Delinquent Saints* (New York, 1956), p. 10.

15. Most historians have fallen prey to this oversimplification when analyzing the interplay of religion and politics. See Perry, *Williamstown and Williams College*, p. 278; Charles B. Kinney, Jr., *Church and State: The Struggle for Separation in New Hampshire, 1630-1900* (New York, 1955), p. 97; John A. Krout, *The Origins of Prohibition* (New York, 1925), p. 85; Jacob C. Meyer, *Church and State in Massachusetts from 1740 to 1833: A Chapter in the Development of Individual Freedom* (Cleveland, Ohio, 1930), p. 137.

16. For some remarks on this competition see Heimart, *Religion and the American Mind*, p. 541. See also the essay of Bertram Wyatt-Brown, "Prelude to Abolitionism: Sabbatarian Politics and the Rise of the Second Party System," *Journal of American History* 58 (September 1971): 321.

17. Quoted in J. Earl Thompson, Jr., "A Perilous Experiment: New England Clergymen and American Destiny, 1796-1826" (Ph.D. diss., Princeton University, 1966), p. 204. In New Hampshire, Massachusetts, and Connecticut, for example, the bulk of the Jeffersonian party remained Congregationalist. The reasons for this are complex and not strictly a part of this narrative. For a superb treatment see McLoughlin, *New England Dissent*, 2:881.

18. Solomon Aiken, *The Rise and Progress of the Political Dissension in the United States* (Haverhill, Mass., 1811), pp. 15-16.

19. For some perceptive remarks on this problem see Richard Hofstadter, *The Idea of a Party System: The Rise of Legitimate Opposition in the United States, 1780-1840* (Berkeley, Calif., 1969), p. ix.

20. James Sabine, *The Great Moral Duties of a Free and Independent People* (Boston, 1826), p. 32.

21. Samuel Miller, *Letters on Clerical Manners, and Habits, Addressed to a Student in the Theological Seminary at Princeton, New Jersey* (New York, 1827), p. 459.

22. Goodrich, *Recollections*, 1:433. See also Stauffer, *New England and the Bavarian Illuminati*, p. 89 n; Dwight, *Travels*, 4:403-4; Ralph H. Gabriel, "Evangelical Religion and Popular Romanticism in Early Nineteenth-Century America," *Church History* 19 (March 1950): 40. A good essay on the push for a Christian civilization is James F. Maclear, " 'The True American Union' of Church and State: The Reconstruction of the Theocratic Tradition," *Church History* 28 (March 1959): 41-62. See Hofstadter, *The Idea of a Party System*, p. ix, for the general notion of parties and conflict.

23. *Personal Reminiscences of the Life and Times of Gardiner Spring* (New York, 1826), pp. 65-66. This quotation is from his journal, September 15, 1814.

24. *Diary of William Bentley*, 4:114-15. Entry for September 6, 1812. For the Federalist view see Asa McFarland, *A Defense of the Clergy of New-England, against the Charges of Interfering in Our Political Affairs, and Condemning the Policy of the Present War* (Concord, N.H., 1814).

25. Thompson, "A Perilous Experiment," p. 203, notes this shift, but attributes it simply to a decline in clerical enthusiasm for political controversy. A more balanced view is in Keller, *The Second Great Awakening*, pp. 64-65. Two issues arose, that of orthodoxy and that of disestablishment. Both were closely entwined, but I have treated the challenge to orthodoxy first. Not until this problem became intense did the Trinitarian-Congregationalists begin to argue for disestablishment.

26. Woods, *Andover*, pp. 28-29, 31-32, 40-41.

27. Joseph Haroutunian, *Piety vs. Moralism: The Passing of the New England Theology* (New York, 1932), p. 62. A full-scale discussion of technical theology is not within the scope of this narrative. If the reader wishes to pursue this further he should turn to Haroutunian's excellent narrative. For an analysis of the situation in Connecticut during the early nineteenth century, see the reflections of the Reverend Joel Hawes in his letter to Leonard Woods, October 12, 1853, in Woods, *Andover*, p. 29. The Massachusetts problem is discussed in Woods, p. 31; letter of the Reverend Thomas Snell to Woods, December 7, 1853. For the subtleties of the change to evangelism, see the discussion in McLoughlin, *New England Dissent*, 2:984.

28. The Reverend Joel Hawes (Hartford, 1830).

29. Ibid., pp. 83-84.

30. Ibid., pp. 185-86.

31. Letter from Dwight to Dr. Jedidiah Morse, July 6, 1805, in Woods, *Andover*, pp. 454-55.

32. Dwight, *Travels*, 1:511; Hawes, *A Tribute*, p. 181. A few historians erroneously contend that this dispute emerged seemingly out of nowhere. See Sidney E. Mead, "Lyman Beecher and Connecticut Orthodoxy's Campaign against the Unitarians, 1819-1826," *Church History* 9 (September 1940): 218. The institutional impact of this change will be discussed in chapter five below. At this juncture I am concerned with the ministerial reaction that eventually led to these institutional changes.

33. Quoted in Sprague, *Life of Morse*, pp. 92-93. For the influence of Boston on the rest of New England, see the *Christian Spectator* 2 n.s. (January 1828): 20.

34. *Diary of Sarah Connell Ayer* (Portland, Maine, 1910), p. 242. Some wealthy lay Trinitarians showed no deep personal commitment. See Ayer's *Diary*, along with Tileston, *Memorials of Mary W. White*. In the latter, see especially the letter from Ruth Hurd to Mary Van Schalkwyck, November 6, 1804, on p. 200.

35. Letter to Edward Beecher, April 16, 1823, in Beecher, *Autobiography*, 1:518.

36. Letter to Dr. Taylor, May 1, 1823, in ibid., p. 544. Travelers throughout the region noted the same disarray. See John M. Duncan, *Travels through Part of the United States and Canada in 1818 and 1819*, 2 vols. (New York, 1823), 1:83, 87; Frances Wright D'Arusmont, *Views of Society and Manners in America; in a Series of Letters from That Country during the Years 1818, 1819, and 1820. By an Englishwoman* (New York, 1821), p. 320; Hodgson, *Remarks during a Journey*, p. 72 (from a letter written in Salem, Mass., February 24, 1821); W. N. Blane, *An Excursion through the United States and Canada during the Years 1822-23. By an English Gentleman* (London, 1824), p. 491.

37. "The Exiled Churches of Massachusetts," *Congregational Quarterly* 5 (July 1863): 224. This is case number 26. The article is a full reprint of the 1833 report. All towns and churches remain anonymous.

38. For a discussion of this problem see McLoughlin, *New England Dissent*, 2: 1193; and Dudley, "Historical Sketch," pp. 247-54 passim.

39. Letter to Mr. Cornelius, January 23, 1821, in Beecher, *Autobiography*, 1:439. For a survey of the legal inroads of Unitarians in Massachusetts, see Leonard Levy, *The Law of the Commonwealth and Chief Justice Shaw* (New York, 1957), pp. 29-42.

40. McLoughlin, *New England Dissent*, 1:661-62. Rhode Island, always peculiar among the New England states, remained outside the mainstream of religious problems and controversy during these years.

41. 3 Mass. 159-83. The quotation is on p. 159.

42. Ibid., p. 172.

43. 6 Mass. 400-17.

44. Ibid., p. 415.

45. For an informed analysis of similar events in New Hampshire, see William McLoughlin, "The Bench, the Church and the Republican Party in New Hampshire," *Historical New Hampshire* 20 (1965): 3-31. See also the letters from "A Baptist" in the *New Hampshire Patriot* during February 1816. As McLoughlin indicates, Federalist courts and Republican politics combined to envision conspiracies on all sides.

46. The most complete study of disestablishment in Vermont is in McLoughlin, *New England Dissent*, 2: 787-832. See also the *Diary of Thomas Robbins*, 1:340 (entry for November 24, 1807).

47. Lyman Beecher, *On the Importance of Assisting Young Men of Piety and Talents in Obtaining an Education for the Gospel Ministry* (Andover, Mass., 1815), p. 1.

48. *The Politics of Connecticut*, pp. 18-19. Unfortunately historians have partly obscured the whole problem of disestablishment. Few have seen it correctly as a local problem. Typical of studies that blame the French Revolution, Jeffersonianism, or some other national or international scheme is Purcell, *Connecticut in Transition*; see especially p. 4. Local histories often reflect this same bias; see White, *History of the Town of Litchfield*, pp. 165-66. A perceptive analysis, though unfortunately brief and somewhat superficial, is in Paul Coons, *The Achievement of Religious Liberty in Connecticut* (New Haven, Conn., 1936), p. 24. The most intensive discussion is in McLoughlin, *New England Dissent*.

49. For a discussion of this problem see Maclear, " 'The True American Union,' " pp. 41-62 passim. It is true that by 1815 several moral reform societies did exist, but their promoters could still find reassurances in the continued existence of a legally established church.

50. Gillett, *The Past and Present*, pp. 21-22; Morse, *A Neglected Period*, p. 125. For a concise history of Connecticut disestablishment see McLoughlin, *New*

England Dissent, 2: 1043-62. In Connecticut, unlike Massachusetts, Unitarians had captured very few established churches.

51. Kinney, *Church and State*, p. 117; McLoughlin, *New England Dissent*, 2:834, 880. McLoughlin notes one unusual political feature in the struggle for disestablishment in New Hampshire. In the Granite State Republicans were not irrevocably aligned against the existing religious structure. Instead they used this establishment as a negative reference group to help unite all dissenters within their own ranks. In the case of New Hampshire, therefore, the onset of disestablishment produced fluidity and turmoil in all segments of society.

52. Goodman, *The Democratic-Republicans of Massachusetts*, p. 165. For a succinct analysis of this divisiveness see Bentley's *Diary*, 3:346; and McLoughlin, *New England Dissent*, 2:1093-1106.

53. In Massachusetts, Trinitarians supported disestablishment in an effort to prevent a Unitarian takeover. The Standing Order in the state had become a Unitarian-Federalist alliance. Thus Trinitarians joined dissenters. For more on Massachusetts see John D. Cushing, "Notes on Disestablishment in Massachusetts, 1780-1833," *William & Mary Quarterly*, 3d series, 26 (April 1969): 169-90.

54. Aiken, *The Rise and Progress of Political Dissension*, p. 13.

55. Calvin Hitchcock, *Knowledge Essential to Religion: A Sermon, Delivered in the Second Parish, Abington, Mass. Sept. 24, 1823* (Boston, 1823), pp. 16-17.

56. *Christian Spectator* 2 n.s. (January 1828): 21.

57. Joshua Bates, *A Discourse, Delivered in Castleton, at the Organization of the Vermont Juvenile Missionary Society, September 16, 1818* (Middlebury, Vt., 1818), pp. 8-9, 11.

58. *Travels*, 4:369.

59. From a letter, September 22, 1809, in Cummings, *Memoir*, 1:186. His attachment to his mother appears to have gone beyond filial devotion.

60. Ibid., p. 304. From a letter to his mother, January 25, 1826. See also Haroutunian, *Piety vs. Moralism*, pp. 180-81.

61. Hawes, *A Tribute*, p. 195

62. Beecher, *Autobiography*, 1:262.

Chapter Five

1. A good summary of this effort is in R. Pierce Beaver, ed., *Pioneers in Mission: The Early Missionary Ordination Sermons, Charges, and Instructions* (Grand Rapids, Mich., 1966), p. 3. For another view see Scott, "Watchmen," pp. 25, 34; George Punchard, *History of Congregationalism*, 2 vols. (Boston, 1881), 2:550. The organizational efforts of Presbyterians are noted in Lois Banner, "Presbyterians and Voluntarism in the Early Republic," *Journal of Presbyterian History* 50 (Fall 1972): 187-205.

2. *Letters on Clerical Manners*, pp. 137-38.

3. Krout and Fox, *The Completion of Independence*, pp. 254-55. See also James Kirker, *Adventures to China: Americans in the Southern Oceans, 1792-1812* (New York, 1970).

4. Lucy E. Guernsey, *School-days in 1800; or, Education as It Was a Century Since* (Philadelphia, 1875), p. 191.

5. Stanley Griswold, *Overcoming Evil with Good: A Sermon, Delivered at Wallingford, Connecticut, March 11, 1801* (Hartford, Conn., 1801), p. 32.

6. Elihu Thayer, *A Sermon, Preached at Hopkinton, at the Formation of the New-Hampshire Missionary Society, September 2, 1801*, (Concord, N.H., 1801), pp. 10-11.

7. Thomas Cary, *A Sermon, Delivered to the First Religious Society in Newburyport, September 27, 1801* (Newburyport, Mass., 1801), p. 12. For encouragement to preach the gospel in foreign lands, see Samuel Spring, *A Sermon, Delivered before the Massachusetts Missionary Society, at Their Annual Meeting, May 25, 1802* (Newburyport, Mass., 1802), pp. 12-13. Other comments on this problem can be found in Asahel Hooker, *The Use and Importance of Preaching the Distinguishing Doctrine of the Gospel. Illustrated in a Sermon, at the Ordination of the Reverend John Keep; to the Pastoral Charge of the Congregational Church, in Blandford, Oct. 30, 1805* (Northampton, Mass., 1806).

8. Samuel Austin, *Christians Bound to Spread the Gospel among All Descriptions of Their Fellow Men: A Sermon, Preached before the Massachusetts Missionary Society, at Their Annual Meeting in Boston, May 24, 1803* (Salem, Mass., 1803), p. 11.

9. Evan Johns, *The Happiness of American Christians: A Thanksgiving Sermon, Preached on Thursday the 24th of November, 1803* (Hartford, Conn., 1804), p. 8. For remarks on the obligations and rewards of feminine involvement in these enterprises see Daniel Dana, *A Discourse Delivered May 22, 1804, before the Members of the Female Charitable Society of Newburyport, Organized June 8, 1803* (Newburyport, Mass., 1804), p. 21.

10. Edward D. Griffin, *The Kingdom of Christ: A Missionary Sermon, Preached before the General Assembly of the Presbyterian Church, in Philadelphia, May 23d, 1805* (Greenfield, Mass., 1808), pp. 24-25.

11. Ibid.

12. Ibid., p. 28.

13. Joseph Lyman, *A Sermon, Preached in Halifax (Vt.) Sept. 17, 1806. At the Installation of Reverend Thomas H. Wood, over the Congregational Church and Society in that Town* (Northampton, Mass., 1807), p. 19.

14. See a recollection of the Haystack meeting in Perry, *Williamstown and Williams College*, p. 361.

15. An excellent expression of these values is in William Lyman, *The Happy Nation: A Sermon, Preached at the Anniversary Election, in Hartford, May 8th, 1806* (Hartford, Conn., 1806), pp. 6, 8, 27.

16. "Survey of New England Churches," *Panoplist* 2 (April 1807): 504.

17. John Reed, *A Sermon, Preached before the Convention of the Congregational Ministers in Boston, May 27, 1807* (Boston, 1807), passim.

18. Joseph Lathrop, *A Sermon, Preached in Putney, (Vt.) June 25, 1807. At the Ordination of Reverend Elisha D. Andrews, over the Congregational Church and Charitable Christian Society, in That Town* (Brattleboro, Vt., 1807), p. 6.

19. Ibid., pp. 4, 14.

20. On the reasons for secrecy see the letter from Dr. Fisk to Samuel Worcester, June 24, 1829, quoted in Worcester, *Life and Labors*, 2:85. In the letter Fisk recalled the early ventures in foreign missions. Another example of this theme is in Timothy M. Cooley, *The Universal Spread of the Gospel: A Sermon, Preached at Northampton, before the Hampshire Missionary Society; at Their Annual Meeting, August 25, 1808* (Northampton, Mass., 1808), pp. 18-19.

21. See Cooley, *The Universal Spread of the Gospel*, p. 15; and Fisk to Worcester, June 24, 1829, in Worcester, *Life and Labors*, 2:85.

22. Nathan Perkins, *The Benign Influence of Religion on Civil Government and National Happiness. Illustrated in a Sermon, Preached before His Excellency Jonathan Trumbull, Esq., Governor: His Honor John Treadwell, Esq. Lieutenant Governor: The Honorable The Council: and House of Representatives of the State of Connecticut, on the Anniversary Election, May 12th, 1808* (Hartford, Conn.,

1808), pp. 8, 18, 30-31, 36, 47, 50. See also William Jenks, *The True Spirit of Missions: A Sermon Delivered before the Maine Missionary Society, at Their Annual Meeting in North Yarmouth (Maine), July 5, 1809* (Hallowell, Maine, 1809), p. 10.

23. For the problem of organization see Ebenezer C. Tracy, *Memoir of the Life of Jeremiah Evarts* (Boston, 1845), p. 61; and Banner, *To The Hartford Convention*, pp. 165-66. The lasting values of forceful preaching are enumerated in Edward D. Griffin, *An Oration Delivered June 21, 1809, on the Day of the Author's Induction into the Office of Bartlet Professor of Pulpit Eloquence, in the Divinity College, at Andover* (Boston, n.d.), pp. 10, 12, and passim. Although many of Griffin's remarks were undoubtedly self-serving, the activities of other pastors indicate a fundamental agreement among his colleagues.

24. "Concern for the Salvation of the Heathen," *Panoplist* 5 (May 1810): 545-46.

25. Timothy Dwight, *The Charitable Blessed: A Sermon, Preached in the First Church in New-Haven, August 8, 1808* (n.p., 1810), p. 12.

26. Joseph Lathrop, *The Importance of Female Influence in the Support of Religion: A Sermon, Delivered to a Charitable Female Association in West-Springfield, May 15, 1810* (Springfield, Mass., 1810), p. 5. For the urging to go forward in this cause see especially Jonathan Grout, *Missionary Societies Called to Go Forward: A Sermon, Preached at Northampton, before the Hampshire Missionary Society, at Their Annual Meeting, August 30, 1810* (Northampton, Mass., 1810), p. 16. The continuing emphasis on the community is reflected in William Emerson, *A Sermon, Preached at the Ordination of the Rev. Samuel Clark, to the Pastoral Care of the First Congregational Society of Christians in Burlington [Vt.], April 19, 1810* (Burlington, Vt., 1810), p. 5.

27. Worcester, *Life and Labors*, 2:123. For a succinct statement on the social condition of women see Gerda Lerner, *The Grimké Sisters from South Carolina* (New York, 1967), p. 33.

28. ABCFM, *An Address to the Christian Public* (n.p., n.d. [1811?], pp. 1, 5-6. The *Panoplist* published a similar appeal; see v. 4 n.s. (June 1811): 4.

29. Van Den Berg, *Constrained by Jesus' Love*, p. 132.

30. Ezekiel Rich's Subscription List, 1811, ABC 8.5, No. 5. Of the $80 he collected, over one-half came from one donor in Greenland, New Hampshire. For Frost, the first ABCFM agent, see Anderson, *Memorial Volume*, p. 177.

31. The *Panoplist* 4 n.s. (September 1811): 185.

32. Ibid. (November 1811): 269-70. He calculated the amount to be about $10 and enclosed that sum as his donation.

33. Foreign Mission Society of Boston and the Vicinity, *Constitution*, ABC 42-5939, No. 3. The *Panoplist* published an announcement of the society's formation, along with the constitution; see v. 4 n.s. (December 1811): 332-34.

34. The Reverend Kiah Bailey to Worcester, November 2, 1811, ABC 10, v.1, No. 68. For a suggestion that other societies be established, see "D. M." to Worcester (no date), ABC 10, v. 2, No. 55.

35. See the letter to the Andover Society of Inquiry, June 12, 1811, in Shedd, *Two Centuries*, p. 66.

36. For the evaluation of foreign missions see the *Panoplist* 4 n.s. (December 1811): 312. Bentley's objections can be found in his *Diary*, 4:49, 75. The highlight of these defensive preparations came in 1811 when the Andover Society of Inquiry reprinted David Bogue's sermon *Objections against a Mission to the Heathen Stated and Considered: A Sermon, Preached at Tottenham Court Chapel, before the Founders of the Missionary Society, 24 Sept. 1795* (Cambridge, Mass.).

37. For examples of these exhortations see Evan Johns, *A Sermon, Preached at Northampton, before the Foreign Missionary Society of Northampton and the Neighboring Towns, at their First Meeting, March 31, 1812* (Northampton, Mass., 1812), p. 17; Diodate Brockway, *A Missionary Sermon, Delivered in the North Presbyterian Meeting House, in Hartford, on the Evening of May 19, 1812. At the Request of the Trustees of the Missionary Society of Connecticut* (Hartford, Conn., 1812), pp. 8, 12, 14. See also Worcester, *Life and Labors*, 2:258. Worcester also notes (p. 269) that the war did interrupt the sending of missionaries, but not the all-important organizational efforts at home.

38. *Panoplist* 4 n.s. (April 1812): 492.

39. Ibid. (February 1812): 431. Samuel T. Armstrong, a wealthy bookseller and theological printer in Boston also spent much of his time and money working for the ABCFM. See Krout, *Origins of Prohibition*, p. 92.

40. Benjamin Wood, *Labourers Needed in the Harvest of Christ: A Sermon, Delivered at Sutton (S.P.) March 18, 1812. As a Preliminary to the Formation of a Society, in the County of Worcester, for the Aid of Pious Young Men, With a View to the Ministry* (Worcester, Mass., 1812), pp. 19-20. See also Joseph Lathrop, *The Angel Preaching the Everlasting Gospel: A Sermon Delivered in Springfield, April 21st, 1812, at the Institution of a Society for the Encouragement of Foreign Mission* (Springfield, Mass., 1812), pp. 13, 18.

41. Letter to Samuel Worcester from David Oliphant and Chauncey Booth, March 25, 1812, ABC 12.1, v. 1, No. 75.

42. *Panoplist* 4 n.s. (May 1812): 560-61. See the issue for March 1812 (p. 446) for the argument that Christians needed to be convinced of the need for foreign missions. A similar exhortation is in Chester Dewey, *A Sermon, Occasioned by the Present Religious Attention in Williams College, Preached May 12th, at the Desire of the Junior Class, as a Substitute for Their Expected Public Exhibition* (Stockbridge, Mass., 1812), p. 17.

43. Abraham Bodwell, *A Sermon, Delivered at the Request of the Female Cent Society, in Sandbornton, New-Hampshire, December 23, 1812* (Concord, N.H., 1813), pp. 11-12. See also Leonard Woods, *A Sermon, Delivered at the Tabernacle in Salem, Feb. 6, 1812, on Occasion of the Ordination of the Rev. Messrs. Samuel Newall, Adoniram Judson, Samuel Nott, Gordon Hall, and Luther Rice, Missionaries to the Heathen in Asia* (Boston, 1812), pp. 5, 15-16.

44. Beecher, *A Reformation of Morals*, pp. 21-22, 35.

45. ABCFM, *Printed Circular to Agents Appointed by the A.B.C.F.M.* (n.p., n.d.), ABC 42-5939, No. 15.

46. ABCFM, *Circular Letter of the Prudential Committee of the American Board of Commissioners for Foreign Missions* (Boston, 1812), ABC 42-5939, No. 13.

47. Beecher to Hooker, Nov. 24, 1812, in Beecher, *Autobiography*, 1:257. For Beecher's efforts to organize a foreign mission society, see p. 291 n. See also Payne K. Kilbourne, *Sketches and Chronicles of the Town of Litchfield, Connecticut, Historical, Biographical, and Statistical* (Hartford, Conn., 1859), p. 187; Hibbard, *History of Goshen*, pp. 250-51.

48. *Constitution and Addresses of the Religious Charitable Society of Worcester, Mass.* (n.p., 1812), 5, ABC 42-5939, No. 7. For the other societies see Lathrop, *The Angel Preaching the Everlasting Gospel*, p. 23; Salem Foreign Missionary Society, Accounts of Subscribers, begun 1812, pp. 1-109, ABC 25, v. 1; *Semi-centennial of the Litchfield County Foreign Mission Society, Celebrated at Litchfield, Oct. 16, 1861* (Hartford, Conn., 1861), p. 11.

49. In Salem, Mass. 78 percent of all donors in 1812 contributed two dollars

or less. Salem Foreign Missionary Society, Accounts of Subscribers, begun 1812, ABC 25, v. 1, pp. 1-109. For efforts at propaganda and encouragement to donate more, see Foreign Mission Society of Northampton and the Neighboring Towns, *Circular Letter* (Northampton, Mass., 1812), ABC 42-5939, No. 4. The question of dues is found in Foreign Mission Society of Northampton and the Neighboring Towns, *Constitution* (Northampton, Mass., 1812), ABC 42-5939, No. 6; *The Fiftieth Anniversary of the Norwich and New London Foreign Missionary Society, Held at Norwich, Oct. 21, 1862* (Norwich, Conn., 1862), p. 13.

50. For New London see the *Panoplist* 5 n.s. (June 1812): 47; *Fiftieth Anniversary*, pp. 9-10. The Norwich officers are listed in the *Panoplist* 5 n.s. (June 1812): 47. For New Haven see the *Panoplist* 4 n.s. (March 1812): 479; and 5 n.s. (November 1812): 286.

51. Massachusetts' societies and officers in 1812 are in the *Panoplist* 4 n.s. (January 1812): 380; (February 1812): 427; (May 1812): 571; 5 n.s. (November 1812): 285. The *Panoplist* also listed officers for the Maine societies. See v. 4 n.s. (February 1812): 427; (March 1812): 479; (May 1812): 570-71; 5 n.s. (June 1812): 47.

52. *Diary*, 4:82.

53. Ibid., pp. 146, 160.

54. See *Diary of Thomas Robbins*, 1:530. In his entry for October 20, 1812, Robbins attacked foreign missions in much the same tone as had Bentley. The next day he preached a sermon against formation of an auxiliary foreign mission society in Hartford.

55. "An Address to the Public on the Subject of Missions," *Panoplist* 9 (October 1813): 320.

56. Timothy Dwight, *A Sermon, Delivered in Boston, Sept. 16, 1813, before the American Board of Commissioners for Foreign Missions, at Their Fourth Annual Meeting* (Boston, 1813), p. 22. See also p. 30. On pretended benevolence see Bennet Tyler, *A Sermon, Preached at Litchfield, before the Foreign Mission Society of Litchfield County, at Their Annual Meeting, February 10, 1813* (New Haven, Conn., 1813), pp. 10-12; and Joshua Spaulding, *The Burden and Heat of the Day, Borne by the Jewish Church: A Sermon, Preached at Shelburne, before the Auxiliary Society for Foreign Missions, at Their Annual Meeting, Oct. 12, 1813* (Boston, 1814), pp. 22-23. For remarks on the duty of working for this cause see Levi Nelson, *The Enlargement of the Church of Christ, and Its Firm and Durable State; Illustrated and Applied in a Sermon, Delivered at Norwich, Chelsea, before the Foreign Mission Society, for Norwich and Its Vicinity, May 18, 1813, at the First Annual Meeting of the Society* (Norwich, Conn., 1813), p. 30.

57. One society even included such a provision in its constitution. See Auxiliary Foreign Mission Society of Middlesex, *Constitution* (Boston, 1813), ABC 42-5939, No. 5. For some examples of these commands see Abiel Holmes, *A Discourse, Delivered at the Old South Church in Boston before the Society for Foreign Missions of Boston and the Vicinity, Jan. 1, 1813* (Cambridge, Mass., 1813). In this sermon Holmes compared pagans and Christians and then concluded with numerous references to duty and the Indian Mission. See especially pp. 6, 10. Also see Samuel Goodrich, *A Missionary Sermon, Delivered in the North Presbyterian Church in Hartford, May 18, 1813. At the Request of the Trustees of the Missionary Society of Connecticut* (Hartford, Conn., 1813), p. 7.

58. See especially the new item on the annual meeting of the Foreign Mission Society of the Eastern District of New Haven County, Connecticut, in the *Panoplist* 9 (September 1813): 237.

59. For figures on contributions see the issues of the *Panoplist* as well as the various annual reports of the foreign mission societies for this period. Also see Joseph Harvey, *A Sermon, Preached at Litchfield, before the Foreign Mission Society of Litchfield County, at Their Annual Meeting, February 15, 1815* (New Haven, Conn., 1815), p. 2; Anderson, *Memorial Volume*, p. 160; Warren Fay, *The Obligations of Christians to the Heathen World: A Sermon, Delivered at the Old South Church in Boston, before the Auxiliary Foreign Mission Society of Boston and Vicinity, at Their Annual Meeting, January 3, 1825* (Boston, 1825), p. 38. For the need to combine missions with commerce and thereby advance the board's efforts, see John Chester, *A Sermon, Delivered before the Berkshire and Columbia Missionary Society, at Their Annual Meeting in Canaan, September 21st, 1813* (Hudson, Mass., 1813), pp. 19-20, 23.

60. These figures are in *Fiftieth Anniversary*, p. 25; *Thirteenth Anniversary of the Auxiliary Foreign Mission Society of Boston and Vicinity, Jan. 3, 1825* (Boston, 1825), pp. 38-39; *Proceedings at the Fourteenth Anniversary of the Auxiliary Foreign Mission Society of Boston and Vicinity, May 26, 1825* (Boston, 1825), p. 36.

61. "Address to the Public," *Panoplist* 10 (January 1814): 4.

62. James Richards, *The Spirit of Paul the Spirit of Missions: A Sermon Preached at New Haven (Con.), before the American Board of Commissioners for Foreign Missions, at Their Annual Meeting, Sept. 15, 1814* (Boston, 1814), pp. 5, 7, 23.

63. Bela B. Edwards, *Memoir of Elias Cornelius* (Boston, 1833), p. 29. See his diary entry for March 14, 1814.

64. Joseph Lathrop, *A Sermon, Preached at Springfield, before the Bible Society, and the Foreign Mission Society, in the County of Hampden, at Their Annual Meeting, August 31, 1814* (Springfield, Mass., 1814), p. 10.

65. Ibid., pp. 7-8.

66. For an evaluation of the New England clergy and the problem of the foreign missionary commitment in 1814, see Samuel Nott, *Reasons Why We Should Pray for the Prosperity of the Redeemer's Kingdom on Earth: A Sermon, Preached at Norwich, First Society, before the Foreign Mission Society for Norwich and Its Vicinity, May 17, 1814, at the Second Annual Meeting* (Norwich, Conn., 1814), pp. 14, 18. This decline in zeal is also noted in the Reverend Miron Winslow, comp., *Memoir of Mrs. Harriet L. Winslow* (New York, 1840), p. 29 (diary entry for August 21, 1814). Efforts of local collectors are noted in the *Report of the Committee of the Auxiliary Foreign Missionary Society in the County of Franklin, Mass. Read and Accepted at Their Annual Meeting, Holden at Ashfield, Oct. 11, 1814* (Greenfield, Mass., 1814), pp. 4, 6.

67. Examples of these exertions are in Daniel Chaplin, *A Sermon, Delivered in Boston, before the Massachusetts Society for Promoting Christian Knowledge; on the Evening of June 1, 1815* (Boston, 1815), p. 15; Jedidiah Morse, *The Gospel Harvest, Illustrated in a Sermon Delivered at the Old South Church in Boston, before the Society for Foreign Missions of Boston and the Vicinity, at Their Annual Meeting, January 2, 1815* (Boston, 1815), p. 26; *A Sketch of the Proceedings of the Society for Foreign Missions of Wiscasset and Its Vicinity, Organized Sept. 14, 1815* (Boston, 1815), pp. 10-11; see also the *Connecticut Courant*, May 17, 1815.

68. Ebenezer Burgess, "Address to the Society of Inquiry," Society of Inquiry, Student Dissertations, v. 1, AN.

69. James Kimball, "The Influence of Foreign Missions upon the Churches at Home," Society of Inquiry, Student Dissertations, v. 8, AN.

70. Thomas Shepard, "What Are the *Improper Motives* by Which a Missionary Is in Danger of Being Influenced by Devoting Himself to *the Heathen?*" pp. 2-18 passim, Society of Inquiry, Student Dissertations, v. 1, AN. This was delivered December 5, 1815. See also Reuben Puffer, *The Widow's Mite: A Sermon Delivered at Boylston, before the Boylston Female Society for the Aid of Foreign Missions, Jan. 8, 1816* (Worcester, Mass., 1816), p. 7.

71. *A Sketch of the Proceedings of the Society for Foreign Missions of Wiscasset and Its Vicinity*, pp. 405, 8, 11. For the urge to unity see Horatio Bardwell, *The Duty and Reward of Evangelizing the Heathen: A Sermon Delivered in Newburyport, Lord's Day Evening, October 22, 1815* (Newburyport, Mass., 1815), pp. 8-9, 11; John Keep, *Motives for Well-Doing: A Sermon, Delivered in Northampton August 24, 1815, before the Hampshire Missionary Society, at Their Annual Meeting* (Northampton, Mass., 1815), p. 13; Robert Forrest, *Great Encouragement to Perseverance in Missionary Labours: A Sermon Delivered before the Northern Missionary Society, at Their Annual Meeting in Lansingburgh, September 6, 1815* (Albany, N.Y., 1815), p. 7; Zebulon Ely, *Revelation Necessary to Salvation: A Sermon, Delivered in Thompson, at a Meeting of the Foreign Mission Society of Windham County, Oct. 4, 1815* (Hartford, Conn., 1815), p. 5.

72. *First Quarterly Circular of the Prudential Committee of the American Board of Commissioners for Foreign Missions* (Boston, 1815), ABC 42-5939, No. 18, p. 3. For an emphasis on the family see Heman Humphrey, "Union Is Strength," in *Miscellaneous Discourses and Reviews* (Amherst, Mass., 1874), p. 23. Some of the board's problems in keeping abreast of economic and political developments are noted in Worcester to Jeremiah Evarts, July 24, 1815, ABC 11, v. 1, No. 131.

73. For the relation of foreign missions to the cause of liberty, see Harvey, *A Sermon, Preached at Litchfield . . . February 15, 1815*, p. 25.

74. Joseph Anderson, *Churches of Mattatuck* (New Haven, Conn., 1892), pp. 50-51; Krout and Fox, *The Completion of Independence*, p. 255.

75. Worcester to Payson (no date), in Anderson, *Memorial Volume*, pp. 177-78; Worcester to Payson, February 28, 1816, Samuel Worcester, Letter Book, 1812-1818, ABC 1.01, v. 1, pp. 66-67. For the *Panoplist's* reprint of the board circular, see v. 12 (January 1816): 41.

76. Chester Wright, *A Sermon, Preached before the Female Foreign Mission Society in Montpelier, 1816* (Montpelier, Vt., 1817), pp. 8-9, 13.

77. Letter to ABCFM agents, January 31, 1816, in Worcester, *Life and Labors*, 2:387-88. Pastors had urged such a step; see Joshua Bates, *A Sermon, Preached at Boston, January 4, 1816, before the Society for Foreign Missions of Boston and the Vicinity* (Dedham, Mass., 1816), p. 17.

78. *Religious Intelligencer* (June 29, 1816): 77; *Connecticut Courant*, July 30, 1816.

79. For the increased feminine commitment to foreign missions, see Winslow, *Memoir*, pp. 71-72, 77. The woes of the local societies are noted in the *Religious Intelligencer* (October 19, 1816): 334, 336; Foreign Mission Society of Tolland County, *An Address to the People of the County of Tolland, Ct.* (Hartford, Conn., 1816), p. 3.

80. A good example of this use of returned missionaries is Samuel Nott, *A Sermon, On the Idolatry of the Hindoos, Delivered Nov. 29, 1816, at the Annual Meeting of the Female Foreign Mission Society, of Franklin, Connecticut. Illustrated by an Appendix* (Norwich, Conn., 1817). For other changes see Foreign Mission Society of Tolland County, *An Address to the People*, pp. 10-11. The

impact of a touring heathen is in Edwin W. Dwight, *Memoirs of Henry Obookiah* (New Haven, Conn., 1818), p. 74.

81. *Connecticut Courant*, April 30, 1816. See also Winslow, *Memoir*, pp. 74, 86. These pages contain her diary extracts for July 17 and November 10, 1816. For the enlarged edition of Buchanan's works see Claudius Buchanan, *The Works of the Rev. Claudius Buchanan* (New York, 1812). Most of Buchanan's other writings on missions had appeared by 1812.

82. Elias Cornelius to Worcester, June 26, 1816, ABC 12.1, v. 1, No. 1. See also Winslow, *Memoir*, p. 73 (diary entry for June 5, 1816).

83. See letters 1-4 in ABC 12.1, v. 2. Because of his early interest and organizing activities, Mills is usually considered the father of American foreign missions.

84. Harvey and Morris to Worcester, June 25, 1816, ibid., No. 7.

85. "On Educating Heathen Youth in Our Country," *Panoplist* 12 (July 1816): 298-99. See also the letter from Harvey, Prentice, and Morris to the ABCFM, August 20, 1816, ABC 12.1, v. 2, No. 8.

86. Harvey, Prentice, and Morris to ABCFM, August 20, 1816, ABC 12.1, v. 2, No. 8.

87. See letter No. 9 in ibid.

88. For the recommendation of Cornelius see Beecher to Worcester, August, 1816, ABC 12.1, v. 1, No. 3. Cornelius's requests are in the *Circular Letter of the Rev. Elias Cornelius to the Clergy of Essex County* (n.p., 1816), ABC 42-5939, No. 21.

89. Harvey to Worcester, October 12, 1816, ABC 12.1, v. 2, No. 10; *Religious Intelligencer* (October 12, 1816): 313-14.

90. Evarts to Morris, Prentice, and Harvey, November 15, 1816, ABCFM Letter Book, 1816-1819, pp. 17-18, ABC 1.01. For estimates of the property value see Harvey to Worcester, October 30, 1816, ABC 12.1, v. 2, No. 12.

91. Cornelius to Worcester, ABC 12.1, v. 1, No. 10.

92. Edwards, *Memoir of Elias Cornelius*, pp. 37, 47; Hibbard, *History of Goshen*, p. 252. Worcester introduced Cornelius to irascible old William Bentley; Bentley was unimpressed. See his *Diary*, 4:425.

93. *Second Quarterly Circular of the Prudential Committee of the American Board of Commissioners for Foreign Missions* (Boston, 1816), ABC 42-5939, No. 9, p. 3.

94. *Third Quarterly Circular of the Prudential Committee of the American Board of Commissioners for Foreign Missions* (Boston, 1816), ABC 42-5939, No. 10, p. 2.

95. James Morris to Worcester, December 9, 1816, ABC 12.1, v. 2, No. 41; Theodore S. Gold, comp., *Historical Records of the Town of Cornwall, Litchfield County, Connecticut* (Hartford, Conn., 1877), p. 30.

96. Morris to Jedidiah Morse, November 25, 1816, ABC 12.1, v. 2, No. 40; Emily C. Hawley, *Introduction of Christianity into the Hawaiian Islands* (Brattleboro, Vt., 1922), pp. 25-26; Starr, *A History of Cornwall*, p. 90. For information about other donations see Morris to ABCFM, September 2, 1817, ABC 12.1, v. 2, No. 44.

97. Morris to ABCFM, September 2, 1817, ABC 12.1, v. 2, No. 44. See also Mitchell, *The Great Awakening*, p. 38; Morris to Morse, November 25, 1816, ABC 12.1, v. 2, No. 40.

98. John Treadwell, *Inaugural Address* (Elizabethtown, N.J., 1819), pp. 5-6. See also Hiram Bingham, *A Residence of Twenty-one Years in the Sandwich Islands* (Hartford, Conn., 1855), p. 58; *Extracts from the Report of the Agents of*

the Foreign Mission School to the American Board of Commissioners for Foreign Mission, September, 1817 (Hartford, Conn., 1817), p. 4.

99. Joseph Harvey, *The Banner of Christ Set Up: A Sermon Delivered at the Inauguration of the Rev. Hermon [sic] Daggett, as Principal of the Foreign Mission School in Cornwall, Connecticut, May 6, 1818* (Elizabethtown, N.J., 1819), p. 24. See also *Extracts from the Report of the Agents . . . 1817*, p. 6. For some evaluations of the Foreign Mission School, see Ralph H. Gabriel, *Elias Boudinot, Cherokee, and His America* (Norman, Okla., 1941), p. 34; Thomas French, *The Missionary Whaleship* (New York, 1961), p. 40.

100. Evarts to James Morris, November 8, 1817, ABCFM Letter Book, 1816-1819, ABC 1.01, v. 2, p. 134.

101. "Address to the Christian Public," *Panoplist* 13 (January 1817): 1.

102. An example of these continuing exhortations is Alexander Proudfit, *The Extent of the Missionary Field. A Call for the Increase of Missionary Labourers: A Sermon, Preached August 19, 1817 before the Middlebury College Charitable Society for Educating Indigent Youth for the Gospel Ministry* (Middlebury, Vt., 1817), p. 25.

103. See Timothy Cooley, *A Sermon, Delivered in Springfield, before the Bible Society, and the Foreign Mission Society, in the County of Hampden, at Their Annual Meeting, August 27, 1817* (Springfield, Mass., 1817), pp. 11, 14; Lyman Beecher, *The Bible a Code of Laws: A Sermon, Delivered in Park Street Church, Boston, Sept. 3, 1817, at the Ordination of Mr. Sereno Edwards Dwight, as Pastor of the Church; and of Messrs. Elisha P. Swift, Allen Graves, John Nichols, Levi Parsons & Daniel Buttrick, as Missionaries to the Heathen* (Andover, Mass., 1818), pp. 7, 25; Jesse Appleton, *A Sermon, Delivered at Northampton, September 18, 1817, before the American Board of Commissioners for Foreign Missions* (Charlestown, Mass., 1817), pp. 17, 26-27.

104. The following letters from the board's agents illustrate this growth (see ABC 12.1, v. 1). Miron Winslow to Worcester, November 11, 1817, (No. 148); Levi Parsons to Prudential Committee, November 6, 1817 (No. 97); Parsons to Prudential Committee, July 4, 1817 (No. 96); Samuel P. Williams to Prudential Committee, April 26, 1817 (No. 89). For the increase in funds see Anderson, *Memorial Volume*, p. 160.

105. A crystallization of this discontent is in *The Politics of Connecticut*, p. 20. For one agent's report see Levi Parsons to Prudential Committee, July 4, 1817, ABC 12.1, v. 1, No. 96.

106. *Religious Intelligencer* (October 11, 1817): 309. For activities of the agents see Jeremiah Evarts to Worcester, July 7, 1817, ABC 11, v. 1, No. 154. Elias Cornelius to Worcester, February 25, 1817, ABC 12.1, v. 1, No. 12.

107. Joseph T. Buckingham, *Personal Memoirs and Recollections of Editorial Life*, 2 vols. (Boston, 1852), 1:93-94.

108. "Address of the Prudential Committee to All Foreign Mission Societies," *Panoplist* 14 (January 1818): 28.

109. For examples of these reminders in 1818 see John Codman, *Idolatry Destroyed, and the Worship of the True God Established: A Sermon Delivered in the Old South Church, Boston, before the Foreign Mission Society of Boston and the Vicinity, Jan. 1, 1818* (Boston, 1818), pp. 15, 27; Lyman Beecher, *A Sermon Delivered at the Funeral of Henry Obookiah, a Native of Owhyee, & a member of the Foreign Mission School at Cornwall, Conn., Feb. 18, 1818* (Elizabethtown, N.J., 1819), p. 8.

110. (Andover, 1818), p. 8. Of course this was probably true, for as American missionaries failed to understand native superstitions, so the natives failed to

comprehend those of the missionaries. Whichever seemed the most frightening and mysterious would eventually triumph.

111. Ibid., p. 66.

112. Ibid., p. 27.

113. For the Masons see Copy of the Circular Letter from the Officers of the Grand Lodge of Massachusetts, ABC 12.1, v. 1, No. 263; see also the letters of Jonathan Greenleaf in the same volume. The appeal to women is in *An Address to Christian Females, in Favour of the Missionary Society* (Andover, Mass., 1818), p. 6.

114. *Addresses by Rev. Jesse Appleton, D.D. Late President of Bowdoin College. Delivered at the Annual Commencements, from 1808-1818; With a Sketch of His Character* (Brunswick, Maine, 1820), p. 151.

115. For these arguments see Bates, *A Discourse . . . September 16, 1818*, p. 5; John Keep, *Nature and Operations of Christian Benevolence: A Sermon, Delivered Oct. 21, 1818, before the Directors of the Domestic Missionary Society, of Massachusetts Proper, at Their First Annual Meeting in Northampton* (Northampton, Mass., 1818), pp. 5, 17-18, 20.

116. Beecher, *Autobiography*, 1:344. The Prudential Committee report is in the *Panoplist* 14 (November 1818): 511. For a rare note of gloom see Evarts to Worcester, December 6, 1818, ABC 11, v. 1, No. 186.

117. *Christian Spectator* 1 (January 1819): 22; (April 1819): 211-15; *Religious Intelligencer* (May 8, 1819): 792.

118. A note on "missionary boxes" is in the *Panoplist* 15 (July 1819): 331. For the progress of the missionary sheep see the *Panoplist* 15 (April 1819): 172-73. Contributions to the Foreign Mission School are enumerated in A List of Articles Given to the Foreign Mission School, ABC 12.1, v. 2, No. 19.

119. Samuel Gile, *A Sermon, Delivered in the Old South Church, Boston, before the Foreign Mission Society of Boston and the Vicinity, Jan. 1, 1819* (Boston, 1819), pp. 9, 21, 26.

120. For comments on missionary support and charity see the *Boston Recorder* (July 10, 1819): 115; and (July 24, 1819): 122. An exchange on publicizing charitable gifts is in the *Christian Spectator* 1 (January 1819): 22; (April 1819): 183. See also Miron Winslow, *A Sermon Delivered at the Old South Church, Boston, June 7, 1819, on the Evening Previous to the Sailing of the Reverend Miron Winslow, Levi Spaulding, and Henry Woodward, & Dr. John Scudder, as Missionaries to Ceylon* (Andover, Mass., 1819), pp. 16-17.

Chapter Six

1. E. S. Thomas, *Reminiscences of the Last Sixty-five Years*, 2 vols. (Hartford, Conn., 1840), 1:42-43; Samuel E. Morison, *Maritime History of Massachusetts, 1783-1860* (Boston, 1921), p. 44.

2. A 1799 letter in the *New York Missionary Magazine*, 1, no. 3 (1800): 240, mentions the possibility of sending a mission to these islands. This is the earliest direct reference that I found and antedates the founding of the ABCFM by eleven years.

3. Samuel E. Morison notes the theatrical performance in "Boston Traders in the Hawaiian Islands, 1789-1823," Massachusetts Historical Society, *Proceedings* 54 (October 1920): 11. The *Salem Gazette* reported the arrival of one youth in 1802. It is reprinted in R. Gerard Ward, ed., *American Activities in the Central Pacific, 1790-1870* (Ridgewood, N.J., 1966), p. 123. For one dreamer see Charles Brewer, *Reminiscences* (Jamaica Plain, Mass., 1884), p. 17.

4. *A Volume of Records Relating to the Early History of Boston, Containing Minutes of the Selectmen's Meetings, 1799 to, and Including, 1810* (Boston, 1904), p. 339.

5. Figures on the growing sandalwood trade are in Morison, "Boston Traders," p. 14. For several newspaper articles see Ward, *American Activities*, pp. 124, 125, 127.

6. Edwards, *Memoir of Elias Cornelius*, pp. 37, 42-43.

7. *Religious Intelligencer* (June 1, 1816): 13-15. One of these early letters is in the same paper (October 19, 1816): 335.

8. *Narrative of Five Youth from the Sandwich Islands* (New York, 1816). These youth were Henry Obookiah, Thomas Hopoo, John Honoree, William Tennooe, and Prince George Tamoree.

9. *Religious Intelligencer* (December 7, 1816): 440. See also the ABCFM's 1816 "Annual Report" in *First Ten Annual Reports*, p. 136.

10. Reprinted in the *Narrative of Five Youth*, p. 35. Tamoree later had his portrait done by Samuel F. B. Morse. By 1807, however, Tamoree had been away from the islands so long that he had forgotten his native tongue. While his countrymen learned English, they had to teach him Hawaiian!

11. Harvey, Prentice, and Morris to the ABCFM, August 20, 1816, ABC 12.1, v. 2, No. 8. For more information about these youth see "On Educating Heathen Youth in Our Country," *Panoplist* 12 (July 1816): 297, 300-301; (August 1816): 358-62.

12. Starr, *History of Cornwall*, pp. 145-47; James Morris to ABCFM, September 2, 1817, ABC 12.1, v. 2, No. 44. Tennooe had a checkered career after leaving Cornwall. Amid two trips to Hawaii he was excommunicated from the church (1819); employed in a saloon; employed as a schoolteacher; made and lost a fortune in the California gold fields; was an irreligious bootblack in San Francisco (1860); became blind; and finally died in Honolulu in 1864.

13. "Report of the Agents of the Foreign Mission School (1817)," in *First Ten Annual Reports*, pp. 166-69.

14. For details on Obookiah's life see Dwight, *Memoirs of Henry Obookiah*, and *Narrative of Five Youth*, pp. 8-12.

15. Perkins to Samuel Worcester, January 21, 1817, ABC 12.1, v. 1, No. 87. For a sketch of Obookiah's life see *Narrative of Five Youth*, pp. 8-18.

16. Quoted in Dwight, *Memoirs of Henry Obookiah*, p. 73.

17. For several estimates of his influence see Payne K. Kilbourne, *Biographical History of the County of Litchfield, Ct.* (New York, 1851), p. 96; *Report of the American Board of Commissioners for Foreign Missions, Compiled from Documents Laid before the Board, at the Seventeenth Annual Meeting* (Boston, 1826), p. 108; Dwight, *Memoirs of Henry Obookiah*, p. 74; Gerould, *A Brief History*, p. 30; Duncan, *Travels*, pp. 179-80; Hibbard, *History of Goshen*, p. 297.

18. Morris to Evarts, February 23, 1818, ABC 12.1, v. 2, No. 46.

19. For a list of pupils see the board's "Annual Report" for 1818 in *First Ten Annual Reports*, p. 200. See also Worcester, "Origins of American Foreign Missions," p. 713.

20. Most accounts of Obookiah's role in the organization of the mission to the Sandwich Islands are saccharine and rhapsodic. Typical examples are Read, *The Hand of God in History*, pp. 138-39, and Belle M. Brain, *The Transformation of Hawaii—How American Missionaries Gave a Christian Nation to the World* (New York, 1898), p. 64.

21. Beecher, *A Sermon Delivered at the Funeral of Henry Obookiah*, p. 32. For some other exhortations see pp. 28, 30.

22. Leverett W. Spring, *A History of Williams College* (Boston, 1917), pp. 84-85.

23. Harvey, *The Banner of Christ Set Up*, pp. 26, 28-29.

24. Daggett to Worcester, May 12, 1818, ABC 12.1, v. 2, No. 48.

25. The controversy over Obookiah's tombstone is in Starr, *History of Cornwall*, p. 140. For expenses of his sickness see Harvey to Worcester, June 27, 1818, ABC 12.1, v. 2, No. 13; and "Account of Foreign Mission School, From May 25 to November 25, 1818," No. 18 in the same volume.

26. Morris and Harvey to the ABCFM, September 10, 1818, ABC 12.1, v. 2, No. 53. Notices of this petition for an agent appeared in the *Religious Intelligencer* (November 21, 1818): 392; *First Ten Annual Reports*, p. 172.

27. Morris and Harvey to the ABCFM, September 10, 1818, ABC 12.1, v. 2, No. 53.

28. Worcester to Daggett, November 6, 1818, Samuel Worcester, Letter Book, 1818-1819, p. 98, ABC 1.01, v. 3.

29. Daggett to Worcester, November 14, 1818, ABC 12.1, v. 2, No. 100.

30. Ibid.

31. Comments on the natives' morals state are in ibid. For Daggett's request to the ABCFM, see Daggett to ABCFM, November 19, 1818, ABCFM Letter Book, 1816-1819, p. 210, ABC 1.01, v. 2.

32. *Christian Spectator* 1 (January 1819): 36-43.

33. Worcester to Harvey, February 2, 1819, Samuel Worcester, Letter Book, 1818-1819, p. 117, ABC 1.01, v. 3.

34. Ibid.

35. Ibid.

36. Harvey to Worcester, February 26, 1819, ABC 12.1, v. 2, No. 20.

37. Worcester to Daggett, April 27, 1819, Samuel Worcester, Letter Book, 1818-1819, p. 143, ABC 1.01, v. 3.

38. There is, unfortunately, no biography of Hiram Bingham. Like the other missionaries, his early life attracted no special attention and consequently little is known about it. It must be pieced together from a number of diverse sources. For Bennington see Thompson, *History of Vermont*, p. 209; and Stilwell, *Migration from Vermont*, p. 139. Hiram Bingham's early life can be assembled from the following sources: "Congregational Necrology," *Congregational Quarterly* 13 (October 1871): 593-96; Anderson, "Survey of the Congregational Churches in the County of Bennington, Vt.," pp. 132-33; Rufus Anderson, *History of the Mission of the American Board of Commissioners for Missions to the Sandwich Islands*, pp. 359-60 (hereafter cited as *Sandwich Islands Mission*); *Dictionary of American Biography*, 2:276; Isaac Jennings, *Memorials of a Century. Embracing a Record of Individuals and Events Chiefly in the Early History of Bennington, Vt. and Its First Church* (Boston, 1869), pp. 291-92; Hawaiian Mission Children's Society (HMCS), *Missionary Album: Portraits and Biographical Sketches of the American Protestant Missionaries to the Hawaiian Islands* (Honolulu, 1939), p. 35; *Memoirs of American Missionaries*, pp. 106-7. A brief survey of the entire family is in the *Vermont State Banner*, December 28, 1855 (taken from a transcript given to me courtesy of the Bennington Museum).

39. For the effects of this revival see Punchard, *History of Congregationalism*, 5:528.

40. Bingham's career in the society can be traced from Biographical Data and Autobiographical Sketches of Members, 32; and Early Records, 9, 36, The Brethren Papers, AN; A Record of Subjects Discussed in the Society of Enquiry [*sic*], Papers of the Society of Inquiry Respecting Missions, AN. Just when he

decided to become a foreign missionary is in doubt and probably irrelevant. All commentators, however, agree that it was during his theological training at Andover. See "Congregational Necrology," pp. 593-94; *Memoirs of American Missionaries*, pp. 106-7; A. W. Wild, "History of the Congregational Churches in Vermont," p. 21, CL.

41. Bingham to ABCFM, December 22, 1818, ABC 6, v. 2, No. 1. In the same volume see also Bingham to Worcester, July 2, 1818 (No. 119); Bingham to Worcester, February 11, 1819 (No. 122b).

42. Bingham, *Residence*, p. 59. Also see Starr, *History of Cornwall*, p. 140.

43. Bingham to Worcester, May 11, 1819, ABC 6, v. 2, No. 121.

44. Anderson, *Sandwich Islands Mission*, p. 360; HMCS, *Missionary Album*, p. 35; the Reverend John H. Lockwood, *Westfield and Its Historic Influences, 1669-1919*, 2 vols (n.p., n.d.), 2:216; Mrs. Titus Coan, *A Brief Sketch of the Missionary Life of Mrs. Sybil Moseley Bingham* (Honolulu, 1895), pp. 3-4; Emerson Davis, *A Historical Sketch of Westfield* (Westfield, Mass., 1826), p. 23; *The Westfield Jubilee* (Westfield, Mass., 1870), p. 192.

45. Her early commitment is noted in *The Westfield Jubilee*, p. 192. For her contributions see the *Panoplist* 12 (December 1816): 560; and Account of the Foreign Mission School, From May 25 to November 25, 1818, ABC 12.1, v. 2, No. 18.

46. Sybil Bingham's dedication is in Coan, *A Brief Sketch*, p. 5; Mrs. Bingham to Evarts, October 23, 1819, ABC 6, v. 2, No. 4; Elias Cornelius to Prudential Committee, August 30, 1820, ABC 12.1, v. 1, No. 67. Hiram Bingham's approach to marriage was influenced by an earlier effort that failed, due to objections from his prospective bride's parents. See Bingham to ABCFM, August 21, 1819, ABC 6, v. 2, No. 2. An account of the meeting between Moseley and Bingham is in Edwin Harris, *A Hero of Fitchburg, Asa Thurston* (Fitchburg, Mass., 1878), p. 19.

47. For Thurston's life see HMCS, *Missionary Album*, p. 181; Mrs. Lucy G. Thurston, *Life and Times of Mrs. Lucy G. Thurston* (Ann Arbor, Mich., 1882), passim; Harris, *A Hero of Fitchburg*, pp. 8-9, 11-12; George A. Hitchcock, "The First Half-Century of the Calvinistic Congregational Church," *Proceedings of the Fitchburg Historical Society and Papers Relating to the History of the Town* (Fitchburg, Mass., 1908), 4:41; Anderson, *Sandwich Islands Mission*, p. 360.

48. The growth of Fitchburg's economy is in Duane Hamilton Hurd, comp., *History of Worcester County*, 2 vols. (Philadelphia, 1889), 1:220, 273, 282-85.

49. Ibid., pp. 246, 252.

50. Ibid., p. 304; *Memoirs of American Missionaries*, pp. 112-13; Harris, *A Hero of Fitchburg*, pp. 12-13; Ebenezer Bailey, "Asa Thurston, The Pioneer Missionary," *Proceedings of the Fitchburg Historical Society and Papers Relating to the History of the Town* (Fitchburg, Mass., 1902), 3:48-49; Brown Thurston, comp., *1635-1880, Thurston Genealogies* (Portland, Maine, 1892), p. 162. An account of his conversion also appeared in the *Boston Recorder*, issue for March 17, 1826.

51. Thurston to ABCFM, August 17, 1819, ABC 6, v. 2, No. 114. His letter asking to be sent to the Sandwich Islands was written August 12, 1819, and is in *Memoirs of American Missionaries*, p. 113. For Thurston's career at Andover see Biographical Data and Autobiographical Sketches of Members, p. 37; and Early Records, p. 9 in The Brethren Papers, AN; Constitution and By-laws, and Records of the Society, 1811-1823, p. 164, in the Papers of the Society of Inquiry Respecting Missions, AN; *Panoplist* 14 (September 1818): 421.

52. Harris, *A Hero of Fitchburg*, pp. 17, 20, notes his friends' opposition. Some friends "had him eaten up by the savages in less than a twelve months." His

commitment is also noted in Wild, "History of the Congregational Churches in Vermont," p. 21, CL; Bingham, *Residence*, p. 59. For the notice of the Yale commencement see the *Boston Recorder*, September 25, 1819, p. 160; Theodore Bingham, comp., *The Bingham Family in the United States, Especially of the State of Connecticut*, 2 vols., (Easton, Pa., 1927), 2:57.

53. Thurston to Worcester, September 7, 1819, ABC 6, v. 2, No. 117.

54. For background on Lucy Thurston see Anderson, *Sandwich Islands Mission*, p. 360; HMCS, *Missionary Album*, p. 181; Charles Hudson, *History of the Town of Marlborough, Middlesex County, Massachusetts, from its First Settlement in 1657 to 1861* (Boston, 1862), p. 371. The marital arrangements are noted in the Reverend and Mrs. Orramel Gulick, *The Pilgrims of Hawaii* (New York, 1918), p. 27; and Thurston, *Life and Times*, pp. 3-5. William Goodell, her cousin, was a missionary of the ABCFM in Turkey. The marriage arrangements were unusual, and her cousin acted as intermediary.

55. Worcester to Evarts, March 26, 1819, ABC 11, v. 1, No. 192; Worcester to Herman Daggett, April 27, 1819, Samuel Worcester, Letter Book, 1818-1819, p. 143, ABC 1.01, v. 3. A series of letters testifying to Chamberlain's piety, good character, and agricultural expertise are in ABC 6, v. 2 (Nos. 145, 146, 147, 149).

56. For Burder's letter see the *Panoplist* 4 n.s. (September 1811): 182.

57. Bingham, *Residence*, pp. 61-62; Harris, *A Hero of Fitchburg*, p. 20.

58. For Westboro in 1819 see Herman DeForest and Edward Bates, *The History of Westborough, Massachusetts* (Westborough, Mass., 1891), pp. 222-23. Family background on the Chamberlains is in Anderson, *Sandwich Islands Mission*, p. 380; HMCS, *Missionary Album*, p. 53; Bingham, *Residence*, p. 61; ABCFM, "Annual Report" for 1819 in *First Ten Annual Reports*, p. 248; Bradford Smith, *Yankees in Paradise: The New England Impact on Hawaii* (Philadelphia, 1956), p. 340; Daniel Chamberlain, Journal, November 21, 1819, to July 22, 1820, typed copy of MS, AAS.

59. A description of Ruggles (along with his wife) and his early commitment is in Sereno Edwards Bishop, *Reminiscences of Old Hawaii* (Honolulu, 1916), p. 23; and Starr, *History of Cornwall*, pp. 356-57. Ruggles's early life can be found in Emily C. Hawley, *Annals of Brookfield, Fairfield County, Connecticut* (Brookfield, Conn., 1929), pp. 132, 259-60, 549; Emily C. Hawley, *Biographical Sketch, Four Early Missionaries to the Hawaiian Islands* (New York, 1908), p. 2; Hawley, *Introduction of Christianity*, pp. 26, 55; and Ruggles to Samuel Worcester, June 7, 1817, ABC 6, v. 2, No. 133. His career at the Foreign Mission School can be pieced together from a number of other sources. See Account of the Foreign Mission School, Cornwall, May 25, 1818, by James Morris and Charles Prentice, ABC 12.1, v. 2, No. 14; and Account of the Foreign Mission School, May 25 to November 25, 1818, No. 18 in the same volume; James Morris to ABCFM, September 2, 1817, ABC 12.1, v. 2, No. 44. See also ABCFM, "Report of the Agents of the Foreign Mission School," in *First Ten Annual Reports*, p. 165. The school's recommendation is in Charles Prentice to Worcester, June 7, 1819, ABC 12.1, v. 2, No. 58. For general information and vital statistics see Anderson, *Sandwich Islands Mission*, p. 380; HMCS, *Missionary Album*, p. 159.

60. This was somewhat unusual for a doctor and was perhaps the first indication of Holman's financial difficulties. The Prudential Committee assumed the debt. See Prentice to Worcester, September 2, 1819, ABC 12.1, v. 2, No. 64. For Holman's early life see Hawley, *Biographical Sketch*, p. 3; Hawley, *Annals of Brookfield*, pp. 426-27; Anderson, *Sandwich Islands Mission*, p. 378; HMCS, *Missionary Album*, p. 107. His offer of services was to Hiram Bingham and is in Bingham to Worcester, May 11, 1819, ABC 6, v. 2, No. 121.

61. Daggett to Worcester, August 6, 1819, ABC 12.1, v. 2, No. 106.

62. Bingham to Evarts, November 2, 1820, ABC 19.1, v. 1, No. 153. None of Holman's troubles at the Foreign Mission School are noted in its records. The public was never told the full extent of the difficulty, as only general references were made publicly to Holman's dismissal from the mission company. Throughout the crisis, full blame fell on Holman, and the board's judgment was not publicly questioned.

63. Daggett to Evarts, September 1822, ABC 12.1, v. 2, No. 140.

64. Thomas Holman died in 1826, whereupon Lucy remarried. For sketches of her life see the *Journal of Lucy Ruggles Holman* (Honolulu, 1931), p. 3; Starr, *History of Cornwall*, pp. 315-16; Hawley, *Biographical Sketch*, p. 3; Anderson, *Sandwich Islands Mission*, p. 378; HMCS, *Missionary Album*, p. 107; Daggett to Worcester, August 6, 1819, ABC 12.1, v. 2, No. 106.

65. I have been able to discover few details concerning his early life. What pieces that were found are in Anderson, *Sandwich Islands Mission*, pp. 380-81; HMCS, *Missionary Album*, p. 131; Starr, *History of Cornwall*, pp. 144-45, 328. For his commitment to the mission see Bingham to Worcester, May 11, 1819 (No. 121), and Loomis to Worcester, September 16, 1819 (No. 129), in ABC 6, v. 2. Notice of his marriage is in the *Boston Recorder*, October 9, 1819, p. 167. Worcester himself wrote Jeremiah Evarts to urge Loomis's appointment. See Worcester to Evarts, October 5, 1819, ABC 11, v. 1, No. 46.

66. The best sources for Whitney's life are Bingham, *Residence*, p. 61; Chauncey Goodrich to Worcester, August 17, 1819 (No. 137), and Whitney to Worcester, August 23, 1819 (No. 139), in ABC 6, v. 2. See also HMCS, *Missionary Album*, p. 189; Anderson, *Sandwich Islands Mission*, p. 360.

67. For examples of these letters see ABC 6, v. 1, Nos. 26, 33, 36, 67. A typical pastoral letter of evaluation and recommendation is in the same volume, letter No. 12. See also Horatio Bardwell, *Memoir of Reverend Gordon Hall, A.M. One of the First Missionaries of the American Board of Commissioners for Foreign Missions, at Bombay* (Andover, Mass., 1834), p. 22.

68. Recollections of these early years can be found in the *Report of the American Board of Commissioners for Foreign Missions, Presented at the Twenty-ninth Annual Meeting* (Boston, 1838), p. 36; and the *Report of the American Board of Commissioners for Foreign Missions, Presented at the Thirtieth Annual Meeting* (Boston, 1839), p. 38.

69. Bingham to Worcester, July 16, 1819, ABC 6, v. 2, No. 123. For his earlier commitment see Bingham, *Residence*, pp. 58, 60. Bingham's views on the importance of religion can be found in Mrs. Sarah E. Ford, *Memoir of Mrs. Sally Fornis, Who Died at Beverly, Massachusetts, July 31, 1817, at 19. Compiled from Private Manuscript Written at the Time by Her Mother. With Remarks by H. Bingham* (Andover, Mass., 1819), pp. 73-74. References to Obookiah's influence on these men are in Dwight, *Memoirs of Henry Obookiah*, p. xi; and Foreign Missionary Society of Northampton and the Neighboring Towns, *The Annual Report of the Committee; Published by Direction of the Society at Their Meeting in Belchertown, Oct. 12, 1819* (Northampton, Mass., 1819), p. 7. Comparison with other companies can be drawn from Clifton J. Phillips, *Protestant America and the Pagan World: The First Half-Century of the American Board of Commissioners for Foreign Missions, 1810-1860* (Cambridge, Mass., 1969), pp. 30-31.

70. The best summaries of missionary motivation are Varg, *Missionaries, Chinese and Diplomats*, pp. vii-viii; and Howard A. Bridgmen, *New England in the Life of the World* (Boston, 1920), p. 11. For academic discussions of missionary life see Hart Talcott, "The Advantages and Disadvantages of Becoming a Mission-

ary While Young," Society of Inquiry, Student Dissertations, v. 4, AN; Robert C. Robbins, "What Constitutes a Call to be a Missionary?" Society of Inquiry, Student Dissertations, v. 6, AN. Despite this commitment Leonard Woods still felt it necessary to utter a disclaimer that these men were misfits with no other prospect for employment. See *A Sermon, Delivered at the Tabernacle in Salem, February 6, 1812*, p. 26.

71. Evarts to Worcester, August 19, 1819, ABC 11, v. 1, No. 200. The board's financial resources received their first jolt when the ship's captain demanded $500 more than the board wanted to pay. Final expenses for passage to the islands amounted to yet another $500.

72. An example of Bingham's requests for more supplies is in Bingham to Evarts, October 24, 1819, ABC 6, v. 2, No. 3. For a breakdown of the mission's expenses, see the board's "Annual Report" for 1820 in *First Ten Annual Reports*, pp. 308, 320-21; ABCFM, *Views of the Missions, Funds, Expenditures and Prospects of the American Board of Commissioners for Foreign Missions* (Boston, 1821), pp. 4-5.

73. Worcester's letter was in the *Boston Recorder*, September 11, 1819, p. 150. See also the *Columbian Centinel*, September 15, 1819; *Panoplist* 15 (September 1819): 428-30; and the *Religious Intelligencer* (September 18, 1819): 242.

74. Arthur Tappan's bequest is in Tappan to Worcester, September 29, 1819, ABC 10, v. 1, No. 182. For Colonel Williams's legacy see the *Panoplist* 15 (November 1819): 526. Notice of one missionary exhibition is in the *Diary of William Bentley*, 4:625 (entry for October 24, 1819). Many of these donations came from the missionaries' hometowns and were directed toward the support of particular individuals. See the *Report of the American Board of Commissioners for Foreign Missions; Compiled from Documents Laid before the Board, at the Eleventh Annual Meeting* (Boston, 1820). The donations are listed in a forty-page appendix. Those earmarked for the Sandwich Islands Mission totaled $2,321.49. Some of the missionaries' efforts are noted on pages 66-67. See also the *Panoplist* 14 (August 1818): 382; 15 (January 1819): 38-39; (August 1819): 380-81.

75. A list of the articles is in the *Panoplist* 15 (December 1819): 567-69.

76. Daggett to Worcester, September 27, 1819, ABC 12.1, v. 2, No. 108.

77. For observations on the ordination see Litchfield County Foreign Mission Society, *Semi-Centennial, Celebrated at Litchfield, October 16, 1861* (Hartford, Conn., 1861), p. 28; Hibbard, *History of Goshen*, pp. 256-57, 259, 261; the *Boston Recorder*, October 9, 1819, p. 167; Stephen L. Baldwin, *Foreign Missions of the Protestant Churches* (New York, 1900), pp. 152-53.

78. Heman Humphrey, *The Promised Land* (Boston, 1819), p. 9.

79. Ibid., p. 10.

80. Perry's charge is in ibid., p. 34. For Humphrey's concluding remarks, see ibid., pp. 26, 28, 32.

81. Thurston, *Life and Times*, p. 17. For a discussion of the earlier meeting see Ethel Damon, *The Stone Church at Kawaiahao, 1820-1944* (Honolulu, 1945), p. 141.

82. For the committee's instructions see Humphrey, *The Promised Land*, especially p. ix. These same sentiments had been expressed less than two weeks earlier at the marriage of Hiram Bingham and Sybil Moseley. See Thomas H. Gallaudet, *An Address, Delivered at a Meeting for Prayer with Reference to the Sandwich Mission, in the Brick Church in Hartford, October 11, 1819* (Hartford, Conn., 1819), p. 8.

83. *Religious Intelligencer* (October 30, 1819): 344. The same notice appeared in an earlier issue of the *Boston Recorder*.

Chapter Seven

1. *Christian Spectator* 1 (December 1819): 631.
2. Beecher, *The Means of National Prosperity*, pp. 21, 24-25.
3. Dwight, *Thy Kingdom Come*, pp. 4, 8. Dwight was pastor of the Park Street Church, Boston. Notice of the meeting appeared in the *Boston Recorder*, January 1, 1820, p. 3. To attract as many persons as possible the notice stated that "Seats will be provided for Ladies, and the room will be rendered warm and comfortable."
4. Dwight, *Thy Kingdom Come*, pp. 12-13.
5. Ibid., p. 28.
6. Evarts to Worcester, March 11, 1820, ABC 11, v. 1, No. 207. For estimates of expenses in 1820 see Evarts to Worcester, March 2, 1820, No. 206, in the same volume. New England's economic conditions are noted in "Address of the Prudential Committee," *Panoplist* 16 (March 1820): 140.
7. "Address of the Prudential Committee," *Panoplist* 16 (March 1820): 141-42.
8. David L. Perry, *The Spiritual Temple: A Sermon, Delivered at the Annual Exhibition of the Foreign Mission School, in Cornwall, May 17, 1820* (Hartford, Conn., 1820), p. 17.
9. Notice of the Northampton plan is in the *Boston Recorder*, May 20, 1820, p. 83. For activity at Andover Theological Seminary see Mrs. Helen C. Knight, *Memorial of Rev. William A. Hallock* (New York, 1882), p. 16 (entry in his diary for March 18, 1820). The letter from Harvey is in the *Religious Intelligencer* (June 17, 1820): 44-45.
10. ABCFM, *View of the Missions, Funds, Expenditures and Prospects of the American Board of Commissioners for Foreign Missions* (Boston, 1820). For an estimate of the impact of Mills's *Memoirs*, see Knight, *Memorial of Rev. William A. Hallock*, p. 15.
11. ABCFM, *Address of the Prudential Committee, of the American Board of Commissioners for Foreign Missions. To All Societies of Every Name, Auxiliary to the Board, and All Patrons, Benefactors, and Friends* (Boston, 1820), pp. 3, 6.
12. Ibid., p. 6.
13. *Panoplist* 16 (September 1820): 424.
14. Ibid., p. 425.
15. Ibid.
16. *Boston Recorder*, November 25, 1820, p. 190.
17. Ibid., December 9, 1820, p. 198. Of 180 scholars at a Sabbath School in Brookfield, Connecticut, the editor commented on two, both natives of the Sandwich Islands. He took particular care fully to quantify their every achievement, while generally ignoring the other students and their accomplishments.
18. Yale College Society for Inquiry Respecting Missions, *A Missionary Catechism, for the Use of Children; Containing a Brief View of the Moral Condition of the World, and the Progress of Missionary Efforts among the Heathen* (New Haven, Conn., 1821), p. iii.
19. Ibid., pp. 15, 16, 25-26, 38, 39.
20. Harvey to Evarts, January 20, 1821, ABC 12.1, v. 2, No. 28.
21. Harvey to Evarts, March 9, 1821, ibid., No. 29.
22. *Boston Recorder*, February 17, 1821, p. 31. For other appeals see the *Christian Spectator* 3 (February 1821): 104; and the *Religious Intelligencer* (February 10, 1821): 594.
23. *Boston Recorder*, April 14, 1821, p. 63.

24. Bingham to Samuel Worcester, May 13, 1820, Hawaiian Historical Society, *Sixteenth Annual Report* (1951), p. 18. The packet of letters actually arrived March 21, 1821, but first appeared publicly in the *Missionary Herald* in April. The *Boston Recorder* had published a small notice of the death of Kamehameha on May 20, 1820, and a longer article on June 20. It had also published a letter from Tamoree, "King of Attooi" to his son George at Cornwall. The king mentioned his intent to burn his idols, but indicated no widespread religious changes. See *Boston Recorder*, September 9, 1820, p. 146. In October a news item appeared which gave the name of the new king as "Reo-Reo." It also expressed relief that "he will maintain his authority under the patronage of the American navy." See *Boston Recorder*, October 21, 1820, p. 170. The *Christian Spectator* preempted the *Missionary Herald* in printing news of the missionaries' arrival, although it had no official correspondence. For extracts of a private letter see 3 (March 1821): 158-61.

25. *Boston Recorder*, April 28, 1821, p. 72. See also the *Christian Spectator* 3 (March 1821): 164.

26. An example of how severely contributions declined is in Salem Foreign Missionary Society, Accounts of Subscribers, Begun 1812, ABC 25, v. 1. Donations from Salem dropped nearly 50 percent from 1820 to 1821.

27. From a joint letter of the missionaries to Samuel Worcester, July 23, 1820, printed in the *Missionary Herald* 17 (April 1821): 113.

28. *Missionary Herald* 17 (May 1821): 142. But only good news appeared. The trials with Dr. and Mrs. Holman, for example, were never fully outlined in print. Hiram Bingham stated the mission's position, and ABCFM officials gave the board's view. The rest remained hidden in private letters and the official journal of the mission. The public had to rest content with guessing at vague allusions from the pages of the *Missionary Herald*.

29. *Boston Recorder*, June 9, 1821, p. 95.

30. Ibid., August 25, 1821, p. 137. These articles were really a pump-priming device to elicit public support for a proposed venture. If no support appeared, the board could drop the idea without ever having publicly committed itself. In this way failures could be hidden.

31. Ibid., July 14, 1821, p. 114.

32. Harvey to Evarts, October 22, 1821, ABC 12.1, v. 2, No. 33.

33. Harvey to Evarts, November 14, 1821, ibid., No. 32.

34. An outstanding example of organization can be found in the efforts of Edward Payson in Portland, Maine. Payson reported that his church was divided into seven districts, each one meeting for prayer and conversation once a month. He also noted, "We have a monthly meeting of all the brethren for business, a church conference every Tuesday evening, a prayer meeting on Friday evening, a monthly prayer meeting for the Sabbath schools, and the monthly union concert for prayer. We have also an inquiry meeting for males, on Sabbath evening, and for females, on Friday afternoon." See his letter, August 17, 1821, in Cummings, *Memoir*, 1:250.

35. *Religious Inquirer* 1 (November 24, 1821): 13.

36. Ibid.

37. Ibid., 1 (January 19, 1822: 47.

38. Ibid., 1 (February 16, 1822): 60.

39. "On the Peculiar Characteristics of the Benevolent Efforts of Our Age," *Christian Spectator* 4 (March 1822): 113-20. A comment on the increasing number of charitable societies is in the *Boston Recorder*, February 23, 1822, p. 81.

40. Evarts to Rufus Anderson, March 30, 1822, ABC 11, v. 1, No. 225. Evarts suggested that this theme be written up in a tract for mass distribution. The *Religious Inquirer* attacked ABCFM efforts constantly and lamented: "Genius of Don Quixote, when wilt thou cease to possess the good people of these States?" See 1 (April 27, 1822): 98.

41. Since news of the Sandwich Islands Mission did not reach the press until April, patrons had only about six months to respond before publication of the board's annual report. The figure for 1820 was $39,949.45; that for 1821 was $49,354.95. See Anderson, *Memorial Volume*, p. 160. The ABCFM devoted thirteen pages of its 1821 report specifically to the Sandwich Islands Mission. See *Report of the American Board of Commissioners for Foreign Missions; Compiled from Documents Laid before the Board at the Twelfth Annual Meeting* (Boston, 1821).

42. Sylvester Burt, *The Importance of True Charity: A Sermon, Delivered at Cornwall, Connecticut; at the Exhibition of the Foreign Mission School, May 15, 1822* (Hartford, Conn., 1822), p. 13. For notices of Sandwich Islands youths see the *Boston Recorder*, April 27, 1822, p. 66. Comments on the privileges of contributing to foreign missions are in a letter to the editor, *Boston Recorder*, April 13, 1822, p. 58. In an April issue, editors of the *Religious Inquirer* forthrightly stated their attitude toward foreign missions: "We are decidedly opposed to missionary societies, on the present plan of draining the country of its resources, to refresh the wilds of Paganism." See 1 (April 27, 1822): 98.

43. *Boston Recorder*, June 29, 1822, p. 103.

44. Daggett to Evarts, June 28, 1821, ABC 12.1, v. 2, No. 127.

45. *Missionary Herald* 18 (July 1822): 213.

46. Outstanding donations to the ABCFM are noted in Joseph Harvey to Evarts, July 14, 1822, ABC 12.1, v. 2, No. 35; *Missionary Herald* 18 (June 1822): 189; (August 1822): 257, 263; *Boston Recorder*, July 13, 1822, p. 111; September 7, 1822, p. 143; Isaac Bird to Worcester, July 9, 1822, ABC 12.1, v. 3, No. 18. For requests for more support see the *Missionary Herald* 18 (August 1822): 272.

47. The large number of candidates who volunteered their services in 1821 is in Register of Candidates for Employment as Missionaries in the Service of the American Board of Commissioners for Foreign Missions, June 8, 1821-December 13, 1821, ABC 6.1. For Plainfield in the early nineteenth century see the Reverend John Lockwood et al., eds., *Western Massachusetts: A History, 1636-1925*, 4 vols. (New York, 1926), 1:321-22; Charles N. Dyer, *History of the Town of Plainfield from Its Settlement to 1891* (Northampton, Mass., 1891), pp. 70-74; Samuel Williston, *William Richards* (Cambridge, Mass., 1938), pp. 6-7. His family background is in Lucius E. Smith, ed., *Heroes and Martyrs of the Modern Missionary Enterprise* (Chicago, 1853), p. 437; Dyer, *Plainfield*, pp. 39, 118-19, 168-69; William Sprague, ed., *Annals of the American Pulpit* (New York, 1859), 2:688; *History of the Connecticut Valley*, 1:432; Williston, *William Richards*, p. 7. William Richards's premissionary career must be pieced together from a great variety of sources, since the only biography is a brief one by his grandson Samuel Williston. See Early Records, Constitution and List of Members, p. 9, and Biographical Data and Autobiographical Sketches of Members, p. 32, The Brethren Papers, AN; Sprague, *Annals of the American Pulpit*, 2:692; *Memoirs of American Missionaries*, pp. 122-23; Anderson, *Sandwich Islands Mission*, p. 361; HMCS, *Missionary Album*, p. 153; *Dictionary of American Biography*, 15:560; John H. Hewitt, *Williams College and Foreign Missions* (Boston, 1914), pp. 96-98, 103. Notice of his marriage is in the *Hampshire Gazette*, November 6, 1822.

48. For Ely's background see Account of Foreign Mission School, May 25 to November 25, 1818, and James Morris to ABCFM, September 2, 1817, ABC 12.1, v. 2, letters 18, 44; Starr, *History of Cornwall*, pp. 295-96; "Report of the Agents of the Foreign Mission School (1817)," in *First Ten Annual Reports*, p. 165. His family background is in George B. Vanderpoel, ed., *The Ely Ancestry* (New York, 1902), pp. 267, 392.

49. Charles Prentice to Samuel Worcester, June 7, 1819, ABC 12.1, v. 2, No. 58.

50. Ely's progress at the Foreign Mission School and efforts to become a foreign missionary are noted in two letters from Herman Daggett to Samuel Worcester, May 18, 1820, and September 20, 1820, ABC 12.1, v. 2, Nos. 115, 117. When the couple left for Hawaii they were still without money. The reason remains a mystery, for Louisa Ely taught school in her hometown of Cornwall for a number of years. The document appointing her for 1816 is in the Connecticut Historical Society, Hartford, Conn. James Ely's request for money to buy clothes prior to departure is in Ely to Evarts, July 27, 1822, ABC 6, v. 4, No. 74. Fragments of Ely's life are also in HMCS, *Missionary Album*, p. 81; and Anderson, *Sandwich Islands Mission*, p. 362.

51. For Stewart's commitment and debts see his letters to Jeremiah Evarts, August 30, 1821, and March 5, 1822, ABC 6, v. 4, Nos. 193, 201. A letter from his wife is included in the same volume, No. 204. She cites the influence of Horne's *Letters* in presenting her case for appointment. Other information on the Stewarts is in HMCS, *Missionary Album*, p. 175; Anderson, *Sandwich Islands Mission*, pp. 361-62; and the Reverend Edward H. Roberts, comp., *Biographical Catalogue of the Princeton Theological Seminary, 1815-1932* (Princeton, N.J., 1933), pp. 14-15.

52. The Bishops' background can be drawn from a number of scattered sources. For Bishop's debts see Bishop to Henry Hill, February 20, 1826, ABC 19.2, v. 1, No. 89; and Bishop to Evarts, March 13, 1822, ABC 6, v. 4, No. 4. His other activities are noted in letters 49-52, ABC 12.1, v. 2; Bishop, *Reminiscences*, p. 4; HMCS, *Missionary Album*, p. 39; Roberts, *Biographical Catalogue*, p. 16; Anderson, *Sandwich Islands Mission*, p. 361.

53. For Goodrich see Wethersfield Congregational Church, *Manual, Comprising Historical and Biographical Memoranda* (Hartford, Conn., 1860), p. 24; William R. Cutter, *Genealogical and Family History of the State of Connecticut*, 4 vols. (New York, 1911), 3:1262-63; Henry R. Stiles, ed., *The History of Ancient Wethersfield, Connecticut*, 2 vols. (New York, 1904), 2:385; HMCS, *Missionary Album*, p. 93; Anderson, *Sandwich Islands Mission*, p. 362. Fragments of his wife's life are in the Reverend Heman R. Timlow, *Ecclesiastical and Other Sketches of Southington, Connecticut* (Hartford, Conn., 1875), p. 20; Smith, *Yankees in Paradise*, p. 342. Little information is available on Abraham Blatchley's early life. For what there is available see *Report of the American Board of Commissioners for Foreign Missions; Compiled from Documents Laid before the Board, at the Fourteenth Annual Meeting* (Boston, 1823), p. 115; HMCS, *Missionary Album*, p. 43; French, *Missionary Whaleship*, p. 68; Anderson, *Sandwich Islands Mission*, pp. 378-79.

54. Levi Chamberlain's early career can be pieced together from several diverse sources. See letters from him in ABC 6.1; Chamberlain to Evarts, September 27, 1821, ABC 6, v. 4, No. 47; *Honolulu Star-Bulletin, 1820-1920. Centenary Number* (Honolulu, 1920), p. 33; HMCS, *Missionary Album*, p. 55; French, *Missionary Whaleship*, p. 69; Anderson, *Sandwich Islands Mission*, p. 381.

55. In Hawaii she quickly became fluent in the native language and taught

native children (but not families of the chiefs). Little has been written about this interesting woman, but see my article "Betsey Stockton: Stranger in a Strange Land," *Journal of Presbyterian History* 52 (Summer 1974): 157-66. See the following letters for her early life: Ashbel Green to (Evarts?), September 3, 1821; Michael Osborn to Evarts, September 5, 1821, ABC 6, v. 4, Nos. 210, 209. Other remarks are in French, *Missionary Whaleship*, pp. 70, 112-17; HMCS, *Missionary Album*, p. 177. A brief sketch of her life appeared with her obituary in the *Freeman's Journal* (November 3, 1865). (Photocopy transcript courtesy of New York State Historical Association, Cooperstown, N.Y.)

56. Goodrich to Morse, April 6, 1821, ABC 6.1. See also Goodrich to Morse, April 6, 1821, ABC 6, v. 4, No. 123.

57. Bishop to Rufus Anderson, April 4, 1821, ABC 12.1.9, v. 1. Two other letters elaborate his commitment: Bishop to Evarts, December 10, 1821, and January 30, 1822, ABC 6, v. 4, Nos. 1, 3.

58. For Ely see "Report of the Agents of the Foreign Mission School (1817)," *First Ten Annual Reports*, p. 165; Joseph Harvey to Evarts, January 22, 1822, ABC 6, v. 4, No. 72. Richards's commitment is noted in two letters: Richards to Prudential Committee, February 2, 1822, ABC 6, v. 4, No. 177; and Rufus Anderson to Evarts, ABC 11, v. 1, No. 323.

59. Samuel Miller, *A Sermon, Delivered in the Middle Church, New Haven, Con. Sept. 1822 at the Ordination of the Rev. Messrs. William Goodell, William Richards, and Artemas Bishop, as Evangelists and Missionaries to the Heathen* (Boston, 1822), pp. 32-33. Efforts to collect money are noted in Richards to Evarts, October 25, 1822, ABC 6, v. 4, No. 181.

60. *Religious Inquirer* 1 (March 16, 1822): 76. There is no indication that the editor knew of the missionaries' many debts.

61. Ibid. (October 12, 1822): 198.

62. Ibid. That there was some discussion at this time too of the need for women to become involved is evidenced by *Letters on Practical Subjects, from a Clergyman of New England, to His Daughter* (Hartford, Conn., 1822). For comments on foreign missions, see especially p. 122.

63. Four natives accompanied the missionaries: William Kummoolah, Richard Kriouloo, and Cooperee of the Sandwich Islands, and Stephen Papohe of the Society Islands. Notices of the detachment's departure are in the *Religious Intelligencer* (November 23, 1822): 414-15; and the *Boston Recorder*, November 30, 1822, p. 190.

64. Anderson, *Memorial Volume*, p. 160. The previous high of $49,354.95 had been set only the preceding year.

65. Joel Hawes, *"What Hath God Wrought!" A Sermon, Delivered in Hartford, on the Last Sabbath of the Year 1822* (Hartford, Conn., 1823), pp. 6-7, 15.

66. Ibid., pp. 18-19.

67. For organization of the new heathen school societies, see Bardwell to Evarts, December 10, 1822, ABC 12.1, v. 2, No. 40. The board had already encouraged donations by allowing persons to support individual heathen youth; in return these youth would bear a name selected by the donor. ABCFM plans for additional auxiliaries are in History of the Organization of Auxiliaries and Associations, December 10, 1844, ABC 8.5, No. 74.

68. James Sabine, *The Relation the Present State of Religion Bears to the Expected Millennium: A Sermon, Delivered in the Old South Church, Boston, before the Foreign Mission Society, of Boston and the Vicinity, Jan. 8, 1823* (Boston, 1823), pp. 4, 19; *Christian Spectator* 5 (January 1823): 50.

69. *Christian Spectator* 5 (February 1823): 99-100, 108.

70. Daggett to Evarts, February 3, 1823, ABC 12.1, v. 2, No. 143. This same volume contains a number of letters indicating the dismissal of several youths. Apparently fighting became a major problem; see the letter from George White-field, a Chippewa Indian at the school to the Reverend Amos Bassett, (n.d.), Litchfield Historical Society, Litchfield, Conn. In its pursuit of money the board even sent agents to England and Scotland. Notice of future systematic efforts appeared in the *Boston Recorder*, May 3, 1823, p. 71. See also Chauncey Eddy to Rufus Anderson, April 4, 1823, ABC 12.1.9, v. 1.

71. Ebenezer Porter, *Signs of the Times: A Sermon Preached in the Chapel of the Theological Seminary, Andover, on the Public Fast, April 3, 1823* (Andover, Mass., 1823), pp. 10, 12, 16-17.

72. A good summary of this view is in Henry Colman, *A Discourse on the Character Proper to a Christian Society, Delivered at the Opening of the Second Congregational Church in Lynn, Massachusetts, 30 April, 1823* (Cambridge, Mass., 1823), p. 9.

73. Nathaniel W. Taylor, *A Sermon, Addressed to the Legislature of the State of Connecticut, at the Annual Election in Hartford, May 7, 1823* (New Haven, Conn., 1823), p. 34. See also William B. Sprague, *A Sermon, Preached in Springfield, August 28, 1823; at the Annual Meeting of the Bible Society, the Foreign Missionary Society, and the Education Society, of the County of Hamp-den* (Springfield, Mass., 1823), p. 24. These restraints apparently did not apply to foreign lands, where merchants pursued their own interests without concern for society or religion. This, of course, led many of them to oppose foreign missions. For warnings of this tendency see the speech of William Ropes, in Foreign Mission Society of Boston and Vicinity, *Special Meeting, Holden at the Pantheon Hall, June 18, 1823* (n.p., 1823), p. 5.

74. Harvey to Evarts, July 26, 1823, ABC 12.1, v. 2, No. 38.

75. *Missionary Herald* 19 (September 1823): 96. Following the meeting the new solicitors chose potential contributors by name (see p. 297).

76. Ibid., p. 297.

77. Another reason for concern about the *Herald* was a conviction that the *Boston Recorder* was too "inefficient." For an analysis of these publications see the letter on the Efficacy of the Missionary Herald, September 16, 1823, ABC 5.4, v. 2.

78. *Missionary Herald* 19 (November 1823): 365-66.

79. Ibid., pp. 366-67.

80. Ibid., p. 367. Students at Andover Theological Seminary had also dis-cussed the need for greater benevolence. See O. Pearson, "How Shall a Student Ascertain His Personal Duty as to Engaging as a Missionary?" p. 22, Society of Inquiry, Student Dissertations, v. 16, AN. This was delivered March 25, 1823.

81. For some alarming observations on the declining state of foreign mission societies, see Elnathan Gridley to Rufus Anderson, December 18, 1823, ABC 12.1, v. 2, No. 60. Funds for 1823 dropped over $4,000 from those collected in 1822. See Anderson, *Memorial Volume*, p. 160.

82. Emmons, "False Zeal," in Ide, *Works of Emmons*, 2:212.

Chapter Eight

1. ABCFM, *The Necessity and Utility of Employing Agents to Solicit Money for the Support of Missions* (Boston, 1824), p. 7. See also pp. 1-2, 3, 6. Exhortations to support the work of these agents is in Benjamin Wisner, *The Moral Condition and Prospects of the Heathen: A Sermon, Delivered at the Old*

South Church in Boston, before the Foreign Mission Society of Boston and the Vicinity, at Their Annual Meeting, Jan. 1, 1824 (Boston, 1824), p. 35. Extensive quotations from Wisner's remarks are in the *Boston Recorder*, March 6, 1824, p. 38.

2. ABCFM, *The Necessity and Utility*, p. 11.

3. ABCFM, *View of the Missions of the American Board of Commissioners for Foreign Missions* (Boston, 1824), pp. 8-10.

4. *Missionary Herald* 20 (January 1824): 21. The board's missionary interests did not apply solely to foreign lands. See its argument linking abolition of privateering with the coming millennium in the *Missionary Herald* 20 (January 1824): 26. For other missionary influences see "The Influence of Missions upon Science and Literature," *Christian Spectator* 6 (February 1824): 57-62; (March 1824): 113-17.

5. Richards to Evarts, December 31, 1824, ABC 12.1, v. 3, No. 76. For the emphasis on Boston see Evarts to H. H. Hill, February 6, 1824, in Tracy, *Memoir*, pp. 190-91. For other societies see the letters of Elnathan Gridley to Evarts, 1823-1824, ABC 12.1, v. 2, Nos. 60-70; Frederick S. Cannon to Evarts, November 13, 1824, ABC 12.1, v. 3, No. 17; Temple, *History of North Brookfield*, p. 279; *Formation of the Auxiliary Foreign Mission Society of the North Brookfield Association* (Brookfield, Mass., 1824), pp. 2-4, 11; Auxiliary Foreign Mission Society of Boston and Vicinity, *Thirteenth Anniversary*, p. 39. Beginning in 1824 each issue of the *Missionary Herald* contains a listing of newly formed associations. For a detailed description of how one society organized its activities, see Foreign Missionary Society of Northampton and the Neighboring Towns, *The Annual Report of the Committee, Published by Direction of the Society at Their Meeting in South Hadley, Oct. 12, 1824* (Northampton, Mass., 1824), p. 6. The situation in Connecticut is summarized in Beecher, *Autobiography*, 2:13.

6. "On the Causes by Which Unitarians Have Been Withheld from Exertions in the Cause of Foreign Missions," *Christian Examiner* 1 (May-June 1824): 184-86, 189. A convenient summary of standard Trinitarian arguments for foreign missions is Enoch Pond, *Short Missionary Discourses, or Monthly Concert Lectures* (Worcester, Mass., 1824).

7. "On the Causes," pp. 189-96 passim. Unitarians still preferred to keep this missionary energy bottled up within the United States. They also quarreled about the course of heathen education and training.

8. For two notices of progress see the reports from the Hampshire Central Association and the Hampden Association, Massachusetts General Association, Report by District Association on the State of Religion in 1824, CL.

9. Fay, *The Obligations of Christians to the Heathen World*, pp. 6-7.

10. Ibid., pp. 7-8, 9.

11. Ibid., p. 30 (italics added).

12. Beecher, *Autobiography*, 2:18-19 (from a letter written to his son Edward, January 1825). Notice of continued pockets of opposition is in the *Boston Recorder*, January 15, 1825, p. 12.

13. Evarts to an agent of the board, February 7, 1825, in Tracy, *Memoir*, p. 213. For the growth of the benevolent empire see Leonard Bacon, *The Social and Civil Influence of the Christian Ministry: A Sermon, Preached at the Sixth Anniversary of the American Education Society of the Young Men of Boston; February 6, 1825* (Boston, 1825), p. 12.

14. J. Walker, "Associations for Benevolent Purposes," *Christian Examiner* 2 (July & August 1825): 241-52 passim.

15. Joshua Bates, *Influence of Christian Truth: A Sermon, Preached in North-*

ampton, Mass., Sept. 21, 1825, at the Sixteenth Meeting of the American Board of Commissioners for Foreign Missions (Boston, 1825), p. 19.

16. *Missionary Herald* 21 (September 1825): 297.

17. Ibid., p. 298.

18. Ibid.

19. For notices of new societies see the pages of the *Missionary Herald*. Also see the Report of the Hampshire Central Association, Massachusetts General Association, Report by District Association on the State of Religion in 1825, CL; the letters from ABCFM agents in ABC 12.1, v. 3 (especially the letter from Ornan Eastman to Evarts, October 5, 1825, No. 48); and George Cowles to Evarts, July 11, 1825, ABC 12.1.9, v. 1; Women's Foreign Mission Society, Jericho Center, Vt., Records of Founding, 1825-32, CL. For other societies see the reports for 1825 and 1826, listed in the bibliography of my original dissertation. The rise in contributions is in Anderson, *Memorial Volume*, p. 160. The Foreign Missionary Society of Northampton and the Neighboring Towns was perhaps the most successful local society. Its contributions jumped from $647.75 in 1824 to $1,315.56 in 1825. See *The Annual Report of the Committee, Oct. 11, 1826* (Northampton, Mass., 1826), pp. 3-4.

20. Keller, *The Second Great Awakening*, p. 221.

21. His address is in the *Proceedings at the Organization of the Auxiliary Foreign Mission Society of Essex County, [Mass.], April 11, 1826* (Salem, Mass., 1826), pp. 9-10.

22. See his address in ibid., p. 26.

23. "Review of *Journal of a Tour around Hawaii, the Largest of the Sandwich Islands. By a Deputation from the Mission on Those Islands,*" *North American Review* 22 (April 1826): 362.

24. Chamberlain to Rufus Anderson, April 28, 1826, ABC 19.1, v. 2, No. 62.

25. Eastern Auxiliary Foreign Mission Society of Rockingham County, New Hampshire, *First Annual Report, Presented at Kingston, June 22, 1826* (Portsmouth, N.H., 1826), p. 7.

26. Rutland County Foreign Missionary Society, *First Report of the Executive Committee, Presented 29th June, 1826* (Castleton, Vt., 1826), pp. 32-33.

27. For Bardwell's address see Auxiliary Foreign Mission Society of Worcester Central Association, *Proceedings at the Second Anniversary, Oct. 18, 1826* (Worcester, Mass., 1826), p. 11.

28. Beriah Green, *A Sermon, Preached at Poultney, June 29, 1826, at the First Annual Meeting of the Rutland County Foreign Missionary Society* (Castleton, Vt., 1826), pp. 5-8, 12-14. Evidence of these changing attitudes is also in the *Boston Recorder*, June 30, 1826, p. 102. The newspaper printed a notice on Sandwich Islanders living in parts of Massachusetts. All cited were gainfully employed and members of some church; a far cry from notices that appeared ten years earlier!

29. Edward D. Griffin, *A Sermon Preached September 14, 1826, before the American Board of Missions, at Middletown, Connecticut* (Middletown, Conn., 1826), pp. 6-7. The sermon was reprinted in the *National Preacher* 1, no. 4 (September 1826): 49-64.

30. The merger was really a takeover, since the ABCFM dominated the union. For notice of its intentions see ABCFM, *An Address to the Christian Public, Especially to the Ministers and Members of the Presbyterian, Reformed Dutch, and Congregational Churches, Throughout the United States, on the Subject of the Proposed Union between the American Board of Commissioners for Foreign Missions, and the United Foreign Missionary Society* (Boston, 1826). A record of

the annual contributions is in Anderson, *Memorial Volume*, p. 160. This increase in funds can also be seen in George Cowles to Rufus Anderson, March 8, 1826, ABC 12.1.9, v. 1; Record of the Formation and Transactions of the Gentlemen's Association in the Town of Bedford, Auxiliary to the American Board of Commissioners for Foreign Missions, (1826-1834), ABC 22, v. 1; *Christian Spectator* 8 (July 1826): 373; *Boston Recorder*, (January 27, 1826), p. 14. Contributions from specific societies can be found in the bibliography in my original dissertation.

31. Evarts to Chapin, July 5, 1825, in Tracy, *Memoir*, pp. 222-23.

32. *Report of the ABCFM . . . Seventeenth Annual Meeting*, p. 105. See also pp. 103-4.

33. Ibid., p. 106. For Indian attitudes see Carolyn T. Foreman, "The Foreign Mission School at Cornwall, Connecticut," *Chronicles of Oklahoma* 7 (September 1929): 258. See also Gold, *Historical Records of the Town of Cornwall*, p. 29; Keller, *The Second Great Awakening*, p. 104.

34. *Missionary Herald* 23 (January 1827): 24-26.

35. The Prudential Committee's message is in the *Missionary Herald* 23 (February 1827): 58. Some persons linked foreign missions with eradication of intemperance, urging all to contribute to religious charities instead of buying liquor. See the *American Quarterly Register* 1, no. 1 (July 1827): 14. Clerical arguments are summarized in two sermons: Alvan Bond, *A Sermon, Preached October 2, 1827 before the Auxiliary Foreign Mission Society of Brookfield Association at Their Fourth Annual Meeting* (Brookfield, Mass., 1827), pp. 10-11, 15-16; Lyman Beecher, "Resources of the Adversary and Means of Their Destruction," in *Sermons Delivered on Various Occasions* (Boston, 1828), pp. 269, 289 (delivered October 12, 1827). Efforts of the auxiliaries are in the pertinent annual reports. A full listing is in the bibliography of my original dissertation. See also *Boston Recorder* (June 29, 1827): 102; and (November 16, 1827): 183. Donations to the ABCFM for 1827 totaled $88,341.89, a jump of nearly $17,000 from 1826. See Anderson, *Memorial Volume*, p. 160.

36. C. J. Tenney, *New England Distinguished: A Discourse Preached in Wethersfield, Nov. 29, 1827, being the Day of Annual Thanksgiving* (Wethersfield, Conn., 1828), p. 4.

37. Evarts to E. Lord, November 30, 1827, in Tracy, *Memoir*, pp. 286-87.

38. 2 vols. (Washington, D.C., 1828).

39. Ibid., 1:164, 165.

40. Ibid., p. 166.

41. Ibid., p. 182. See also pp. 167, 172-73.

42. For a view of the system and the work of agents, see the *Missionary Herald* 24 (January 1828): 5. A promise that no novices would be sent abroad is in the same issue, p. 30. For a summary of missionaries' training, see the *American Quarterly Register* 1, no. 3 (January 1828): 42. Other comments are in Tracy, *Memoir*, p. 293.

43. *Missionary Herald* 24 (March 1828): 91.

44. Ibid., pp. 91-92. See also ABCFM, *An Appeal to the American Churches in Behalf of Missions* (Boston, 1828), p. 1.

45. *Missionary Herald* 24 (July 1828): 228-29.

46. Ibid., (September 1828): 294.

47. *Christian Spectator* 2 n.s. (November 1828): 569, 571. A good example of the standard clerical argument is in David L. Ogden, *The Excellence of Liberality: A Sermon Delivered at Farmington, before the Auxiliary Foreign Mission Society of Farmington and Vicinity, Oct. 22, 1828* (New Haven, Conn., 1828). See

especially pp. 6, 14. The annual reports for many auxiliaries dwelled on the need for energy in 1828. See especially those for the Brookfield Association, Essex County and Franklin County in Massachusetts; Hartford County in Connecticut; and Rockingham County in New Hampshire.

48. See the *Missionary Herald* 24 (February 1828): 60; Osgood Herrick to Rufus Anderson, July 2, 1828, ABC 12.1, v. 3, No. 57. Circulation figures are in ABCFM, *A Brief View of the American Board of Commissioners for Foreign Missions, and Its Operations* (Boston, 1829), p. 4. See also ABCFM, *The Missionary Herald; A Monthly Publication of the American Board of Commissioners for Foreign Missions* (Boston, 182[?]). This is Missionary Paper No. 8.

49. They reached $102,009.64. See Anderson, *Memorial Volume*, p. 160.

50. Statistics on the growing number of associations are in the *American Quarterly Register* 2 (August 1829): 26; and ABCFM, *A Brief View*, pp. 3, 26-27. Reasons for a drop in funds can be found in the 1829 annual reports for Franklin County, Essex County, Barnstable County-West, and the Brookfield Association.

51. William Ellery Channing, "Associations," *Christian Examiner* 7 (September 1829): 106.

52. Ibid., p. 118. See also pp. 111-12.

53. Lyman Beecher, "Propriety and Importance of Efforts to Evangelize the Nation," *National Preacher* 3 (March 1829): 154, quoted in Sidney Mead, "The Rise of the Evangelical Conception of the Ministry in America: 1607-1850," in *The Ministry in Historical Perspective,* ed. H. Richard Niebuhr and Daniel D. Williams (New York, 1956), p. 225.

54. From a speech printed in Auxiliary Foreign Mission Society of Essex County, *Proceedings at the Fourth Annual Meeting, Held at Andover, April 14, 1830* (Salem, Mass., 1831), pp. 19-20. The speaker's name has been lost to history. For some perceptive comments on the use of propaganda, see J. O. Oliphant, "The American Missionary Spirit, 1828-1835," *Church History* 8 (June 1938): 126-27.

55. McLoughlin, *New England Dissent*, 2:1144.

56. Jenks, *The True Spirit of Missions*, p. 7. For the universal application of Christianity, see Woods, *A Sermon . . . Feb. 6, 1812,* p. 18. A model of this insecurity is in Kai Erikson, *Wayward Puritans: A Study in the Sociology of Deviance* (New York, 1966), p. 52.

57. Francis Wayland, *The Moral Dignity of the Missionary Enterprise: A Sermon Delivered before the Boston Baptist Foreign Mission Society, on the Evening of October 26, and before the Salem Bible Translation Society on the Evening of November 4, 1823* (Boston, 1824), p. 12. See also pp. 21-22. For comments on Americans' superior intelligence, see Auxiliary Foreign Mission Society of Hampden County, *Seventh Annual Report, Presented Oct. 14, 1831* (Springfield, Mass., 1832), p. 11. Some perceptive general remarks on the use of the gospel are in Niebuhr, *The Kingdom of God*, pp. 8-9.

Chapter Nine

1. Bingham, *Residence*, p. 81. A survey of letters reveals that most of Bingham's compatriots felt the same way.

2. "God Never Forsakes His People" (November 1800), in Ide, *Works of Emmons*, 2: 179-80.

3. Those at home who wished for success, of course, often did so for other reasons. See the *Boston Recorder*, January 27, 1820, p. 14, for the argument that by Christianizing the islands the missionaries would advance American com-

mercial interests. The missionaries, however, did not hold this view. Their instructions clearly convey the emphasis on piety and harmony; see ABCFM, *Instructions to the Missionaries* (1823), p. 4.

4. For a perceptive, and parallel, treatment of this theme in another cause, see Aileen Kraditor, *Means and Ends in American Abolitionism* (New York, 1967), pp. 238-39.

5. From his journal, November 26, 1820; quoted in Gulick, *Pilgrims of Hawaii*, p. 85.

6. Almost every issue of the *Missionary Herald, Boston Recorder*, and *Religious Intelligencer* carried such reports. They were especially graphic during the early years of the mission, from 1820 to 1824.

7. *Residence*, p. 169.

8. For comments from British missionaries see the Reverend Daniel Tyerman and George Bennett, *Journal of Voyages & Travels in the South Sea Islands, China, etc.*, 2 vols. (Boston, 1832), 2: 78-79. Gilbert Mathison, a trader friendly to the spread of Christianity, also visited the islands in 1822. See his *Narrative of a Visit to . . . the Sandwich Islands* (London, 1825), p. 372. Other observations are in speeches delivered before local foreign mission societies. Excerpts are reported in *Proceedings at the Fourteenth Anniversary of the Auxiliary Foreign Mission Society of Boston and Vicinity, May 26, 1825*, p. 19; and *Special Meeting of the Foreign Mission Society of Boston and Vicinity* (1823), p. 5.

9. *Residence*, p. 149.

10. Quoted in Williston, *William Richards*, pp. 10-11.

11. Worcester to S. I. Mission, August 14, 1820, S. Worcester, Letter Book, 1820, p. 187, ABC 1.01, v. 4.

12. See Noah Emerson, "How Should a Missionary Station Be Conducted?" Society of Inquiry, Student Dissertations, v. 2, p. 94, AN.

13. Bingham, *Residence*, p. 101.

14. Ibid., pp. 107-8.

15. Journal of the Mission, January 1, 1821, p. 147, ABC 19.1, v. 1.

16. See letters Nos. 114, 121, 123, 130, and the Journal of the Mission, pp. 55-56, in ABC 19.1, v. 1, for efforts to influence the chiefs; as well as the *Boston Recorder*, April 28, 1821, pp. 69-70.

17. *Missionary Herald* 19 (February 1823): 41.

18. This assumption of stewardship is clearly noted in ABC 1.01, v. 4, letters Nos. 176 and 230. Bingham wanted one of the missionaries to accompany the king on his upcoming visit to England. The full narrative of Hawaiian history during this time is in Ralph Kuykendall, *The Hawaiian Kingdom*, 3 vols. (Honolulu, 1938), vol. 3. See also the *Missionary Herald* 19 (April 1823): 100.

19. These efforts are noted in the *Missionary Herald* 20 (April 1824): 110-11; L. Chamberlain to Evarts, July 22, 1824, ABC 19.1, v. 2, No. 44.

20. Aarne Koskinen, *Missionary Influence as a Political Factor in the Pacific Islands* (Helsinki, Finland, 1953), p. 83.

21. Bingham's narrative of these events provides striking evidence of missionary purpose. See his *Residence*, pp. 279-80.

22. See Mathison, *Narrative*, pp. 428-29. All progress, however slight, was reported in the New England press. See the *Boston Recorder*, April 14, 1821, p. 63; February 9, 1822, p. 23. The missionaries also created a Hawaiian orthography.

23. Hitchcock, *Knowledge Essential*, p. 19. For this progress in education see Bingham, *Residence*, pp. 156-57.

24. Bingham to Evarts, October 27, 1823, ABC 19.1, v. 1, No. 171.

25. Bingham, *Residence*, p. 215.

26. L. Chamberlain to Evarts, November 8, 1824, ABC 19.1, v. 2, No. 46. See also William D. Westervelt, comp., "Copy of the Journal, Hawaii 1824-1826, of Elisha Loomis," University of Hawaii, 1937, p. 32.

27. See his address before the Auxiliary Foreign Mission Society of Boston and Vicinity, in *Proceedings . . . May 26, 1825*, p. 18.

28. Koskinen, *Missionary Influence*, p. 89.

29. See the minutes of the Prudential meetings for 1826 in ABC 19.3, v. 2, p. 36 (typed copies of the originals).

30. Ibid., p. 37 (italics added).

31. Ibid., p. 38 (italics added).

32. Koskinen, *Missionary Influence*, p. 57.

33. Journal of the Mission (April 5, 1820), p. 41, ABC 19.1, v. 1.

34. The course of this change can be seen in Westervelt, "Copy of the Journal," pp. 22, 45-46, 51-52. For some of the violence see C. O. Paullin, *Diplomatic Negotiations of American Naval Officers, 1778-1883* (Baltimore, Md., 1912), p. 338.

35. See the letter from William Richards, August 13, 1824, in the *Missionary Herald* 22 (August 1826): 240. Other laws are noted in the *Herald* 18 (July 1822): 205, and in Bingham, *Residence*, p. 213. A more hostile opinion is in Alexander Simpson, *The Sandwich Islands* (London, 1843), p. 8.

36. This missionary influence is stoutly defended in Bingham, *Residence*, passim. See especially pp. 269, 281-82.

37. See ABC 19.3, v. 2, pp. 33, 40, for discussion of this issue. The resolution is in the *Christian Advocate* 6 (May 1828): 236.

38. Bingham, *Residence*, pp. 300-301.

39. ABC 19.3, v. 2, p. 40. Unlike their descendants, these early missionaries had little interest in acquiring land; see Jean Hobbs, *Hawaii: A Pageant of the Soil* (Stanford, Calif., 1935).

40. An excellent discussion of this process is in Koskinen, *Missionary Influence*, pp. 51, 55-56. The Constitution is in Charles Wilkes, *Narrative of the United States Exploring Expedition*, 5 vols. (Philadelphia, 1845), 4:22.

41. Bingham letter, December 15, 1827, in *Missionary Herald* 24 (July 1828): 210.

42. Journal of the Mission (January 14, 1821), p. 153, ABC 19.1, v. 1.

43. Bingham, *Residence*, pp. 108, 117.

44. For the retention of idolatry see Tyerman and Bennett, *Journal of Voyages*, 1:382. Native behavior is noted in the Journal of the Mission (May 20, 1820), p. 67, ABC 19.1, v. 1; Mathison, *Narrative*, pp. 378, 427-28, 432.

45. Bingham to Evarts, October 12, 1822, ABC 19.1, v. 1, No. 162; Damon, *The Stone Church*, pp. 8, 12.

46. See the notices from the Journal of Goodrich and Ruggles in the *Missionary Herald* 21 (May 1825): 142. The *Boston Recorder* also carried extracts of missionary correspondence in every issue, and these clearly indicate the problems to be found in Christianizing the native islanders.

47. The prevalence of this fear is, of course, understandable, for the missionaries prayed for the sick and dying—many of whom did not recover. For the chiefs see Westervelt, "Copy of the Journal," p. 37.

48. Bingham, *Residence*, pp. 255-56.

49. Ibid., p. 249; Journal of William Richards, July 3, 1826, in the *Missionary Herald* 24 (May 1828): 149-50.

50. *Missionary Herald* 24 (March 1828): 77. See also the minutes of the

Prudential meeting at Honolulu, April 29, 1828, pp. 68-69, ABC 19.3, v. 2.

51. For discussion of this point see the *North American Review* 22 (1826): 362.

52. See Ellis's memoranda of a conversation, April 25, 1825, ABC 8.5, No. 26.

53. Ibid.

54. Chamberlain to Evarts, November 14, 1820, ABC 19.1, v. 1, No. 218. See letters Nos. 231-34 for Holman's protests of innocence and Nos. 264-68 for Bingham's command of the mission. The Journal of the Mission noted this conflict—see November 28, 1820, p. 136—but this section was not published in the *Missionary Herald*. The Reverend Elijah Waterman, Holman's minister, read the transcript of the case and thought the doctor correct. See Waterman to Chamberlain, April 12, 1824; and Chamberlain to Evarts, July 20, 1824, ABC 10, v. 3, Nos. 104, 105. Bingham's judgments on his colleagues were also bluntly stated; see Bingham to Evarts, October 27, 1823, ABC 19.1, v. 1, No. 172.

55. *Missionary Herald* 21 (April 1825): 123-24.

56. Otto von Kotzebue, *A New Voyage Round the World, in the Years 1823, 24, 25, and 26*, 2 vols. (London, 1830), 2: 254-56.

57. Ibid., p. 257. Kotzebue had high praise, however, for Charles Stewart.

58. "Sandwich Islanders," *Westminster Review* 35 (1827): 438. Other comments are in Lieutenant Hiram Paulding, *Journal of a Cruise of the United States Schooner Dolphin among the Islands of the Pacific Ocean*, reprint ed. (London, 1970), pp. 197, 206; *Missionary Herald* 23 (July 1827): 203. Favorable remarks are in Mathison, *Narrative*, pp. 363-69, 419; and Charles S. Stewart, *A Visit to the South Seas in the U.S. Ship Vincennes*, 2 vols., reprint ed. (New York, 1970), 2: 77-78, 259-60. Bingham attacked his critics throughout his history of the mission. See *Residence*, passim.

59. Jones to Marshall and Wildes (Boston commercial firm), March 9, 1823, in Morison, "Boston Traders," p. 46. Jones also formed a friendship with Thomas Holman, which undoubtedly prejudiced his opinion of Bingham.

60. Auxiliary . . . Worcester Central Association, *Proceedings . . . Oct. 17, 1827*, pp. 7-9. See also the *Sag Harbor Watchman*'s (Maine) reply to the *Westminster Review* in the *Boston Recorder* (July 6, 1827), p. 106.

61. *Boston Recorder*, August 24, 1827, p. 134. The editor hoped, however, that the United States would not attempt to meddle in island politics or annex the area.

62. William Richards, *Memoir of Keopuolani, Late Queen of the Sandwich Islands* (Boston, 1825). The first edition was published at Lahaina in 1824.

63. Ibid., pp. 44-45.

64. *Missionary Herald* 23 (August 1827): 242.

65. Ibid., 22 (October 1826): 308; *Christian Spectator* 8 (November 1826): 606; Bingham to Evarts, March 20, 1823, ABC 19.1, v. 1, No. 133.

66. A perceptive discussion of these problems is in Koskinen, *Missionary Influence*, p. 49.

67. For critical comments on this transposition, see Sylvester K. Stevens, *American Expansion in Hawaii, 1842-1898* (Harrisburg, Pa., 1945), p. 9; Father Reginald Yzendoorn, *History of the Catholic Mission in the Hawaiian Islands* (Honolulu, 1927), p. 26; and Peter Buck, *Anthropology and Religion* (New Haven, Conn., 1939), pp. 93-94.

68. Bingham, *Residence*, p. 23.

69. Some observations on this utility are in Thompson, "A Perilous Experiment," p. 20; Lowe, "The First American Foreign Missionaries," p. 160.

BIBLIOGRAPHICAL ESSAY

Source material for early nineteenth-century American social history is plentiful but scattered, and few monographs exist to direct the inquiring scholar. This essay seeks to describe those primary sources most useful to this study. It does not attempt to discuss the enormous range of secondary materials relevant to the topic. Although voluminous, this material is frequently quite thin and must be sifted carefully for nuggets. These sources are enumerated in the chapter notes and need not be repeated here. A full listing is in John A. Andrew III, "Rebuilding the Christian Commonwealth: New England Congregationalists and Foreign Missions, 1800-1830" (Ph.D. diss., University of Texas, 1973).

Manuscript sources, of course, provide the core of any serious research. The central repository for manuscript material on foreign missions is the Archives of the American Board of Commissioners for Foreign Missions at Houghton Library, Harvard University. The ABCFM Archives are well organized and a pleasure to use. They are also very extensive and provide a wide range of material on all aspects of the early nineteenth century. Especially useful are the various letterbooks relating to the board members and their activities, along with the several volumes entitled Miscellaneous Domestic Letters. The letterbooks and personal papers of Samuel Worcester and Jeremiah Evarts highlight the collection for these years.

Material on foreign missions can be found in several volumes: the Letters and Testimonials of Missionaries, records of the Foreign Mission School, and the voluminous records of the Sandwich Island Mission. Several scattered records of local foreign missionary societies provide an occasional glimpse at local conditions.

A second and even less explored resource is the Congregational Library in Boston, Massachusetts. Both the archives and the library are rich in material dealing with New England Congregationalism for this period. Especially useful is the six-volume typescript of the Reverend Emerson Davis. This contains biographical sketches for virtually all New

England Congregational ministers through the nineteenth century. Also of significance is the lengthy manuscript history of the Congregational churches in Vermont by the Reverend Azel W. Wild. The reports on the state of religion to the Massachusetts General Association provide a sample of religious activity in the various districts of the Commonwealth and offer a mild corrective to the optimistic public comments from the clergy. Scattered records of local religious and mission societies can also be found among the library's holdings.

Andover-Newton Theological Seminary, Newton Centre, Massachusetts, houses the records of the student foreign mission societies that stimulated much of the foreign missionary activity throughout the early nineteenth century. Both the Brethren Papers and the Papers of the Society of Inquiry Respecting Missions provide insight into these groups. Also at Andover are the eighteen volumes of Student Dissertations for the Society of Inquiry. These proved invaluable for probing the types of activity and the nature of the commitment emanating from this institution.

The Connecticut Historical Society in Hartford, Connecticut, offered two or three letters of some value relative to the Foreign Mission School at Cornwall, along with a letter from James Ely on board the *Thames* en route to the Sandwich Islands.

The Papers of Betsey Stockton, the young mulatto woman who accompanied the first reinforcement to Hawaii, are at the New York State Historical Association in Cooperstown, New York. These papers are skimpy, and the best source for Stockton remains her letters that Ashbel Green reprinted in the *Christian Advocate*.

The American Antiquarian Society in Worcester, Massachusetts, yielded typescripts of two journals of Daniel Chamberlain, along with a vast selection of newspaper material that reflected changing social conditions in New England during these years.

Among the many printed primary sources that comprised the backbone of this study, printed sermons were often the most revealing. Although they undoubtedly reflect a certain bias of most "literate" sources, these sermons also indicate what the congregations across the region wanted and expected to hear from their clergy. As such, they mirror the tensions of the times better than many critics have contended. I sampled more than 150 of these sermons, concentrating on those that related in some way to foreign missions. A full list is in Andrew, "Rebuilding the Christian Commonwealth," cited above.

Second in importance to the sermons were the reports of the various foreign mission societies from towns throughout New England. These are scattered in libraries across the country and are often difficult to find, although an especially good collection is in the Congregational Library, Boston, Massachusetts. They exhibit a certain sameness as to approach and format, but in aggregate reveal a steady pattern of growth as well as changing membership patterns. The same is true with the reports of the ABCFM. Circulated for informational and propaganda purposes, these reports provide a unique glimpse at the public face of this remarkable organization. They are products of their time and supporters and as such are extremely valuable.

The New England region is blessed with a vast array of printed memoirs, diaries, and autobiographies for this period. Not all are of value, but some are quite remarkable. All must be used with care, for they usually reflect biases that may not be apparent at first glance. Among the most famous is the four-volume travelogue of Timothy Dwight, *Travels in New England and New York* (Cambridge, Mass., 1969). Equally famous and much more cutting is the four-volume *Diary of William Bentley* (Salem, Mass., 1911). But almost every traveler of note kept a detailed tour record and then published it as a guide to the curious. Aside from the many observations they record, these guides are a testimonial to the curiosity of New Englanders about their region and the world at large. It was this same curiosity that fueled the foreign mission movement. Others, especially the many autobiographies and diaries, reflect the considered self-importance of the author. Most document the rapid social, political, economic, and religious change that swept the region after 1800, and many stem from some single experience that seemed so overwhelming as to point the way to the future. In this respect, short autobiographies of Baptist elders take their place alongside the lengthier narratives of Congregational pastors. None can be considered accurate by itself, but together they form a priceless mosaic that captures the whirlwind of change.

Particularly revealing about the nature of religion are several clerical reminiscences from various denominations: George Allen, *Reminiscences of the Reverend George Allen of Worcester* (Worcester, Mass., 1883); H. P. Arms, *A Brief Sketch of the Life of Reverend H. P. Arms, As Written by Himself for His Children* (Boston, 1882); Lyman Beecher, *Autobiography*, 2 vols. (New York, 1864); *Diary of Reverend Moses How* (New Bedford, Mass., 1932); and James Hooper, *Life and Senti-*

ments of James Hooper, Minister of the Gospel (Paris, Me., 1834). Among Baptist accounts of the Second Great Awakening and the accompanying religious change are Mark Fernald, *Life of Elder Mark Fernald* (Newburyport, Mass., 1852); Ariel Kendrick, *Sketches of the Life and Times of Eld. Ariel Kendrick, Being a Short Account of His Birth, Conversion, Call to the Ministry, and His Labors as a Gospel Minister* (Ludlow, Vt., 1847); John Leland, *The Writings of the Late Elder John Leland* (New York, 1845); and John Peak, *Memoir of Elder John Peak* (Boston, 1832). Ray Potter, *Memoir of the Life and Religious Experience of Ray Potter* (Providence, R.I., 1829), reveals the tribulations of a common folk caught up in this maelstrom of change. A more everyday view of the same process is in Asa Sheldon, *Life of Asa G. Sheldon: Wilmington Farmer* (Woburn, Mass., 1862). Also see Peter Young, *A Brief Account of the Life and Experience, Call to the Ministry, Travels, and Afflictions of Peter Young, Preacher of the Gospel* (Portsmouth, N.H., 1817).

The early thrust toward foreign missions stems from several writings, including Gordon Hall and Samuel Newall, *The Conversion of the World* (Andover, Mass., 1818); Joel Hawes, *A Tribute to the Memory of the Pilgrims, and A Vindication of the Congregational Churches of New England* (Hartford, Conn., 1830); *The Works of the Reverend Claudius Buchanan* (New York, 1812); Melville Horne, *Letters on Missions; Addressed to the Protestant Ministers of the British Churches* (Andover, Mass., 1815); and Joseph Tuckerman, *A Letter on the Principles of the Missionary Enterprise* (Boston, 1826). Central to the entire Congregational drive toward voluntarism is Noah Worcester, *Impartial Inquiries Respecting the Progress of the Baptist Denomination* (Worcester, Mass., 1794). Several periodicals, including the *Christian Examiner*, the *Christian Spectator*, and the *Panoplist* document the yearly advances of these efforts.

For the Sandwich Islands Mission Hiram Bingham's *A Residence of Twenty-one Years in the Sandwich Islands* (Hartford, Conn., 1855) remains essential. Although defensive of the author, it shows Bingham's importance to the mission and narrates the problems of the missionaries. The *Journal of Lucy Ruggles Holman* (Honolulu, 1931) and the reminiscences of various ship captains at the islands complete the picture of missionary arrival and enterprise. The *Missionary Herald* reprinted valuable letters and reports, and measures what the ABCFM directors wanted the public to know about mission activities.

The story of the New England clergy and the problem of permanency and social change illustrate the kind of detective work necessary to fit together much of this story. Statistics on clerical tenure are available in the *American Quarterly Register*, and have been listed separately in the Appendix. Careful reconstruction of clerical terms and examination of the reasons for a ministerial change drawn from many sources (manuscript records, local histories, contemporary newspapers and journals) produced the charts found in chapter three. These charts then served as primary data for the interpretive framework that follows in the narrative. We still need to know much more about this process, and the problems encountered here indicate the magnitude of the undertaking. A total picture of social and religious change probably cannot emerge until the records of every local municipality and parish have been examined, recorded, and then translated into similar charts. All this must then be correlated with demographic change and the political alteration of town boundaries. This essay has hopefully provided a small guide as to where to begin.

INDEX